HISTORICAL ATLAS OF THE 20TH CENTURY 1900 1999

JOHN HAYWOOD

with

EDWARD BARRATT
BRIAN CATCHPOLE

MetroBooks

Project director	Peter Furtado
Cartographic manager	Richard Watts
Advisory editors	Jeremy Black
	Professor of History, University of Exeter, UK
	K.M. Chaudhuri
	Vasco da Gama Professor of European Exploration, European University Institute, Florence, Italy
	Barry Cunliffe
	Professor of European Archaeology, University of Oxford, UK
	Brian M. Fagan
	Professor of Anthropology, University of California, Santa Barbara, USA
	J.E. Spence
	Associate Fellow, Royal Institute of International Affairs, UK
Academic advisors	J.I. Catto
	Oriel College, University of Oxford, UK
	Professor Robin Cohen
	University of Warwick, UK
	Professor J.H. Elliott
	Regius Professor of Modern History, University of Oxford, UK
	Professor Harold James
	Princeton University, New Jersey, USA
	Professor Maldwyn A. Jones
	University of London, UK
	Dr Stuart Kewley
	University of Cambridge, UK
	Dr Stewart Lone
	Australian Defence Force Academy
	Dr Oswyn Murray
	Balliol College, University of Oxford, UK
	Professor A.J.S. Reid
	The Australian National University
	Professor Francis Robinson
	Royal Holloway, University of London, UK
	Professor John K. Thornton
	Millersville University, Pennsylvania, USA

This page:
Yuri Gagarin, Soviet cosmonaut

Opposite above left:
Vladimir Ilych Lenin, Bolshevik leader

Opposite centre right:
Symbol of the US National Recovery
Administration, c.1933

Opposite centre left:
US marines on Iwo Jima, 1945

Opposite below right:
Woodcut by Chinese artist Li Hua

Following page:
Martin Luther King, civil rights activist

Art director	Ayala Kingsley
Art editor	Martin Anderson
Cartographic editor	Tim Williams
Editors	Susan Kennedy
	Peter Lewis
(Encyclopedic dictionary)	BCS Publishing
Cartographer	Nathalie Johns
Picture research	Claire Turner
Production	Clive Sparling
Editorial assistance	Marian Dreier
Typesetter	Brian Blackmore
Illustrations	Charles Raymond
Proof reader	Lynne Elson
Index	Ann Barrett

AN ANDROMEDA BOOK

Produced and prepared by
Andromeda Oxford Ltd
11–13 The Vineyard
Abingdon
Oxfordshire OX14 3PX

www.andromeda.co.uk

© 1998 by Andromeda Oxford Ltd

This edition published by MetroBooks,
an imprint of Friedman/Fairfax
Publishers, by arrangement with
Andromeda Oxford Ltd

2001 MetroBooks

ISBN 1-58663-239-6

Printed and bound in Spain by
Graficromo S.A., Córdoba

10 9 8 7 6 5 4 3 2 1

Contents

INTRODUCTION

Many of those who went into battle in August 1914 thought the war would be short and glorious. World War I, though, tested human endurance to the limit. The combatant states had the ideological, bureaucratic and technological capabilities, as well as the nationalistic fervor, to mobilize vast human and material resources.

The postwar settlement was built on the principle of national self-determination. But this settlement was partial: totalitarian governments appeared in Germany, Italy and Russia, using the state's resources to foster a virulent nationalism, and committed to revising the precarious status quo.

Germany's invasion of Poland in September 1939 led to a war that soon became truly global and total. Each side sought the unconditional surrender of the other, and the distinction between soldier and civilian collapsed as air power provided the means to strike at the enemy's heartland. This strategy culminated in the atomic destruction of the Japanese cities of Hiroshima and Nagasaki, and the devastation of the social and economic fabric of Germany. Meanwhile six million Jews perished in the Holocaust, a demonstration of the modern totalitarian state's ability to combine ideology, technology and bureaucracy in systematic mass extermination.

The two wars had one positive outcome: the recognition that the propensity of states to destroy one another had to be restrained by means of international institutions to reinforce the rule of law. The League of Nations, created in 1919, failed, but its successor the United Nations raised expectations that a concert of victorious powers could deter and defend against aggressive states.

The Cold War between the United States and the Soviet Union was perhaps a product of misperception: each assumed the other was bent on aggression. A precarious order ensued, at times threatened by crises in which nuclear disaster was sometimes only narrowly averted. There were, though, other trends in the postwar years whose influence shaped international relations for many years.

First, the United States committed itself to restoring western Europe's battered economies, and equally to the defense of Europe – a reversal of its isolationism after 1919. NATO gave western Europe the confidence to begin economic integration; the European Economic Community was set up in 1957–58. Second, the independence of India, Pakistan and Ceylon from British imperial rule set a precedent for anticolonial struggle elsewhere. By 1968 fifty African states had joined the United Nations. China, too, began a long march to great power status after the Communist victory in 1949. Third, the principle of domestic jurisdiction slowly dissolved, bringing an expansion in the legal competence of bodies such as the UN to intervene when human rights were abused. South Africa's policy of *apartheid* was the catalyst, as new norms entered the vocabulary of inter-state discourse.

The relative stability provided by the threat of "mutually assured destruction" was bought at the expense of the Third World. Nehru in India, Sukarno in Indonesia, Nkrumah in Ghana and Nasser in Egypt hoped to build a third force in international affairs, committed to redressing the inequalities between the rich northern states and the poorer south. Some victories were won: the legal establishment of human rights; the isolation of *apartheid*-ridden South Africa; the recognition that Third World states needed aid and technical assistance to provide a decent life for their peoples.

But the Cold War years also saw wars by proxy fought in Third World states such as Angola, Ethiopia, Somalia and Vietnam, as the superpowers vied to support rival factions in civil wars. And as détente, or relaxation of superpower tension, took hold, the influence of the "nonaligned movement" began to wane, especially as many Third World states failed to deliver social and economic benefits to their people.

Meanwhile, led by Japan, the "tiger" economies – South Korea, Singapore, Taiwan, Malaysia, Hong Kong – underwent an economic miracle via export-led growth and a mix of government intervention and private enterprise. China, too, encouraged market liberalization, though under the strict control of the ruling Communist Party.

In contrast, the Soviet Union was unable to deliver both "guns and butter" to its people. The economy was hamstrung by obsolete state controls, and the arms race of the 1980s placed great burdens on the economy just when conservative western governments – especially in the United States and Britain – were successfully employing free market solutions to boost productivity. Attempts at reform merely led to revolt in several of the Soviet republics and the satellite states of east and south Europe. The fall of the Berlin Wall – symbol of Cold War division – in 1989 heralded a new era, one in which economic activity was global, and free-market capitalism was enshrined as the chief ideology for economic development throughout the world.

As the millennium approached, all governments were constrained by global economic forces. Conventional attack by a neighbor often seemed less threatening than organized crime, drugs and arms trafficking, illegal migration, terrorism and environmental degradation: dangers a nation-state was ill-equipped to cope with. Pressure mounted for the establishment of wider groupings of states, and it seemed possible that such regional associations would be the building blocks for a "new world order" for the twenty-first century ■

USING THIS ATLAS

This atlas is part of a six-volume chronological set covering the Ancient (1), Classical (2), Medieval (3), Early Modern (4), 19th Century (5), and Modern (6) worlds. To help the user pinpoint straight away which era any particular map relates to, pages are numbered first by volume, and then by 2-page spread within that volume. Thus, map spread 14 in volume 6 is identified by the page number 6.14.

World map spreads outline global history on the date shown. Different typographical categories (see table opposite) denote different kinds of political or social entity. The text on these spreads includes many cross-references to other relevant spreads. The timelines here are organized by region.

Regional map spreads cover a part of the world over a specific period. Maps for a continent or major region are grouped in a section, named in the heading on the right-hand side of the spread. These sections also appear in the Contents page.

Maps are shown in true cartographic projections. North is generally at the top of the page. Some distortion is evident in those maps that cover huge areas of the world (e.g. Asia). Where necessary location maps have been included.

Each regional map has certain standard features: thick grey lines denote major borders, thin grey lines internal borders. Campaigns or journeys are shown by lines with arrowheads; thicker grey arrows are used for mass movements of people. Trade routes are thinner lines, with arrowheads when the trade is one-way. All map-key items are referred to in text. The main text explains and amplifies the information on the map.

The timelines on regional maps are arranged in geographical or thematic sections. Civilizations, cultures, and dynasties are shown with colored bands; broad historical phases (such as "Bronze Age") are indicated with grey bands. Every regional map also has several numbered "pointers", whose captions offer further historical detail on the places marked. Finally, the panel bottom right cross-refers to other spreads with related information, listing their numbers and themes.

A substantial encyclopedic section at the end of the book contains an A–Z guide to the people, places, and events of the period. It is cross-referenced both within the section and to the information that appears on the map spreads.

The index provides detailed references to the text, timelines, pointer captions and map keys. Space constraints have precluded indexing every location on the maps themselves.

TYPOGRAPHICAL CONVENTIONS	
World maps	
FRANCE	state or empire
Belgian Congo	dependency or territory
Mongols	tribe, chiefdom or people
Anasazi culture	cultural group
Regional maps	
HUNGARY	state or empire
Bohemia	dependency or territory
Slavs	tribe, chiefdom or people
ANATOLIA	geographical region
✗	battle
•	site or town

At the beginning of the 20th century the world was dominated by
Europe's imperial powers. British sovereignty encompassed the globe,
with important colonies and dominions in every continent. Czarist Russia,
which had already annexed much of central Asia by the end of the 19th
century, now turned its gaze east to Mongolia and Manchuria. Germany,
a latecomer to the scramble for overseas possessions, vigorously sought
to gain footholds in Africa and the Far East. Yet the period of European
preeminence was fast drawing to a close; World War I spelled the end of
the moribund Austro-Hungarian and Ottoman empires (▷ 6.06), replaced
autocratic rule in Germany with a fragile democracy, and sparked the
revolutionary overthrow of the ancient czarist system in Russia (▷ 6.15).
Even among the victors, the manpower and financial resources of Great
Britain and France were drained by four years of costly conflict.

In their place, in both the East and the West, new powers arose that
were ultimately to take center stage in the latter years of the century.
The recently industrialized state of Japan thwarted Russian
ambitions in East Asia, inflicting a crushing defeat on the
czar's armies and navies in Manchuria in 1904–05 and
annexing Korea in 1910. Japan's rise was mirrored
by the decline and fall of the Manchu empire in China
(▷ 6.18). After military defeat by Japan in 1894–95, humiliation
by the West for the anti-foreign Boxer Uprising of 1900–01, and a
long civil war, the Qing dynasty was finally overthrown in 1911.

The United States had emerged as an imperial power in the Spanish–
American War of 1898, when it seized the transoceanic remnants of
Spain's empire – Cuba, Puerto Rico, Guam, and the Philippines. Thus it
was finally able to realize the "manifest destiny" implicit in the Monroe
Doctrine of 1823 – to bring the Western Hemisphere within its sole
sphere of influence, and if necessary enforce its will by military
intervention. When war engulfed Europe in 1914, the United
States consolidated its position as the world's foremost
financial and industrial nation, thanks to the boost given to
its commerce by Allied orders. The country's entry into the
war in 1917 marked its first direct involvement in European
affairs. Fresh US troops and supplies were decisive factors in
the Allied victory, and its politicians and diplomats played a key
role in shaping the peace accords at Versailles and elsewhere in 1919–20.

The break-up of old empires led to the creation of new European states –
Czechoslovakia, Yugoslavia, and the revival of an independent Poland
(▷ 6.07). In an attempt to prevent future global conflict, the main peace broker,

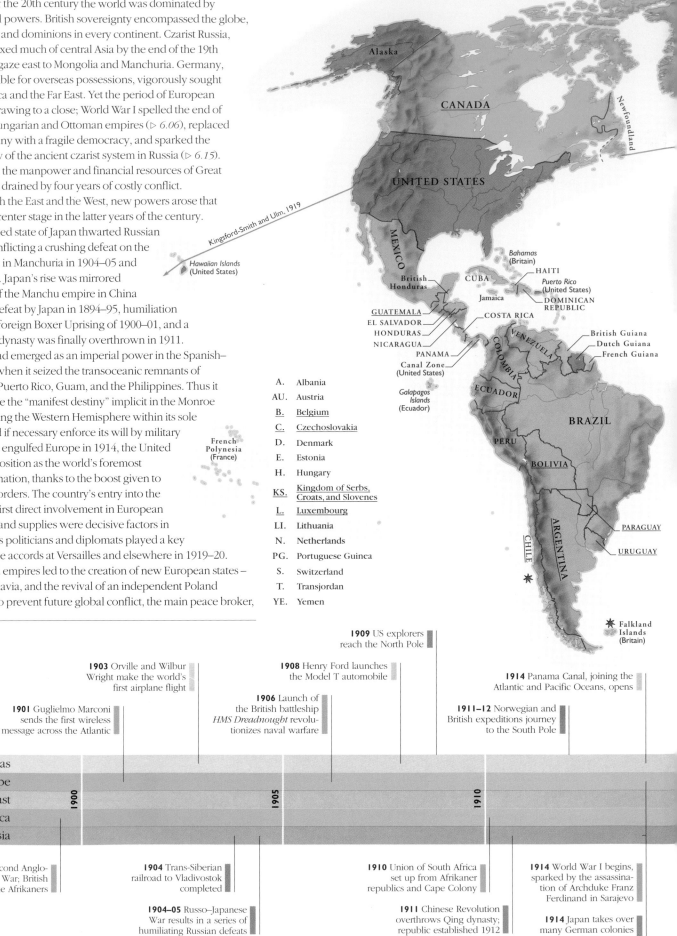

A.   Albania
AU. Austria
B.   **Belgium**
C.   **Czechoslovakia**
D.   Denmark
E.   Estonia
H.   Hungary
KS. **Kingdom of Serbs,**
     Croats, and Slovenes
L.   **Luxembourg**
LI. Lithuania
N.   Netherlands
PG. Portuguese Guinea
S.   Switzerland
T.   Transjordan
YE. Yemen

1909 US explorers
reach the North Pole

1903 Orville and Wilbur
Wright make the world's
first airplane flight

1908 Henry Ford launches
the Model T automobile

1914 Panama Canal, joining the
Atlantic and Pacific Oceans, opens

1901 Guglielmo Marconi
sends the first wireless
message across the Atlantic

1906 Launch of
the British battleship
HMS Dreadnought revolu-
tionizes naval warfare

1911–12 Norwegian and
British expeditions journey
to the South Pole

TIMELINE

The Americas		
Europe		
Middle East	1900	1905	1910
Africa		
Asia and Australasia		

1899–1902 Second Anglo-
Boer War; British
overcome Afrikaners

1904 Trans-Siberian
railroad to Vladivostok
completed

1910 Union of South Africa
set up from Afrikaner
republics and Cape Colony

1914 World War I begins,
sparked by the assassina-
tion of Archduke Franz
Ferdinand in Sarajevo

1904–05 Russo–Japanese
War results in a series of
humiliating Russian defeats

1911 Chinese Revolution
overthrows Qing dynasty;
republic established 1912

1914 Japan takes over
many German colonies
in the Pacific

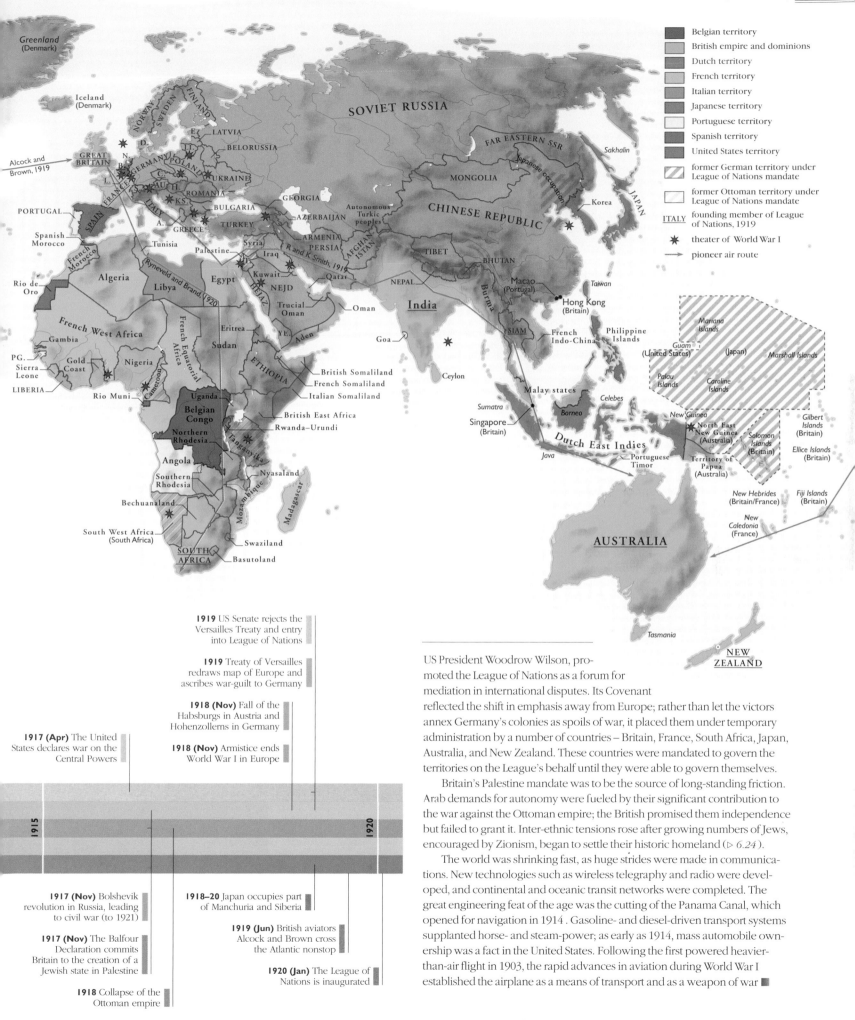

Belgian territory
British empire and dominions
Dutch territory
French territory
Italian territory
Japanese territory
Portuguese territory
Spanish territory
United States territory
former German territory under League of Nations mandate
former Ottoman territory under League of Nations mandate
ITALY founding member of League of Nations, 1919
✱ theater of World War I
→ pioneer air route

1919 US Senate rejects the Versailles Treaty and entry into League of Nations

1919 Treaty of Versailles redraws map of Europe and ascribes war-guilt to Germany

1918 (Nov) Fall of the Habsburgs in Austria and Hohenzollerns in Germany

1917 (Apr) The United States declares war on the Central Powers

1918 (Nov) Armistice ends World War I in Europe

1917 (Nov) Bolshevik revolution in Russia, leading to civil war (to 1921)

1918–20 Japan occupies part of Manchuria and Siberia

1917 (Nov) The Balfour Declaration commits Britain to the creation of a Jewish state in Palestine

1919 (Jun) British aviators Alcock and Brown cross the Atlantic nonstop

1920 (Jan) The League of Nations is inaugurated

1918 Collapse of the Ottoman empire

US President Woodrow Wilson, promoted the League of Nations as a forum for mediation in international disputes. Its Covenant reflected the shift in emphasis away from Europe; rather than let the victors annex Germany's colonies as spoils of war, it placed them under temporary administration by a number of countries – Britain, France, South Africa, Japan, Australia, and New Zealand. These countries were mandated to govern the territories on the League's behalf until they were able to govern themselves.

Britain's Palestine mandate was to be the source of long-standing friction. Arab demands for autonomy were fueled by their significant contribution to the war against the Ottoman empire; the British promised them independence but failed to grant it. Inter-ethnic tensions rose after growing numbers of Jews, encouraged by Zionism, began to settle their historic homeland (▷ 6.24).

The world was shrinking fast, as huge strides were made in communications. New technologies such as wireless telegraphy and radio were developed, and continental and oceanic transit networks were completed. The great engineering feat of the age was the cutting of the Panama Canal, which opened for navigation in 1914. Gasoline- and diesel-driven transport systems supplanted horse- and steam-power; as early as 1914, mass automobile ownership was a fact in the United States. Following the first powered heavier-than-air flight in 1903, the rapid advances in aviation during World War I established the airplane as a means of transport and as a weapon of war ■

The international order which emerged from World War I failed to match the intentions of allowing for national self-determination for all, and left a deep resentment in Germany, which was made to carry the blame for the war. As a result, stability was not achieved, and the post-Versailles order was overturned by extremist powers which by 1942 dominated much of the globe. The Axis powers, Germany and Japan, exploited the political vacuum left by the withdrawal of the United States and Russia from world affairs after the war, and by the effects of the depression on Britain and France. However, although 1942 marked the zenith of Axis power, their attacks on the two nascent superpowers made their eventual victory unlikely.

Soviet Russia emerged from its civil war of the early 1920s and turned in on itself as Stalin tried to build "socialism in one country" (▷ 6.15). The attempt to entrench Soviet power and catch up with the west was partially successful but extremely costly, as Stalin unleashed famine and terror on the Soviet Union.

In Europe, economic recovery was built on American loans. The US stock exchange crash of 1929 precipitated the global economic collapse known as the Great Depression. Its effect was to increase the appeal of fascist or extreme rightwing schemes of national regeneration in countries dissatisfied with the outcome of the peace settlements of 1919–23 (notably Germany). Governments everywhere looked to protect their interests by erecting tariff barriers and closed trading blocs, which further depressed the world economy.

The United States became isolated from international affairs as it tried to resolve its internal problems, and Britain and France were left to try to contain fascist expansion. But, although the depression began to lift in the late 1930s, both were economically too weak and too preoccupied by their global commitments to act effectively (▷ 6.07). They feared the prospect of fighting on three fronts – against Germany in Europe, Italy in the Mediterranean, and Japan in Asia. Their empires were potentially unstable – especially British India, where the nationalist Congress Party was growing in strength (▷ 6.18) – as were their domestic economies and societies.

The League of Nations reacted impotently to a series of crises in the 1930s – an Italian invasion of Ethiopia and German invasions of the Rhineland, Austria, Czechoslovakia – and thereby lost its credibility. France and Britain tried but failed to preserve peace through negotiation, alliances

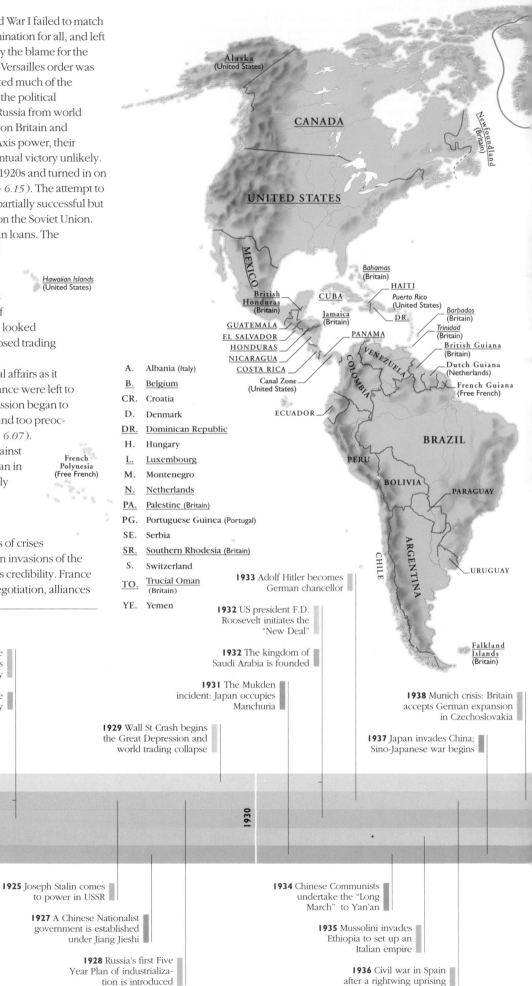

A.	Albania (Italy)
B.	Belgium
CR.	Croatia
D.	Denmark
DR.	Dominican Republic
H.	Hungary
L.	Luxembourg
M.	Montenegro
N.	Netherlands
PA.	Palestine (Britain)
PG.	Portuguese Guinea (Portugal)
SE.	Serbia
SR.	Southern Rhodesia (Britain)
S.	Switzerland
TO.	Trucial Oman (Britain)
YE.	Yemen

TIMELINE

The Americas
Europe
Middle East
Africa
Asia and Australasia

1920 — 1930

1923 France occupies the Ruhr; hyperinflation results in Germany

1923 Foundation of the modern republic of Turkey

1921 The Russian civil war ends with a Bolshevik victory

1929 Wall St Crash begins the Great Depression and world trading collapse

1931 The Mukden incident: Japan occupies Manchuria

1932 The kingdom of Saudi Arabia is founded

1932 US president F.D. Roosevelt initiates the "New Deal"

1933 Adolf Hitler becomes German chancellor

1938 Munich crisis: Britain accepts German expansion in Czechoslovakia

1937 Japan invades China; Sino-Japanese war begins

1922 Mussolini marches on Rome, establishing the first Fascist government

1925 Joseph Stalin comes to power in USSR

1934 Chinese Communists undertake the "Long March" to Yan'an

1922 Washington Naval Agreement limits Japanese naval power in the Pacific

1927 A Chinese Nationalist government is established under Jiang Jieshi

1935 Mussolini invades Ethiopia to set up an Italian empire

1928 Russia's first Five Year Plan of industrialization is introduced

1936 Civil war in Spain after a rightwing uprising against the government

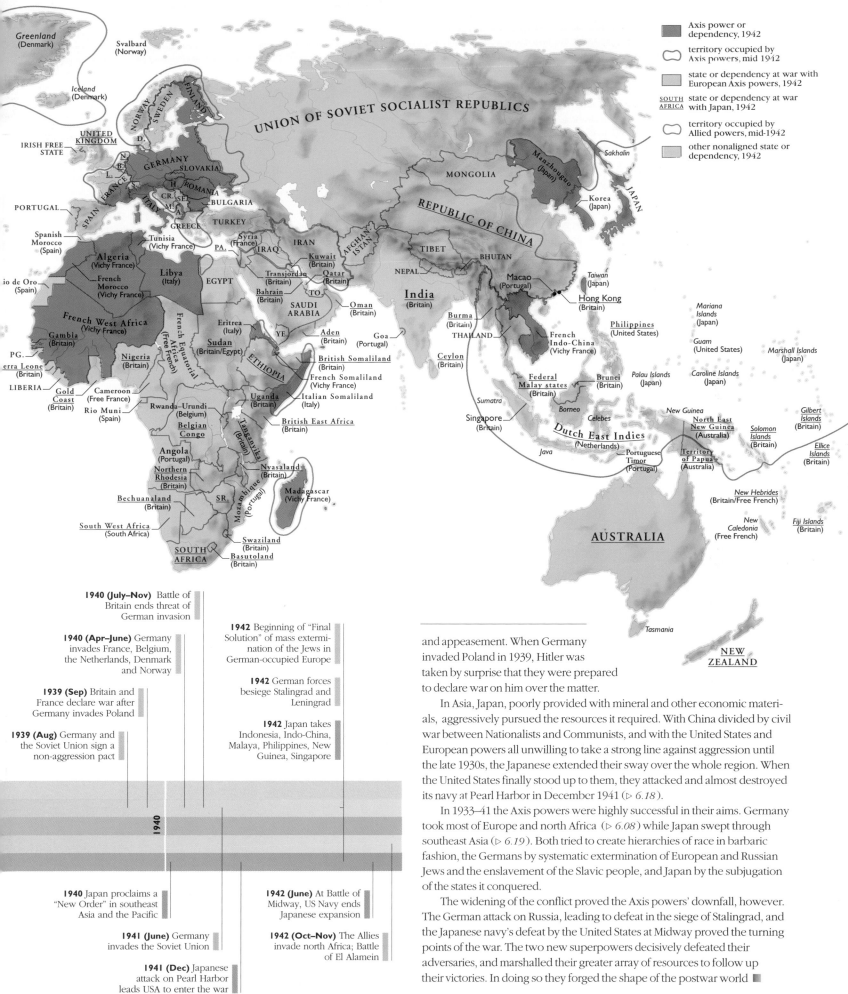

Legend:
- Axis power or dependency, 1942
- territory occupied by Axis powers, mid 1942
- state or dependency at war with European Axis powers, 1942
- SOUTH AFRICA — state or dependency at war with Japan, 1942
- territory occupied by Allied powers, mid-1942
- other nonaligned state or dependency, 1942

1940 (July–Nov) Battle of Britain ends threat of German invasion

1940 (Apr–June) Germany invades France, Belgium, the Netherlands, Denmark and Norway

1939 (Sep) Britain and France declare war after Germany invades Poland

1939 (Aug) Germany and the Soviet Union sign a non-aggression pact

1940 Japan proclaims a "New Order" in southeast Asia and the Pacific

1941 (June) Germany invades the Soviet Union

1941 (Dec) Japanese attack on Pearl Harbor leads USA to enter the war

1942 Beginning of "Final Solution" of mass extermination of the Jews in German-occupied Europe

1942 German forces besiege Stalingrad and Leningrad

1942 Japan takes Indonesia, Indo-China, Malaya, Philippines, New Guinea, Singapore

1942 (June) At Battle of Midway, US Navy ends Japanese expansion

1942 (Oct–Nov) The Allies invade north Africa; Battle of El Alamein

1940

and appeasement. When Germany invaded Poland in 1939, Hitler was taken by surprise that they were prepared to declare war on him over the matter.

In Asia, Japan, poorly provided with mineral and other economic materials, aggressively pursued the resources it required. With China divided by civil war between Nationalists and Communists, and with the United States and European powers all unwilling to take a strong line against aggression until the late 1930s, the Japanese extended their sway over the whole region. When the United States finally stood up to them, they attacked and almost destroyed its navy at Pearl Harbor in December 1941 (▷ 6.18).

In 1933–41 the Axis powers were highly successful in their aims. Germany took most of Europe and north Africa (▷ 6.08) while Japan swept through southeast Asia (▷ 6.19). Both tried to create hierarchies of race in barbaric fashion, the Germans by systematic extermination of European and Russian Jews and the enslavement of the Slavic people, and Japan by the subjugation of the states it conquered.

The widening of the conflict proved the Axis powers' downfall, however. The German attack on Russia, leading to defeat in the siege of Stalingrad, and the Japanese navy's defeat by the United States at Midway proved the turning points of the war. The two new superpowers decisively defeated their adversaries, and marshalled their greater array of resources to follow up their victories. In doing so they forged the shape of the postwar world ∎

T he United States had entered World War II at the end of 1941 to prevent the domination of Europe and Asia by totalitarian regimes. Yet by 1950 the world was again polarized. The split of the wartime Allies (the United States, the Soviet Union and Britain) created power blocs whose rivalry was consolidated by the outbreak of war in Korea, a conflict by proxy between the democratic capitalist "west" and authoritarian Communist "east".

The Axis powers were in retreat from 1942. Japan was pushed across the Pacific by American military and naval might (▷ 6.19); Germany was beaten by the Soviet Union at Stalingrad and Kursk; British and American troops landed in Italy and Normandy as their airforces pounded German cities (▷ 6.09). When the war ended after the dropping of atomic bombs on Hiroshima and Nagasaki, 50 million people, mostly civilians, had died.

As the tide of war turned, the patterns of the postwar world were being laid down. The United Nations Organization (UNO), a new body for resolving international disputes, was set up, but it was clear that the United States and Soviet Union would be the world's strongest powers. The United States and Britain tried to win the trust of the USSR, which had forced the Germans from eastern Europe. They also accepted the incorporation of the Baltic states into the Soviet Union, the annexation of Polish territory and the forced repatriation of Soviet prisoners of war.

The Soviet Union soon become involved in the internal affairs of the states of eastern Europe, however, and the wartime lines of demarcation became the boundaries of a divided postwar Europe. The United States supplied massive aid to prevent the devastated countries of western Europe from succumbing to Communism. In response the Soviet Union created Comecon, a system of interstate economic planning designed to strengthen its hold on eastern Europe. Germany remained divided, a division reinforced by the Soviet blockade of the western zones of Berlin in 1948–49, when Britain and the United States kept the city supplied by air (▷ 6.10).

American aid to Europe followed the Truman doctrine of 1947, which committed the United States to supporting "free peoples" in the struggle against totalitarianism. Initially the struggle against Communism was a European one: in much of Asia, the immediate struggle was for independence from colonial rule.

A.	Albania
AU.	Austria (Allied occupied)
B.	Belgium
C.	Czechoslovakia
D.	Denmark
EG.	East Germany
H.	Hungary
L.	Luxembourg
N.	Netherlands
PG.	Portuguese Guinea (Portugal)
SR.	Southern Rhodesia (Britain)
S.	Switzerland
TO.	Trucial Oman (Britain)
WG.	West Germany (Allied occupied)
YE.	Yemen
YU.	Yugoslavia

1944 (June) D-Day: a huge Allied force invades northern France

1943 June) Allied forces land in Italy

1942–43 (Jan) Defeat at Stalingrad ends German expansion to the east

1945 (Oct) The United Nations Organization (UNO) is created

1945 (July) Churchill loses British election; Labour wins power

1945 (May) Germany surrenders, ending war in Europe

1947 (Mar) The "Truman Doctrine" is announced

1947 The United States withdraw from China

1948 (Apr) Organization of American States is founded

TIMELINE

| The Americas |
| Europe |
| Middle East |
| Africa |
| Asia and Australasia |

1944   1946   1948

1943 (May) Axis forces are evacuated from north Africa

1943 (July) Soviet forces defeat Germans at Kursk

1944 (July) The International Monetary Fund (IMF) is founded

1945 (Aug–Sep) Japan surrenders after atomic bombs are dropped at Hiroshima and Nagasaki

1945 (Sep) North and South Korea independent

1945 (Oct) The Arab league is founded

1946 (July) The Philippines gain their independence

1947 (June) US "Marshall Aid" to assist recovery in western Europe proposed

1947 (Aug) India and Pakistan gain independence from Britain

1948 (Feb) A Communist coup takes place in Czechoslovakia

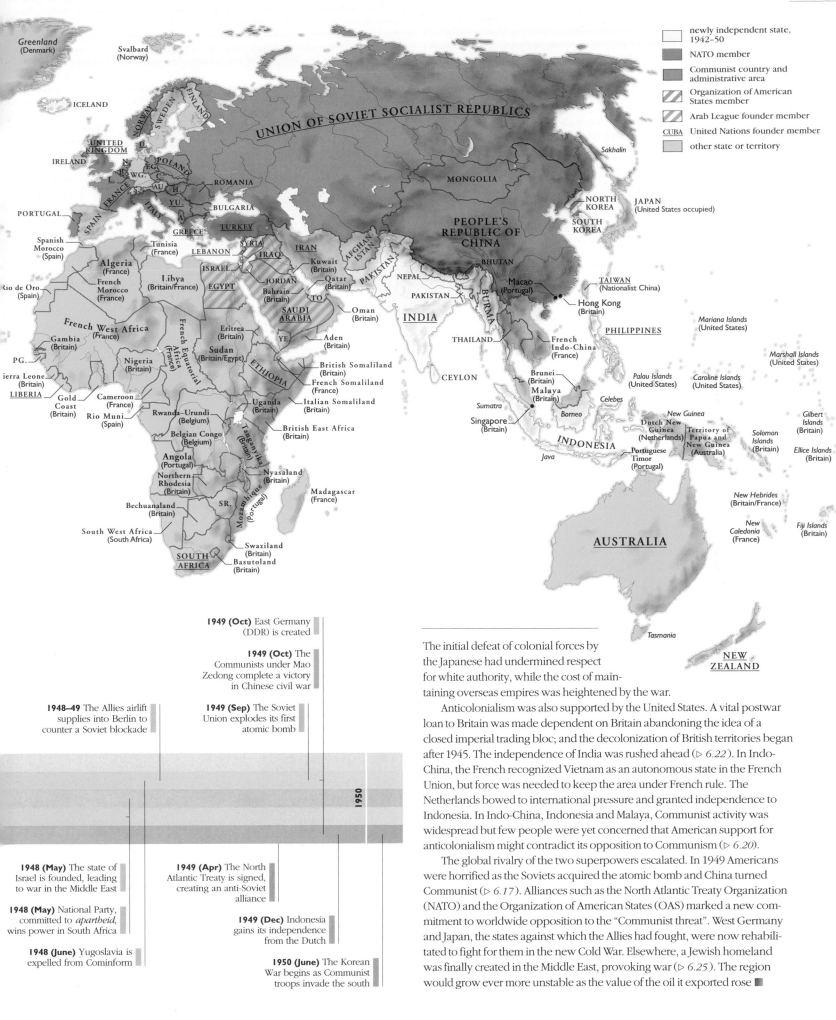

newly independent state, 1942–50

NATO member

Communist country and administrative area

Organization of American States member

Arab League founder member

CUBA **United Nations founder member**

other state or territory

1949 (Oct) East Germany (DDR) is created

1949 (Oct) The Communists under Mao Zedong complete a victory in Chinese civil war

1948–49 The Allies airlift supplies into Berlin to counter a Soviet blockade

1949 (Sep) The Soviet Union explodes its first atomic bomb

1950

1948 (May) The state of Israel is founded, leading to war in the Middle East

1948 (May) National Party, committed to *apartheid*, wins power in South Africa

1948 (June) Yugoslavia is expelled from Cominform

1949 (Apr) The North Atlantic Treaty is signed, creating an anti-Soviet alliance

1949 (Dec) Indonesia gains its independence from the Dutch

1950 (June) The Korean War begins as Communist troops invade the south

The initial defeat of colonial forces by the Japanese had undermined respect for white authority, while the cost of maintaining overseas empires was heightened by the war.

Anticolonialism was also supported by the United States. A vital postwar loan to Britain was made dependent on Britain abandoning the idea of a closed imperial trading bloc; and the decolonization of British territories began after 1945. The independence of India was rushed ahead (▷ 6.22). In Indo-China, the French recognized Vietnam as an autonomous state in the French Union, but force was needed to keep the area under French rule. The Netherlands bowed to international pressure and granted independence to Indonesia. In Indo-China, Indonesia and Malaya, Communist activity was widespread but few people were yet concerned that American support for anticolonialism might contradict its opposition to Communism (▷ 6.20).

The global rivalry of the two superpowers escalated. In 1949 Americans were horrified as the Soviets acquired the atomic bomb and China turned Communist (▷ 6.17). Alliances such as the North Atlantic Treaty Organization (NATO) and the Organization of American States (OAS) marked a new commitment to worldwide opposition to the "Communist threat". West Germany and Japan, the states against which the Allies had fought, were now rehabilitated to fight for them in the new Cold War. Elsewhere, a Jewish homeland was finally created in the Middle East, provoking war (▷ 6.25). The region would grow ever more unstable as the value of the oil it exported rose ■

By 1974 rivalry between the Soviet Union and the United States still dominated international affairs. The USSR guarded its European satellite states jealously. When, in 1956, Hungary tried to break free from the Soviet-dominated Warsaw Pact, the Red Army crushed the revolution. In 1961 the Berlin Wall was erected to enforce Soviet control over East Germany. And in 1968, Warsaw Pact forces ended the Czech attempt to introduce "socialism with a human face" (▷ 6.10). Yet Yugoslavia, Albania and Romania all won some independence from Soviet control.

In western Europe, institutions were set up to integrate the economies of the main industrial nations. The European Economic Community (EEC) was seen as a step to political union and the creation of a European superstate, but most countries (France was the main exception) still relied on the United States membership of NATO for security from possible Soviet aggression.

It was in America's "backyard" that superpower rivalry was most apparent. The Cuban missile crisis of 1962 brought a real threat of nuclear war until the Soviet Union withdrew its missiles from within range of the American mainland (▷ 6.14). Anxiety for the spread of Communism also lay behind the United States involvement in southeast Asia. Fearing that neighboring countries would fall to Communism (the "domino effect"), the United States sent men and dollars to prop up an unpopular regime in South Vietnam. It was another war by proxy but, unlike Korea, American withdrawal from Vietnam led to the collapse of South Vietnam and the descent of Cambodia into civil war (▷ 6.21).

Conflict between China and the Soviet Union, underlain by centuries of mutual suspicion, showed that America's opponents were not a unified bloc, however. The Chinese version of Communism was different from the Soviet, as China tried to develop a locally-based economy centered on communes, in contrast to the centralized bureaucracies of the Soviet Union. Chinese Communism was more applicable to non-industrial societies; Communist insurgents worldwide, especially in southeast Asia where rapid decolonization was followed by political upheaval, turned to it for inspiration and support. Eventual American recognition of the Sino-Soviet split led in the early 1970s to an attempt to exploit it and brought a new era of détente (▷ 6.20).

In Africa, opposition to imperial rule was the driving force. The Suez crisis of 1956 showed the weakness of the old imperial powers, and a wave of

A.   Albania
AU. Austria
B.   Belgium
CAR. Central African Republic
C.   Czechoslovakia
D.   Denmark
DR. Dominican Republic
DY. People's Democratic Republic of Yemen
EG. East Germany
H.   Hungary
LE. Lebanon
L.   Luxembourg

N.   Netherlands
NV. North Vietnam
S.   Switzerland
U.   United Arab Emirates
WG. West Germany
YA. Yemen Arab Republic
YU. Yugoslavia

TIMELINE

1956 Hungarian revolt is crushed by the Warsaw Pact

1956 Egypt nationalizes the Suez Canal; Britain's invasion attempt fails

1955 The Warsaw Pact is created as a Soviet-bloc opponent of NATO

1962 Cuban missile crisis, as US president Kennedy insists on withdrawal of Soviet nuclear missiles

1961 The Nonaligned Conference is founded: OPEC is founded

1961 The Berlin Wall is built

1965 US troops are sent to Vietnam, and open bombing of the North begins

1965 India–Pakistan war

The Americas
Europe
Middle East
Africa
Asia and Australasia

1955   1960   1965

1951 USA, Australia and New Zealand, sign a defense treaty

1954 Algerian uprising begins against French rule

1954 Laos, Cambodia, South and North Vietnam gain independence

1957 The European Economic Community (EEC) is created

1957 The Soviet Sputnik II, the first artificial satellite, is launched

1958 Mao initiates the "Great Leap Forward" in China

1960 Fifteen African countries gain their independence

1962 US military advisors are sent to assist the South Vietnam regime

1963 Sino–Soviet split as Mao and Khrushchev determine different paths

1966-70 Mao Zedong leads the Cultural Revolution in China

1967 Israel defeats Egypt and the other Arab nations in the Six Day War

newly independent state, 1950-74

NATO member

Communist country and administrative area

Warsaw Pact member

Arab League member

GABON OPEC member

other state or territory

Greenland (Denmark)

Svalbard (Norway)

ICELAND

NORWAY SWEDEN FINLAND

UNITED KINGDOM

IRELAND

UNION OF SOVIET SOCIALIST REPUBLICS

D.

N.

B.

WG.

EG.

C.

AU.

L.

FRANCE

POLAND

ROMANIA

H.

YU.

A.

BULGARIA

PORTUGAL

SPAIN

ITALY

MALTA

GREECE

TURKEY

Gibraltar (Britain)

MOROCCO

TUNISIA

CYPRUS

LE.

SYRIA

IRAQ

KUWAIT

ISRAEL

JORDAN

QATAR

BAHRAIN

U.

SAUDI ARABIA

YA.

OMAN

DY.

Western Sahara (Morocco)

ALGERIA

LIBYA

EGYPT

MAURITANIA

MALI

NIGER

CHAD

SUDAN

CAPE VERDE

SENEGAL

UPPER VOLTA

GAMBIA

GUINEA BISSAU

GUINEA

SIERRA LEONE

LIBERIA

IVORY COAST

GHANA

BENIN

TOGO

NIGERIA

CAMEROON

CAR.

ETHIOPIA

French Somaliland (France)

SOMALIA

EQUATORIAL GUINEA

GABON

CONGO

UGANDA

RWANDA

ZAIRE

BURUNDI

KENYA

TANZANIA

Comoros (France)

MALDIVES

Angola (Portugal)

ZAMBIA

RHODESIA

MALAWI

Mozambique (Portugal)

MADAGASCAR

MAURITIUS

BOTSWANA

South West Africa (South Africa)

SWAZILAND

SOUTH AFRICA

LESOTHO

AFGHANISTAN

IRAN

PAKISTAN

NEPAL

BHUTAN

INDIA

BANGLADESH

BURMA

MONGOLIA

PEOPLE'S REPUBLIC OF CHINA

Sakhalin

NORTH KOREA

SOUTH KOREA

JAPAN

Macao (Portugal)

Hong Kong (Britain)

TAIWAN

N.V.

LAOS

SRI LANKA

THAILAND

SOUTH VIETNAM

CAMBODIA

PHILIPPINES

Mariana Islands (United States)

Marshall Islands (United States)

Brunei (Britain)

MALAYSIA

Palau Islands (United States)

Caroline Islands (United States)

Sumatra

SINGAPORE

Borneo

Celebes

New Guinea

Papua New Guinea (Australia)

NAURU

Solomon Islands (Britain)

Gilbert Islands (Britain)

Ellice Islands (Britain)

INDONESIA

Java

Portuguese Timor (Portugal)

New Hebrides (Britain/France)

FIJI

New Caledonia (France)

TONGA

AUSTRALIA

Tasmania

NEW ZEALAND

1974 US president Nixon resigns following the Watergate scandal

1972 US president Nixon visits Beijing and Moscow

1972 Arms Limitation Treaty between the United States and Soviet Union

1971 East Pakistan secedes to become Bangladesh

1969 The US space agency NASA puts the first men on the Moon

1970

1968 Student risings take place in France, the United States and other western countries

1968 "Prague Spring" reforms in Czechoslovakia are crushed by Warsaw Pact forces

1973 US-backed coup against an elected Marxist government in Chile

1973 Arab states fail to defeat Israel in the Yom Kippur War

1973 OPEC restricts flow of oil to world markets

decolonization arose in the 1960s as Britain and France gave up their possessions. Instability and disorder frequently ensued while novice administrations tried to cope with mounting problems in countries that had often been arbitrarily defined by the colonial powers themselves. Civil war was a feature of this era for many African nations, the worst in the Congo (Zaire) and Nigeria. To some, Communism seemed to provide answers, but by 1974 only Ethiopia had an avowedly Marxist government (▷ 6.27). Even the more experienced governments of India and Pakistan faced difficulties in adjusting to decolonization (▷ 6.22).

The "nonaligned movement" was founded in 1961 by those countries that did not wish to be superpower clients. The United Nations, too, had some success in speaking for the world's newer countries. Another power center emerged when the oil-producing nations – organized as OPEC – restricted oil supplies and raised prices in response to western support for Israel. While the Arab states had little success in using Soviet arms against Israel, this economic weapon made them important players on the world stage (▷ 6.25).

The oil crisis disrupted the developing countries most severely, as their debt burden rose sharply. Its effects were also profound in Europe and the United States where the cost of state welfare provision grew ever higher, while the economies of the Soviet bloc were also under strain. In 1974, the United States and the Soviet Union were unquestionably still the superpowers but assumptions about national and international politics were being rethought ■

The years from 1975 saw seismic shifts in world politics. The end of the Cold War permitted longstanding problems in Europe, the Middle East and Africa to be addressed. Fears of imminent nuclear, environmental or demographic disaster, widely predicted in the preceding decades, abated by the late 1990s, though the world's future political shape was still uncertain.

Central to these changes was the collapse of the Soviet Union. Under Leonid Brezhnev the country stagnated, and the *détente*, or cooling of the international tension, of the 1970s came to an end with a Soviet invasion of Afghanistan. The United States emerged from its post-Vietnam crisis of confidence under the tough-talking president Ronald Reagan, changing the mood in the early 1980s. The soaring costs of arms production, combined with the Soviet Union's technological deficit, led the new leader Mikhail Gorbachev to try to improve superpower relations and liberalize the Soviet system. In doing so he unleashed disintegrative forces he could not control (▷ 6.16).

Gorbachev did not resist the demands for increased independence from many of the USSR's eastern European satellites. In 1989–90 the peoples of eastern Europe took the opportunity to overthrow their Communist governments. In the Soviet Union itself the separate republics seceded from the Union and formed the Commonwealth of Independent States. The old order was not so easily replaced in Yugoslavia, which was ripped apart by ethnic conflict (▷ 6.11).

Meanwhile, greater centralization was occurring in western Europe, where the European Community (later the European Union) expanded in size, abolished many border restrictions and initiated moves toward political and economic union.

The collapse of the Soviet Union led to change in Africa, where problems of decolonization and debt had been exacerbated by superpower conflict. South Africa's role in opposing the spread of Communism vanished, and as American support for the regime was withdrawn the burden of upholding *apartheid* grew. South Africa ceased interfering in the politics of other countries of the region, and in 1994 achieved majority rule under the charismatic president Nelson Mandela (▷ 6.28).

In the Middle East, both the west and the Soviet Union felt vulnerable to the threat posed by renascent Islam to oil supplies and the loyalty of the Muslim areas of the USSR. The Islamist takeover of Iran in 1979 complicated the politics of the Middle East: Iraq was supported in a long war with

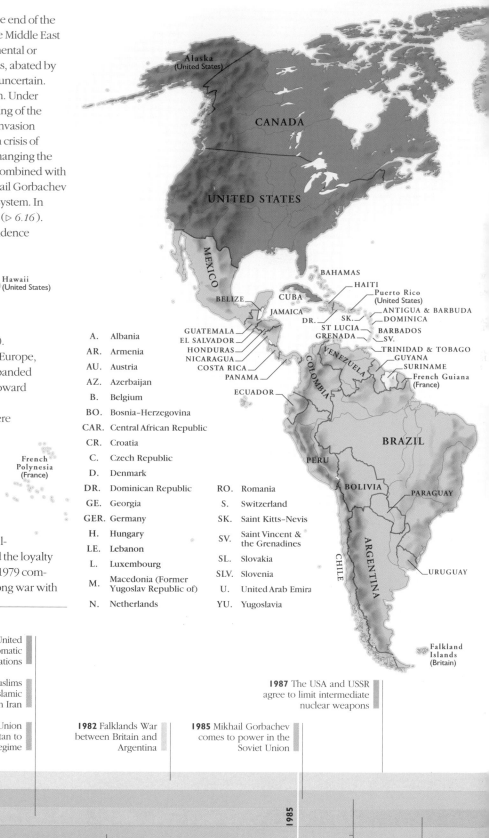

A.	Albania		
AR.	Armenia		
AU.	Austria		
AZ.	Azerbaijan		
B.	Belgium		
BO.	Bosnia–Herzegovina		
CAR.	Central African Republic		
CR.	Croatia		
C.	Czech Republic		
D.	Denmark		
DR.	Dominican Republic	RO.	Romania
GE.	Georgia	S.	Switzerland
GER.	Germany	SK.	Saint Kitts–Nevis
H.	Hungary	SV.	Saint Vincent & the Grenadines
LE.	Lebanon		
L.	Luxembourg	SL.	Slovakia
M.	Macedonia (Former Yugoslav Republic of)	SLV.	Slovenia
		U.	United Arab Emira
N.	Netherlands	YU.	Yugoslavia

TIMELINE

The Americas
Europe
Middle East
Africa
Asia and Australasia

1975 — 1985

1979 China and the United States establish diplomatic relations

1979 Shiite Muslims lead an Islamic revolution in Iran

1975 The Helsinki Agreement between the USA and USSR establishes an atmosphere of détente

1979 The Soviet Union invades Afghanistan to support the Marxist regime

1982 Falklands War between Britain and Argentina

1987 The USA and USSR agree to limit intermediate nuclear weapons

1985 Mikhail Gorbachev comes to power in the Soviet Union

1975 Angola and Mozambique gain independence

1980 Zimbabwe wins independence under majority rule

1986 A nuclear plant at Chernobyl, USSR, explodes, causing damage throughout northern Europe

1975 The US-backed South Vietnam regime falls

1984 Indian prime minister Indira Gandhi is assassinated by Sikh bodyguards

1986 The United States bombs Libya

1977 Egypt's president Sadat visits Israel, initiating the Middle Eastern peace process

1988 Iran and Iraq end the First Gulf War (begun 1980)

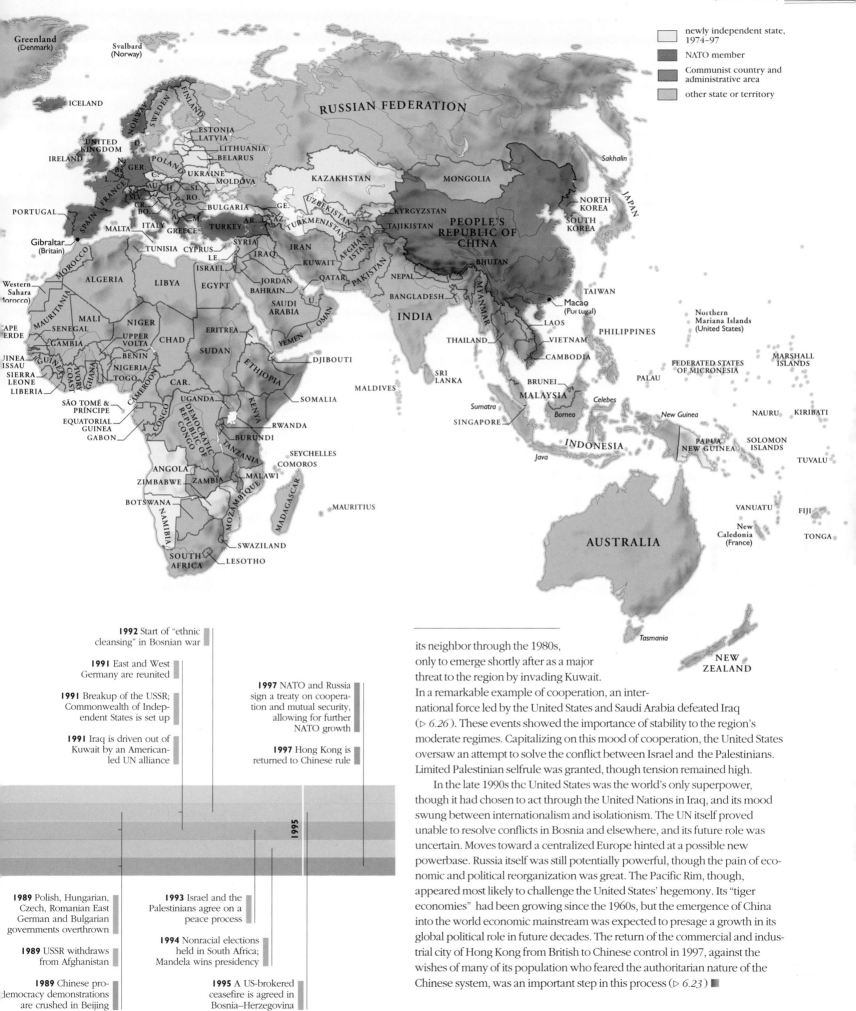

newly independent state,
1974–97

NATO member

Communist country and
administrative area

other state or territory

1992 Start of "ethnic
cleansing" in Bosnian war

1991 East and West
Germany are reunited

1991 Breakup of the USSR;
Commonwealth of Independent States is set up

1991 Iraq is driven out of
Kuwait by an American-led UN alliance

1997 NATO and Russia
sign a treaty on cooperation and mutual security,
allowing for further
NATO growth

1997 Hong Kong is
returned to Chinese rule

1995

1989 Polish, Hungarian,
Czech, Romanian East
German and Bulgarian
governments overthrown

1989 USSR withdraws
from Afghanistan

1989 Chinese prodemocracy demonstrations
are crushed in Beijing

1993 Israel and the
Palestinians agree on a
peace process

1994 Nonracial elections
held in South Africa;
Mandela wins presidency

1995 A US-brokered
ceasefire is agreed in
Bosnia–Herzegovina

its neighbor through the 1980s,
only to emerge shortly after as a major
threat to the region by invading Kuwait.
In a remarkable example of cooperation, an international force led by the United States and Saudi Arabia defeated Iraq
(▷ 6.26). These events showed the importance of stability to the region's
moderate regimes. Capitalizing on this mood of cooperation, the United States
oversaw an attempt to solve the conflict between Israel and the Palestinians.
Limited Palestinian selfrule was granted, though tension remained high.

In the late 1990s the United States was the world's only superpower,
though it had chosen to act through the United Nations in Iraq, and its mood
swung between internationalism and isolationism. The UN itself proved
unable to resolve conflicts in Bosnia and elsewhere, and its future role was
uncertain. Moves toward a centralized Europe hinted at a possible new
powerbase. Russia itself was still potentially powerful, though the pain of economic and political reorganization was great. The Pacific Rim, though,
appeared most likely to challenge the United States' hegemony. Its "tiger
economies" had been growing since the 1960s, but the emergence of China
into the world economic mainstream was expected to presage a growth in its
global political role in future decades. The return of the commercial and industrial city of Hong Kong from British to Chinese control in 1997, against the
wishes of many of its population who feared the authoritarian nature of the
Chinese system, was an important step in this process (▷ 6.23) ∎

Before 1914, Europe had enjoyed unprecedent-ed prosperity, the fruit of industrialization and a century without a general war. Yet two alliances, the Allied powers (the United Kingdom, France and Russia), and the Central powers (Germany, Austria–Hungary and, later, the Ottoman empire), were pre-paring for war. The main reason was the ambition and the instability of Germany, Europe's newest, and strongest, industrial and military power.

Germany had enjoyed a period of rapid industri-alization, replacing Britain as the main motor of Europe's economy. Furthermore, its strength in iron, steel and coal production, and in the new electrical and chemical industries, was matched by a military machine second to none. In peace, Germany's geo-graphical position enabled it to exploit Europe's extensive rail and sea networks. In wartime, how-ever, it faced the prospect of fighting on two fronts.

Germany's rulers believed that its political stand-ing did not match its commercial and imperial ambi-tions. One of its oldest ambitions (one which brought it into conflict with Russia) was to expand eastward. Germany believed it was encircled by hostile powers and was intent on protecting its inter-ests, and those of Austria–Hungary, in southern Europe, the Ottoman empire and the Middle East.

In a long war, the strain of fighting on two fronts would inevitably tell. Military planners sought to combat this by launching a knockout blow against France and then transporting troops to the east to face the Russian army. But the plan failed when, in August 1914, war broke out following a crisis over Austrian and Russian influence in the Balkans. The exhausted German army was halted 80 kilometers (50 miles) short of Paris. The French army was swiftly mobilized and the transport network used shrewdly – even the Parisian taxi cabs were pressed into service to take soldiers to the front. Stalemate followed on the Western Front; the war was bogged down in trench warfare, as the defensive capabilities of the machine gun dominated the war until

Map labels

Orkney Islands · Scapa Flow · Cromarty · Glasgow · Rosyth · Edinburgh · Belfast · UNITED KINGDOM 9.5m · Newcastle · Dublin · Liverpool · Hull · Birmingham · Cardiff · London · Harwich · Lusitania sunk by U-boat, May 1915 · Plymouth · Portsmouth · Dover · Dunkirk · Calais · Cherbourg · Portland · La Havre · Amiens · Reims · Brest · Paris · Nantes · FRANCE 8.2m · Bordeaux · Toulouse · Bilbao · Santander · Marseille · Toulon · Zaragoza · SPAIN · Barcelona · Madrid · PORTUGAL Allied power Mar 1916 · Lisbon · Valencia · Córdoba · Seville · Cádiz · Tangier · Gibraltar to Britain · Spanish Morocco to Spain · Algiers · Algeria to France · Tunis · Tunisia French protectorate

North Sea · Bergen · Christiania · SWEDEN · Stockholm · NORWAY · Göteborg · Copenhagen · DENMARK · Memel · Gumbinnen Aug 1914 · Königsberg · Danzig · Jutland May–June 1916 · Dogger Bank Jan 1915 · Heligoland · Kiel · Hamburg · Stettin · Tannenberg Aug 1914 · Warsaw Sep–Nov 1914 · Bremerhaven · Wilhelmshaven · Bremen · Berlin · Lodz Nov 1914 · Amsterdam · Hanover · Oder · Kraków · Hook of Holland · NETHERLANDS · Essen · GERMAN EMPIRE 13.25m · Dresden · Brussels · Cologne · Gorlice-Tarnow May 1915 · BELGIUM 0.38m · Frankfurt · Prague · Limanowa Dec 1914 · LUXEMBOURG · AUSTRO-HUNGARIAN EMPIRE 9.0m · Munich · Vienna · Basel · Salzburg · Budapest · SWITZERLAND · LIECHTENSTEIN · Trento 1918 · Caporetto Oct–Nov 1917 · Geneva · Lyon · Milan · Battles of the Isonzo June 1915–Sep 1917 · Vittorio Veneto Oct–Nov 1918 · Trieste · Turin · Venice · Pola · Belgrade Dec 1914 · Genoa · Bologna · SAN MARINO · Bosnia–Herzegovina · Corsica to France · Florence · ITALY Allied power Apr 1915 5.6m · Sarajevo · MONTENEGRO capitulated to Central powers Jan 1916 0.05m · Rome · Cattaro · Durazzo · Sardinia to Italy · Naples · Taranto · Brindisi · Balearic Islands to Spain · Palermo · Messina · Sicily · Malta to Britain

1914–19 · 1918 · 1914 · 7 · 5 · 6 · 1 · Baltic Sea · Ebro · Douro · Tagus · Guadiana · Loire · Rhine · Elbe · Danube · ANDORRA

TIMELINE

General

1914 (28 June) Assassination of the Austrian Archduke Franz Ferdinand by a Serb nationalist at Sarajevo

1914 (Aug) Germany declares war on Russia and France; Britain, France and Russia on Germany and Austria–Hungary

1915 (Apr) Allied landings at Gallipoli

1915 (Apr) Italy joins the Allied war effort

1915 (May) US liner *Lusitania* is sunk by a German U-boat

1916 (Apr) Easter Rising in Dublin against British rule in Ireland

1916 (May) The British and German fleets meet at Jutland

1917 (Mar) Czar Nicholas II abdicates in Russia

1917 (Apr) The USA declares war on the Central powers

1917 (Nov) Bolshevik revolution in Russia

1918 (Jan) US president Wilson publishes a 14-point peace plan

1918 (Nov) The Kaiser abdicates and an armistice is signed between Germany and the Allies

Western Front

1914 (Aug) Germans launch Schlieffen plan

1914 (Sep) Germans halted at the Battle of the Marne

1916 (Feb–Dec) German offensive at Verdun

1916 (July–Nov) Expensive British offensive on Somme

1917 (July) Third Battle of Ypres (Passchendaele)

1917 (Nov–Dec) Tanks used by British at battle of Cambrai

1918 (Mar) Germans threaten Paris in Ludendorff offensive

1918 (Aug) Allies break through German lines

Eastern Front

1914 (Aug) The Russian advance into Germany is halted at Tannenberg

1915 (Oct) Austria-Hungary invades Serbia

1916 (Sep) Central powers defeat Romania

1916 (Oct) The Russian Brusilov offensive ends

1917 (July) Last Russian offensive of the war

1917 (Dec) Bolsheviks sign an armistice with Germany

1918 (Mar) Treaty of Brest-Litovsk ends war in Russia

1915 · 1916 · 1917 · 1918

1 The assassination of the Austrian Archduke Franz Ferdinand on 28 June 1914 by a Serbian began the descent into war. Austria declared war on Serbia; Russia mobilized; Germany declared war on Russia and France, and Britain on Germany, by 4 August.

2 The German offensive in the west began with the reduction of the Belgian fortresses around Liège.

3 The French stopped the German advance on Paris on the Marne in September 1914.

4 The unsuccessful Allied landings at Gallipoli were intended to win control of the Dardanelles and secure a sea route to Russia.

5 The sinking of the passenger liner *Lusitania* by a German U-boat in 1915 did much to turn American sentiment in favor of the Allies.

6 The war on the Eastern Front never declined into trench warfare and strategic mobility was preserved; casualties, though, were as heavy as in the west.

7 Although Britain's fleet suffered heavier losses than Germany's, the Battle of Jutland confirmed Britain's control of the seas.

new offensive tactics, using tanks and artillery more intelligently, were developed in 1917. Despite early victories against the Russians, the Germans now had to cope with war on two fronts.

In the Balkans, victories by the Central powers over Serbia and Romania (and the entry of the Ottomans into the war in 1915) seemed to create the kind of central European political and trading empire that Germany wanted. In 1917 czarist Russia collapsed, its economy and political system exhausted by the demands of the war. Early in 1918, its revolutionary Bolshevik government withdrew entirely from the war, leaving Germany in control of much of the Ukraine and southern Russia. German colonial ambitions in Europe seemed satisfied at last.

Yet the Central Powers could not match the Allies for men, materiel, wealth or opportunities. During 1916 Allied economic power began to assert itself. Britain developed a war economy, supplying munitions and other war materiel manufactured at home or imported from the United States and the British empire. Britain's financial superiority allowed it to bankroll the Allied war effort. The German navy tried to break Allied lines of supply by torpedoing British shipping; but when unrestricted submarine warfare began in 1917, the United States was prompted to join the war on the Allied side – though more significantly as a supplier of munitions rather than as a belligerent. The Allies blockaded German ports, intensifying German economic difficulties.

The years 1916–17 saw several desperately costly battles on the Western Front – notably Verdun, the Somme, Ypres – made possible by the huge buildup of arms on the Allied side. The Central powers decided to make a tactical withdrawal on the Western Front and to militarize the economy at home. The result was disastrous. By November 1918, the German army had not retreated to within its own borders (it had in fact made large advances the previous spring), but it was in clear disarray, while food and fuel shortages led to the country collapsing from within. Kaiser Wilhelm II abdicated, as did the emperor of Austria–Hungary. The Allies were clearly in a position to dictate the terms of the peace.

Legend:

borders, 1914

Allied powers and associates, June 1917

Central powers, June 1917

Central power capitulating before Nov 1918

neutral state

furthest advance of Central powers

furthest advance of Russian forces

Armistice line, 11 Nov 1918

Western Front

front line, 5 Sep 1914

front line, 29 Dec 1914

front line, 11 Nov 1918

German offensive, 16 Aug–5 Sep 1914

German offensive, 5 Apr–17 July 1918

furthest extent of German advance, 17 July 1918

Allied counteroffensive, 26 Sep–10 Nov 1918

Russian territory lost at the Treaty of Brest-Litovsk

main area of U-boat activity, 1915–18

naval base

Allied naval blockade

armaments, engineering and metal industry

chemical industry

shipbuilding industry

9.5m maximum mobilized forces (millions)

railroad

shipping route to United States and Canada

0   600 km
0   400 mi

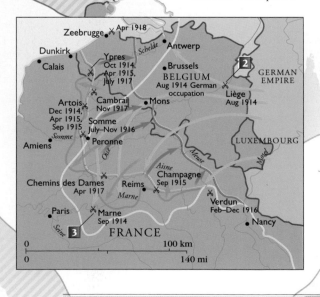

0   100 km
0   140 mi

See also 6.01 (the war outside Europe);
6.07 (Europe between the wars)

World War I destroyed the old order in central and eastern Europe: the fall of the Romanovs (Russia), Habsburgs (Austria–Hungary) and Hohenzollerns (Germany) brought political instability that compounded the economic and social dislocation of the war. Extremism flourished across central Europe, with Marxist revolutions in several major cities being countered by a rightwing backlash.

The peace treaties failed to create a lasting settlement, and provided instead the grounds for future discontent. United States president Wilson hoped that ethnically homogeneous nation-states could eradicate the nationalist rivalries and squabbling over territory that appeared to have caused the war; but this proved impossible. Two new states (Czechoslovakia and the Kingdom of the Serbs, Croats and Slovenes – later Yugoslavia) and one reconstituted one (Poland) assembled many ethnic groups within arbitrary borders, and nationalist groups were often disappointed in disputed areas. Everywhere populations were on the move. Italy, its promises from the Allies for territory unfulfilled, set out to take the territory it claimed by force, as did Poland.

The Treaty of Versailles forced Germany to admit guilt for starting the war and to pay huge reparations to the Allies. It was forbidden to ally with Austria and was divided by the Polish Corridor, while three million ethnic Germans remained outside the state.

The League of Nations, set up to resolve the disputes that were bound to arise from the settlement, was hamstrung as the United States, the only power capable of giving weight to its decisions, declined to join. With Russia preoccupied with domestic affairs, Britain and France were left to deal with European issues alone. They were faced with the prospect of a renascent Germany avenging its grievances and filling the power vacuum created by the fall of the imperial monarchies. Both Britain and France were economically weak following the war and they sought to keep Germany weak as well. France occupied the Ruhr in 1923 to enforce payment of reparations, but the hyperinflation that ensued provided fertile ground for extremist groups in Germany. With

Legend:

area temporarily independent
—— border, 1921

dictatorships by 1 Sep 1939
Communist
fascist
other
1924 date of introduction of dictatorship

democracies, 1939
British territories and mandates
French territories and mandates
other

German gain, 1935–1 Sep 1939
Hungarian gain, 1938–39
Italian gain, Apr 1939
Turkish gain, 1923
Nationalist-held Spain, late 1936
Nationalist gain by Dec 1938
demilitarized zone, 1919–35
area of economic revival
area of economic decline
SPAIN country experiencing civil war, with date
☼ strike, riot or other protest action
✳ Communist uprising, 1919–23
✳ international incident
✳ incident of Polish aggression, 1920
✡ city with large Jewish population
supply route for Spanish civil war
emigration of more than 200,000 refugees

0   600 km
0   400 mi

	1920		1930		1940
International affairs	**1919–20** Treaties of Versailles, St Germain, Neuilly, Trianon create the postwar settlement in Europe	**1925** The European powers guarantee Germany's eastern European borders at Locarno	**1932** German postwar reparations are abolished	**1936** The Rome–Berlin Axis is formed	
		1928 The antiwar Kellogg–Briand pact is signed in Paris	**1932** France and the USSR sign a nonaggression treaty	**1938** Munich agreement on Germany's occupation of the Sudetenland	
	1922 Germany and USSR sign a treaty at Rapallo				
			1934 Yugoslavia, Romania, Turkey, Greece sign a Balkan pact against Hitler and Stalin		
	1924 The Dawes plan reduces German reparations	**1929** Beginning of the Great Depression		**1939** The Nazi–Soviet pact is signed	
Western Europe	**1920** Abortive Communist revolutions in Germany	**1926** General strike in Britain, led by the miners	**1931** The Republicans win a landslide victory in Spanish elections; the king flees	**1936–39** The Spanish Civil War follows an attempted rightwing coup by Franco	
	1921 The Irish Free State is set up in southern Ireland	**1926** Germany enters the League of Nations			
			1933 Adolf Hitler is elected chancellor of Germany	**1939** Britain and France declare war on Germany	
	1923 France occupies the Ruhr; hyperinflation in Germany	**1929** Lateran treaties between Italy and the Papacy ensure the Vatican's independence		**1936** German army reoccupies the Rhineland	
Eastern Europe	**1920–22** War between Greece and Turkey	**1924–29** Joseph Stalin consolidates his power in USSR	**1934** Austrian chancellor Dollfuss is murdered by Nazis	**1938** German invasion of Austria (Anschluss)	
	1920–21 Poland and the Soviet Union are at war	**1926** Josef Pilsudski comes to power in Poland	**1934** King Alexander of Macedonia is assassinated	**1939** Germany and Soviet Union invade Poland	
	1920		1930		1940

TIMELINE

Map labels (Europe, 1900–1997):

Trondheim · Umeå · Lake Onega · Lake Ladoga · FINLAND independent 1917/20 · NORWAY · Bergen · Sundsvall · Gävle · Oslo (Christiania) · SWEDEN · Stockholm · Turku · Helsinki · Russians · Leningrad (Petrograd) · Tallinn (Revel) · ESTONIA independent 1918 **1933** · Lake Peipus · Pskov · Moscow · Göteborg · Baltic Sea · Vänern · Vättern · LATVIA independent 1918 **1934** · Riga · Western Dvina · Vitebsk · Smolensk · UNION OF SOVIET SOCIALIST REPUBLICS 1917–21, 1917 · DENMARK · Copenhagen · 1933 Schleswig · Memel 1939 to Germany · LITHUANIA independent 1918 **1926** · Königsberg · Kaunas · Vilna · Minsk · Belorussia independent 1919–21 · Lübeck · Gdynia · Danzig (free city) 1919 · East Prussia to Germany · Cuxhaven · Kiel · Rostock · Stettin · Polish Corridor · Germans · Poles · Brest-Litovsk · The Curzon Line 1920 · Hamburg · Bremen · 1919–23, 1930–33 · German Jews · Berlin · Warsaw · Poles · 1919–23, 1930–33 · Kiev · Kharkov · GERMANY · Essen **1933** · Magdeburg · Lodz **1936** · POLAND **1926** · Düsseldorf · Cologne · Leipzig · 1938 to Germany · Oder · 1936 · Lvov · Dnieper · Dnepropetrovsk (Yekaterinoslav) · Frankfurt · 1939 to Germany · Sudetenland · Breslau · Krakow · Teschen 1936 · 1939 to Hungary · Ukraine independent 1917–20 · LUXEMBOURG · Nuremberg · Bohemia · Prague · Moravia · CZECHOSLOVAKIA 1938–39 · Dniester · Strasbourg · Bavaria · Vienna · Slovakia · 1938 to Hungary · Iasi · Kishinev · Munich · 1919–23, 1930–33 · AUSTRIA **1934** 1938 to Germany · Budapest · HUNGARY **1931–35** · Hungarians · Odessa · Berne · SWITZERLAND · LIECHTENSTEIN · Zagreb 1935–38 · ROMANIA **1938** · Geneva · Locarno · Trieste · Timisoara · Black Sea · Milan · Bergamo · Venice · Fiume 1919 · Ploiesti · Bucharest 1934 · Turin 1919–22 · Bologna 1919–22 · Zara 1920 to Italy · Belgrade 1935–38 · Danube · Genoa · SAN MARINO · Kragujevac · 1921–34 · BULGARIA **1934** · Varna · KINGDOM OF THE SERBS CROATS AND SLOVENES (Yugoslavia from 1931) **1929** · Sofia · Plovdiv · Burgas · MONACO · Florence · 1937 · Skopje · Edirne · 1919–1922 to Greece, 1923 to Turkey · Istanbul · ITALY **1925** · Tiranë · Thessalonica 1934 · Chanak 1922 · Ankara · TURKEY **1924** · 1919–22 · Corsica to France · Rome 1919–22 · ALBANIA 1939 to Italy · Sakarya River 1921 · Sardinia to Italy · Naples 1919–22 · Bari 1919–22 · 1923 Corfu to Greece · GREECE **1936** · Turks · Izmir · Greeks · 1922 · 1919–22 to Greece, 1923 to Turkey · Palermo · Sicily · Patras · Athens 1933, 1935 · Rhodes · Dodecanese 1920 to Greece, 1923 to Italy · Cyprus to Britain · Tunis · Crete · Malta to Britain · Mediterranean Sea · Tunisia French protectorate · Tripoli · Benghazi · Alexandria · Cairo · Tripolitania to Italy · Cyrenaica to Italy · EGYPT 1922 independent

alliance system
- French
- German
- Italian
- Locarno treaty, 1925
- Balkan Entente, 1934
- Baltic Entente, 1922

Inset map labels: ESTONIA · FINLAND · LATVIA · UNITED KINGDOM · BELGIUM · GERMANY · POLAND · UNION OF SOVIET SOCIALIST REPUBLICS · FRANCE · AUSTRIA · CZECHOSLOVAKIA · ROMANIA · HUNGARY · ITALY · YUGOSLAVIA · ALBANIA · GREECE · TURKEY

Britain and France tried to buy them off by conceding small territorial claims (the policy of "appeasement"), but the dictators demanded more. Italy escaped virtually unpunished for invading Ethiopia in 1935 as Britain and France tried (unsuccessfully) to preserve Mussolini as an ally against Germany. Hitler, as well as initiating his anti-Jewish policies, began to challenge the Treaty of Versailles: in 1935 Germany began to rearm and then reoccupied the Rhineland. Further steps to extend German power and territory followed, with the *Anschluss* with Austria (1938) and the partition of Czechoslovakia (agreed with Britain and France at Munich in 1938).

By now Britain and France had lost all credibility. Germany invaded Czechoslovakia in 1939 and the French and British guaranteed the security of several other European states, but to little avail. A French strategy of fencing the Germans in with the "Little Entente" in eastern Europe had already been weakened by a German–Polish non-aggression treaty in 1934. The democracies failed to secure an alliance with the Soviet Union and Stalin, believing Britain and France to be encouraging Hitler to expand to the east, signed a Nazi–Soviet pact in August 1939. Hitler and Stalin partitioned Poland between them, but Hitler failed to anticipate a sea-change in British and French opinion after his annexation of Czechoslovakia. Unexpectedly he had to fight in the west before pursuing his primary objectives in the east.

1 Budapest saw a Communist takeover in March 1919 under Bela Kun. Hungary then invaded Slovakia and Transylvania; Kun fled abroad in August 1919.

2 Following a plebiscite in 1920, Schleswig was divided between Germany and Denmark.

3 Ireland was divided in 1921: the mainly Protestant north elected to stay in the United Kingdom, the south became the Irish Free State. Civil war ensued in the south (1922–23), where many rejected partition.

4 The Saar became a League of Nations mandate under French rule in 1919, but returned to Germany by plebiscite in 1935.

5 The town of Guernica was destroyed by German bombers in the first massive aerial attack on civilians.

6 The Sudetenland of northwest Czechoslovakia, which had a large German minority, was annexed by Hitler following the Munich agreement in 1938.

See also 6.06 (World War I); 6.08 (World War II); 6.15 (the Soviet Union to 1941)

Germany's prosperity essential for European well-being, reparations were reduced and a limited recovery followed, funded by American loans.

Germany's grievances might have been resolved peacefully. The Locarno pact (1925) guaranteed its western borders and showed that foreign minister Stresemann would work peacefully to revise the Treaty of Versailles while the Kellogg–Briand pact of 1928 officially, if implausibly, renounced war.

The depression of the early 1930s, caused in part by the withdrawal of American loans, shattered the illusion of stability. Democracy was weakly established in many countries: massive unemployment and protest were now seen, followed by a return to authoritarian government. The dictator Pilsudski had upheld Catholicism in Poland since 1926; now Franco did the same in Spain after a three-year civil war. This bloody conflict showed how polarized politics in Europe was, and became a war by proxy between the Soviet-supplied republic and German- and Italian-supported right. Royal dictatorships also flourished in Bulgaria, Romania and Yugoslavia.

The radical new phenomenon of fascism now threatened the peace. Promising national renewal and fueled by grievances over the peace settlement, Mussolini's movement in Italy had established itself as a totalitarian regime in 1925. Fascist parties formed across Europe and in 1933 Hitler's Nazi party won power in Germany, its appeal magnified by mass unemployment and fear of Communism.

The British and French governments continued to be cautious. In Germany the Nazis eliminated unemployment by means of public work schemes, but in Britain the principles of classical economics still applied. Some economists, led by J.M. Keynes, advocated kick-starting the economy through government spending, but heavy industry did not recover until the armaments boom at the end of the 1930s (newer industries, such as electronics, motor and aircraft production did, however, show rapid growth).

The same caution applied to foreign policy. Unwilling to destabilize the international economy with wars or sanctions, the League proved unable to take a firm line with Germany and Italy in the 1930s.

The declaration of war on Germany by Britain and France in 1939 took Hitler by surprise; he was now forced to deal with the threat to Germany's western flank in order to avoid fighting the war on two fronts. His primary objective, though, remained the conquest of the Soviet Union.

Germany and the Soviet Union divided Poland between them as they had agreed in the Nazi–Soviet pact of 1939, both sides deporting large numbers of people. The USSR later absorbed the Baltic states with the exception of Finland, which preserved its independence in the "Winter War" of 1939–40. A "phoney war" ensued, the first break in the inactivity being the German invasion of Denmark and Norway in April 1940. The Allies had planned to seize Narvik to deny Germany access to the only port capable of handling the exports of vital Swedish iron ore; however, the rapid and well-planned German advance resulted in a hurried Allied withdrawal.

Soon after, Winston Churchill took over as British prime minister, but Allied resistance was ineffectual during the German attack on the Low Countries and France in May. France surrendered within six weeks. Germany occupied the north, while a collaborationist regime at Vichy controlled the south; Belgium and the Netherlands became satellites in the German industrial complex. Britain evacuated most of its forces from northern France, but in the Battle of Britain of 1940 (the first decisive battle to be fought in the air) stifled plans for a seaborne invasion by denying air superiority to the Luftwaffe (German air force). Italy chose this point to enter the war. The Mediterranean was closed to British shipping and fighting began in north and east Africa.

While the air offensive continued against Britain and escalated into the Blitz, Hitler turned his attention to the east. By the summer of 1940 he was planning the Barbarossa campaign – an invasion of the Soviet Union which he had planned for the mid-

1940s, but which was now brought forward by the success of the German war effort and the rapid rearmament of the other powers.

In April 1941 German, Bulgarian and Italian forces invaded Greece and Yugoslavia to secure their southern flank for Barbarossa. Italy had been defeated in Greece the previous year but now the Axis forces overran all opposition, driving British troops first to Crete and then to Egypt. German

success had been based on *blitzkrieg* or lightning war. With limited access to raw materials, Germany could not afford a long war. Tanks, dive-bombers and motorized infantry destroyed defenses before reserves could be mobilized or a war of attrition develop. Barbarossa was expected to last six weeks, but by November 1941 the campaign was bogged down by the weather. Hitler had ignored advice to seize Moscow, preferring to advance on all fronts. His forces were now dangerously stretched.

Stalin launched an offensive in the spring of 1942, but the Germans occupied more territory in the summer. It became clear, however, that they could not launch a knockout blow: the vast size of the

Legend

- Germany, 1 Sep 1939
- territory gained by USSR, 1939–40
- western frontier of USSR, June 1941
- area of population and industry evacuated to Siberia, 1941–42
- borders, June 1942
- Axis power, June 1942
- ally of Axis power, June 1942
- under Axis occupation, June 1942
- Vichy territory, June 1942
- under Allied control, June 1942
- furthest Axis advance, 1941
- front lines, end Nov 1942
- Maginot line
- bombed city, 1940–42
- U-boat base
- siege
- atrocity or mass murder
- **Lidice** reprisal killing
- death camp
- concentration camp
- Axis airborne operation
- British commando raid
- Allied withdrawal
- Axis offensive
- Allied offensive
- main convoy route, 1941–42

TIMELINE

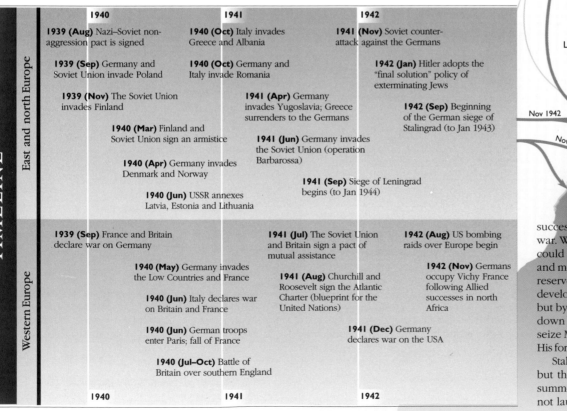

East and north Europe

1940	1941	1942
1939 (Aug) Nazi–Soviet non-aggression pact is signed	**1940 (Oct)** Italy invades Greece and Albania	**1941 (Nov)** Soviet counter-attack against the Germans
1939 (Sep) Germany and Soviet Union invade Poland	**1940 (Oct)** Germany and Italy invade Romania	**1942 (Jan)** Hitler adopts the "final solution" policy of exterminating Jews
1939 (Nov) The Soviet Union invades Finland	**1941 (Apr)** Germany invades Yugoslavia; Greece surrenders to the Germans	**1942 (Sep)** Beginning of the German siege of Stalingrad (to Jan 1943)
1940 (Mar) Finland and Soviet Union sign an armistice	**1941 (Jun)** Germany invades the Soviet Union (operation Barbarossa)	
1940 (Apr) Germany invades Denmark and Norway	**1941 (Sep)** Siege of Leningrad begins (to Jan 1944)	
1940 (Jun) USSR annexes Latvia, Estonia and Lithuania		

Western Europe

1940	1941	1942
1939 (Sep) France and Britain declare war on Germany	**1941 (Jul)** The Soviet Union and Britain sign a pact of mutual assistance	**1942 (Aug)** US bombing raids over Europe begin
1940 (May) Germany invades the Low Countries and France	**1941 (Aug)** Churchill and Roosevelt sign the Atlantic Charter (blueprint for the United Nations)	**1942 (Nov)** Germans occupy Vichy France following Allied successes in north Africa
1940 (Jun) Italy declares war on Britain and France	**1941 (Dec)** Germany declares war on the USA	
1940 (Jun) German troops enter Paris; fall of France		
1940 (Jul–Oct) Battle of Britain over southern England		

summer route to Murmansk and Archangel

1 London and other cities suffered aerial bombardment from September 1940 to May 1941. The "Blitz" failed to break British industry or civilian morale.

2 A surprise amphibious attack in April 1940 allowed Germany to take Norway before British support could arrive. Only in Narvik did the plan falter temporarily.

3 The defense of Greece in April 1941 was poorly coordinated and quickly overrun; the British forces were evacuated to Crete, and soon after to Alexandria.

4 After the Soviet invasion of November 1939, the Finns caused heavy losses but sued for peace in March 1940. Though nominally neutral, Finland favored Germany against the USSR.

5 Vichy, a spa town, was seat of the collaborationist French government from 1940 to November 1942.

6 Britain's strategic naval base at Malta endured more than 1,200 air raids during World War II.

country and its population, and the safety of the industrial areas evacuated east of the Urals meant that the USSR had huge capacity. By the end of 1942, a turning point was approaching.

The United States had already been supplying Britain and the Soviet Union with materiel through the "lend–lease" scheme, and its entry into the war as a full belligerent in December 1941 gave the Allies a major boost. From then on Allied superiority in men and arms, and Hitler's lack of strategic vision were to lead to German defeat.

Disruption of the supply routes from America had become of central concern to the western Allies. The United States was keen to invade western

Europe as quickly as possible, but U-boat attacks on convoys in the Atlantic hampered the transport of men and materiel. A minor invasion of north Africa, occupied by Italian and Vichy forces backed up by General Rommel's Afrika Korps, met with rapid success. If the Battle of the Atlantic could not be won, though, United States numerical and industrial power would count for little in the battle for Europe.

In eastern Europe the Germans undertook the enslavement and murder of the subject populations. Executions of civilians were commonplace in the invasion of Poland, and during Barbarossa mass murder was a tool of occupation policy. Hitler hoped to create a "new order" based on the Nazi idea of the

"historic conflict" between the Aryans (Germans) and the other "inferior races". Millions of Slavs and Gypsies were shot, deported, starved or enslaved to create a "living space" for Germans. In what was called the "final solution", mass shootings and gassings were used to exterminate the Jews. Death camps were built and by the end of 1942 almost the entire Jewish population of Poland, the Baltic states, and the USSR as far east as the Caucasus – about three million people – had been killed.

See also 6.07 (Europe between the wars); 6.09 (World War II to 1945); 6.19 (World War II in Asia)

The end of 1942 marked a turning point, but two more years of fighting were needed before the war in Europe ended. The German surrender at Stalingrad was a major blow to Hitler, who was committed to holding the city and supplying it by air. In July the Soviet army repulsed the Germans at Kursk in the war's biggest land battle; then drove westward, its next victory being at Kharkov.

In May 1943, the Germans capitulated in north Africa. By mid-1943 Germany had also lost the crucial Battle of the Atlantic, where the Allied use of long-range aircraft made Germany's submarine assault on transatlantic convoy routes less effective. The German war effort intensified with the announcement of total war (the complete mobilization of the economy). The Allies invaded Sicily, Mussolini was deposed and the Italians sued for peace; however Germany immediately occupied north and central Italy and made further Allied progress very difficult through the mountainous terrain.

The Allies' Italian campaign was a relatively minor response to success in north Africa, though it dragged on until the end of the war. The main action in the west – the "second front" that Stalin had long demanded – was to be the Allied landing in Normandy, as the Allied leaders had agreed at their meeting in Tehran in November 1943. Even before this was launched, however, Hitler had to withdraw troops from the east to strengthen the western defenses. Allied bombing increased in strength and effectiveness as the US joined the British in attacking German cities in force: the first 1,000-bomber raid took place against Cologne in 1943. The bombing campaign directed German resources from the other fronts and weakened the war economy.

When the Normandy landings finally came in June 1944, they met with stiff resistance. The Allies liberated France and Belgium before halting briefly. Meanwhile in east and southeast Europe the Red Army took advantage of the increased pressure on Germany in the west, and defeated both Romania and Bulgaria. Germany pulled out of Greece but Hungary was kept in the war by a Nazi coup after initially surrendering to the Soviet Union; fierce fighting broke out around Budapest.

Political as well as military considerations had held back United States president Roosevelt from supporting British prime minister Churchill's plan to invade southeast Europe. Unlike Roosevelt, Churchill had little faith in Stalin's postwar intentions, and made an agreement with Stalin which stipulated the influence that Britain and the Soviet Union would each have in the region. Soviet action in Poland and elsewhere did not engender confidence. As the Red Army advanced toward Warsaw, a fullscale rising against the German forces occurred in the city. Despite surrounding the city Stalin did not assist the rebels, and when the Germans eventually quashed the revolt as many as 250,000 people were killed.

Across Europe guerrilla partisan forces fought the Axis powers. Many were divided on ethnic or political lines, and their activities provoked bloody reprisals. A revolt in Slovakia at the same time as the Warsaw rising was brutally put down, but in Yugoslavia the Communist-dominated partisans enjoyed

Legend:
- borders, 1943
- Axis power or ally
- Axis occupied, Mar 1943
- Allied control, Mar 1943
- front line, Dec 1943
- front line, Aug 1944
- front line, Dec 1944
- front line, Apr 1945
- defensive line
- heavily bombed city
- siege
- area of partisan activity
- German reprisal killing
- death camp
- concentration camp
- Allied airborne operation
- conference of Allied leaders, with date
- London V-weapon target zone
- 26 Aug 1944 date of capitulation
- Axis withdrawal
- Axis offensive
- Allied offensive
- Soviet deportation, 1944-45

CIVILIANS, including women, were universally important to the war effort by working in the factories. This poster was from Britain.

TIMELINE

	1943	1944	1945
East and north Europe	1943 (Jan) German army surrenders at Stalingrad	1944 (Jan) The siege of Leningrad ends after 900 days	1945 (Jan) Red Army enters Budapest, Warsaw, Auschwitz
	1943 (Apr) Jews of Warsaw stage a revolt; 60,000 die	1944 (Apr) The Red Army retakes the Crimea	1945 (May) Berlin surrenders to the Red Army
	1943 (June–Aug) Russians defeat a German offensive in a vast tank battle at Kursk	1944 (July) Soviet forces enter Poland; (Aug) Warsaw second rising	
	1943 (Nov) The Russians retake Kiev	1944 (Oct) Soviet troops liberate Belgrade	
		1944 (Oct–Nov) Allied forces liberate Greece	
Western Europe	1942 (Oct) US bombers destroy Lille railyards in northern France	1943 (July) Allied forces land in Sicily	1944 (June) D-Day: Allied forces land in Normandy	1945 (Mar) Allied forces cross the Rhine
		1943 (Sep) Italy surrenders to the Allies; German forces occupy Milan and Rome	1944 (Aug) Allied forces liberate Paris	1945 (May) Germany surrenders
		1943 (Oct) Italy declares war on Germany		1945 (Feb) Huge Allied bombing raid on Dresden
Other	1942 (Oct–Nov) British army defeats Germans at el Alamein	1943 (Nov) Roosevelt, Stalin and Churchill meet at Tehran		1945 (Feb) Roosevelt, Stalin and Churchill meet at Yalta to discuss the postwar division of Germany
		1943 (Jan) Roosevelt and Churchill meet at Casablanca		
	1943	1944	1945

Map labels:
ICELAND, Reykjavik, Faroe Islands to Denmark, Shetland Islands to Britain, Glasgow, Edinburgh, Belfast, Newcastle, UNITED KINGDOM, IRELAND, Dublin, Liverpool, Manchester, Birmingham, Lincoln, Coventry, Cambridge, Oxford, Reading, Londo, Southampton, Plymouth, June 1944, Portsmouth, Le Havr, NORMANDY, Caen, July 194, Paris, Brest, Falaise, Aug 1944, Le Mans, ATLANTIC OCEAN, Nantes, Loire, Aug 1944, Oradour-sur-Glane, Bordeaux, FRANCE liberated by Sep 194, Bilbao, Toulous, Ebro, ANDORRA, Douro, Barcelona, PORTUGAL, SPAIN, Madrid, Tagus, Balearic Islands to Spain, Guadiana, Valencia, Lisbon, Seville, Algiers, Cádiz, Tangier, Gibraltar to Britain, Oran, Spanish Morocco to Spain, Algeria Free French, Fez, Casablanca Jan 1943, French Morocco Free French

1 Hitler's attack on the Soviet defenses at Kursk (June 1943) led to a conflict between the Soviet light but nimble T-34 tanks, and the heavy German Tiger tanks. Despite huge losses, the Red Army broke through.

2 Some 640 villagers, including 200 women and children, were burned to death in a church at the village of Oradour-sur Glane in June 1944.

3 When the Germans retreated to their prewar defenses – the Siegfried Line – in September 1944, the Allies attacked via the Netherlands. The line was broken in February 1945.

4 Peenemünde was the site of research into rocketry by the Germans under Werner von Braun. Allied intelligence knew of it from 1939.

5 Auschwitz was the largest of the Nazi death camps, established in 1940. Well over a million Jews and Poles died there before liberation in January 1945.

6 Churchill, Stalin and Roosevelt met at Yalta in February 1945 to coordinate strategy and agree spheres of influence in postwar Europe.

considerable success and formed the basis of Tito's postwar government; in Prague, a popular rising helped the Soviet advance on the city. In Greece, the Communists, who dominated the rural resistance movement, defied the British who sought to reestablish the monarchy after the Germans had withdrawn in October 1944; the result was a civil war which ended only with the collapse of the Communists in 1949. Resistance in Poland and countries incorporated into the Soviet Union also continued after the war, but it was now directed against the USSR.

Hitler always believed that providence would save him. He tried to stop the Allied bomber assault on Germany by firing rocket-powered V-bombs at Britain, but the forces ranged against him were too

great. The last German offensive, through the Ardennes at the end of 1944, was a failure and after Hitler's suicide, Germany surrendered (8 May 1945).

The implementation of Nazi policies of genocide continued right up until the liberation of the death camps by Allied troops. As the Soviets marched westward, many inmates of camps in Poland were moved to Germany to join prisoners-of-war and other forced foreign labor; by 1944 there were almost eight million foreigners at work in Germany. Some Axis countries – Hungary, Bulgaria and Italy – refused to release many or all of their Jewish population to the Nazis, but the attempt to exterminate the Jews of Europe still proceeded. By the end of the war some six million had been killed, along with

millions of other nationalities including Ukrainians, Poles, Balts, Belorussians, Russians and Gypsies.

Of the 5.5 million Soviet soldiers captured by the Germans, 3.3 million had died; as the Red Army advanced it took its revenge. Ten million ethnic Germans were expelled from their homes in central and eastern Europe; perhaps two million died. The USSR deported five million of its subject nationalities for alleged collaboration; returning prisoners-of-war often faced exile or death. By 1945 much of Europe was destroyed, its peoples dead or homeless.

See also 6.08 (World War II to 1942);
6.10 (postwar Europe); 6.19 (World War II in Asia)

The wartime cooperation of the Allies quickly broke down and two blocs emerged: the western democratic countries which were oriented toward the United States, and the eastern Communist countries dominated by the Soviet Union. Europe lived in the shadow of the superpowers.

Blame for the deterioration of international relations and the drawing of the "iron curtain" across Europe has been laid with both sides, and little is known of Soviet motives. It is clear, however, that US hopes of an "open" Europe were misplaced. Stalin never considered giving up the Soviet Union's new influence in eastern Europe and, though he probably did not envisage invading the west either, there was a real fear that the rest of the continent would succumb to Communism. As a result, with Europe devastated and trying to cope with millions of refugees, the United States produced a massive cash injection ("Marshall Aid") in 1947, becoming the counterweight to Soviet power in the east.

Crucial to the division of Europe was the partition of Germany. The economic and military powerbase of the continent was occupied jointly by the Allies, neither side being willing to risk losing overall control to the other. In 1948 the Soviets blockaded western-occupied West Berlin and in 1949 the republics of West and East Germany were formally constituted. The same year the North Atlantic Treaty was signed, binding the western states and America in an anti-Soviet alliance (NATO), and Comecon was formed to incorporate the east European countries in a system of Soviet-dominated interstate economic planning. In 1950 US troops returned to Europe as part of NATO after the outbreak of war in Korea; the Soviet-led Warsaw Pact was founded five years later.

Thereafter west and east Europe developed on different lines. The western countries soon recovered their prosperity, creating economic areas to increase trade. The Benelux Customs Union of 1948 was followed by the creation of the European Coal and Steel Community (ECSC), which laid the basis for the European Economic Community (EEC) in 1958. A looser affiliation, the European Free Trade Area (EFTA), also existed but the EEC was the more important, later becoming the European Community (EC), aspiring to a political as well as economic role.

The EEC was intended to transcend national boundaries, prevent the strife that had characterized Europe's history and assist Europe to become an independent player on the world stage. The French president Charles de Gaulle twice vetoed Britain's application to join, on the grounds of Britain's "special relationship" with the United States. De Gaulle deplored US involvement in Europe, and withdrew France from NATO, yet the idea of an independent European Defense Community proved unworkable. The United States encouraged western European integration but American troops remained essential. Britain and France established independent nuclear capability; West German chancellor Willy Brandt negotiated cooperation agreements between West and East Germany. But given the Soviet Union's military might, Europe could not be independent until the iron curtain was raised.

In eastern Europe the influence of the Soviet Union was deeply resented. Eastern European countries did not enjoy the "economic miracle" seen in West Germany, and felt their national identities to be compromised by Soviet interference. Yugoslavia and Albania preserved their traditions of independent Communism as, to a lesser extent, did Romania. Hungary (1956) and Czechoslovakia (1968) tried more radical escapes from the Soviet bloc but were brought back into line by force.

Following the Helsinki agreement of 1975 under which the borders of the German Democratic Republic (East Germany) were recognized and the governments of eastern Europe accepted the principle of observing human rights, dissident activity grew more intense. In 1980 the Polish trade union Solidarity was set up and long-standing popular resentment (kept alive by the Catholic church and the accession of John Paul II as the first Polish pope) was manifested in widespread industrial disputes.

Protest in western Europe was directed both against the United States (over the Vietnam war or the presence of US-controlled nuclear missiles) or against individual governments. The Paris riots of 1968 were part of a general revolt of youth

TIMELINE

Western Europe

1945 Potsdam conference of the great powers agrees the postwar position in Germany

1947 USA provides Marshall Aid to western Europe

1948–49 The Berlin airlift follows a Soviet blockade of the city's western zone

1949 North Atlantic Treaty is signed; NATO is set up

1955 Allies end occupation of West Germany and Austria; West Germany joins NATO

1957 The Treaty of Rome sets up the European Economic Community (EEC), from Jan 1958

1966 France withdraws from NATO

1967 French president de Gaulle vetoes UK entry to EEC for the second time

1968 Students riot in Paris and almost bring down the government; unrest is felt in West Germany and Britain

1974 Turkey invades northern Cyprus

1974 Portugal's rightwing government is overthrown

1977 Spain's first postwar elections take place following the death of Franco in 1975

1979 Conservative leader Margaret Thatcher is elected prime minister in Britain

1986 Portugal and Spain join the EC

Eastern Europe

1947–48 Sovietization of the governments of eastern Europe

1949 Comecon is set up to integrate eastern Europe's economies

1956 An anti-Soviet revolt takes place in Hungary

1961 The Berlin Wall is built to prevent emigration from East to West Germany

1968 Czechoslovak "Prague spring" ends with Warsaw Pact invasion

1970–72 *Ostpolitik* agreements for East and West German cooperation

1975 Helsinki agreement on Germany's borders and human rights in east Europe

1980 Solidarity, Polish trade union, is founded

1989 The Berlin Wall is taken down; regimes in Hungary, Poland, East Germany, Bulgaria, Czechoslovakia, Romania fall

against authority, as was the Baader–Meinhof terrorist group in West Germany.

In the 1970s, the economic downturn caused by inflation, high public spending and the rise in oil prices led to unemployment and industrial militancy. British prime minster Margaret Thatcher's response to these problems after 1979 marked a radical departure from the consensus politics of the postwar period, which had stressed cooperation between employers, workers and the state. The introduction of free-market economics and revision of labor legislation brought a year-long miners' strike (1984–85). Elsewhere, terrorism and violence fueled by economic dislocation flared in areas of nationalist tension. Basque separatists mounted a bombing campaign in Spain (where the Catalans gained internal autonomy), and the British province of Ulster simmered on the brink of civil war.

In the late 1980s the disparity in living standards between east and west and the moral and economic bankruptcy of Communism led the new Soviet leader, Mikhail Gorbachev, to slacken the ties binding eastern Europe in an effort to free up the east's economy. It was soon clear that he had unleashed forces beyond his control. Revolutions ensued, first in Poland and then East Germany, Hungary, Czechoslovakia, Bulgaria and Romania. The old order crumbled, with exhilaration mixed with apprehension at the new shape Europe would take.

1 Divided Berlin was a focus for Cold War tension. In 1948-49 the western zone was supplied by air after Soviet forces surrounded the city; in 1961 the Berlin Wall was built to stop refugees leaving the East.

2 The Nuremberg war crimes trials of 1946 indicted many leading Nazis but lesser ones were unpunished; a strong West Germany was needed as a cornerstone of the rebuilding of western Europe.

3 Hungary (1956) and Czechoslovakia (1968) looked to break away from the Communist bloc but both were forced back into line by Warsaw Pact invasions.

4 Yugoslavia remained neutral thanks to its tradition of independent Communism. Its unity was maintained to the 1980s by its Croat leader Tito.

5 The Gdansk shipyards were the center of popular resistance in Poland, which led the way in the later opposition to Communism in eastern Europe.

6 The Treaty of Rome – signed by France, Italy, West Germany, Belgium, the Netherlands and Luxembourg – in 1957 formed the basis for the integration of western Europe under the EEC (later EC and EU).

7 The prolonged attempt by Nikolai Ceauçescu to collectivize the peasantry in Romania was one example of the introduction of Stalinism to eastern Europe, and met with great opposition.

8 The "Forest Brethren" partisans in the Baltic states resisted incorporation into the USSR after 1945.

See also 6.09 (World War II); 6.11 (Europe in the
1990s); 6.16 (the Soviet Union)

When Communist control over eastern Europe collapsed in 1989, tension between the North Atlantic Treaty Organization (NATO) and the Warsaw Pact dissolved. However, many former Soviet satellite countries and, from 1991, the old Soviet republics, suffered problems of social restructuring, while the western countries faced disagreements over how to cooperate politically and economically.

The rapid reunification of Germany signaled the end of the bi-polar Europe and demonstrated many of the problems inherent in the creation of a new one. There were fears that a resurgent Germany at the geographical center of the continent would dominate Europe and create an instability similar to that which existed before 1914. In the short term, however, the price of German reunification was high. To achieve its political aims, the former West Germany was faced with a huge bill for taking over East Germany's backward economy. Germany's dominance in European finance meant that the costs of reunion were felt beyond its own borders. Interest rates rose across Europe, and in 1992 Britain and others were forced to leave the Exchange Rate Mechanism (ERM), which had been introduced to guarantee economic stability in the European Union (EU) and lead to eventual monetary union.

The failure to maintain the integrity of the ERM called into question the creation of more unified financial structures within the European Union (EU; formerly EC). This failure caused doubts to resurface in several member-states about the need for, and price of, a single European currency, planned for introduction in the late 1990s. Parallel with the debate about "deepening" the union was the question of "widening" it to include countries that had formerly chosen or been forced to stay outside. While many of the formerly Soviet-dominated countries were clamoring to join the Union, some countries (including Britain and Denmark) saw vociferous anti-EU campaigns, and a referendum on joining led to a "no" vote in Norway. As fears rose of migration, international terrorism and drug smuggling, doubts arose of the wisdom of the agreement to allow free movement of goods, people and services across the EU from 1992. In 1995 several countries abolished border controls between them, though others viewed this decision with disquiet.

Western Europe's division over such questions was heightened by instability in the east. The euphoria surrounding the demise of communism was soon replaced by uncertainty. The new governments of eastern Europe and the states of the former Soviet Union faced unprecedented difficulties in turning state-run "command economies" into market-driven ones. The nascent democracies often appeared fragile, not least in Russia itself where Boris Yeltsin, a president of authoritarian instincts but failing health, was faced with powerful forces both of reaction and radical reform, and problems of high unemployment and inflation, potent organized crime, alarming ethnic conflict and resurgent Russian nationalism.

Meanwhile, war was seen within Europe for the first time since 1945. Resurgent nationalism led to ethnic conflicts in Armenia and Azerbaijan, then engulfed Europe's heart as Yugoslavia tore itself apart. Here as elsewhere, different nationalities had been held together by the shackles of authoritarian

borders, 1997
member state of EU, 1997
associated state of EU
member state of EFTA
state with EU cooperation agreement
SPAIN   member state of NATO
1989   year of application for EU membership
former boundary of Warsaw Pact
implementation of "open frontier" Schengen agreement, 1995
☆   area of ethnic/nationalist tension

ethnic composition of Bosnia–Herzegovina, pre-1991
more than 60 percent Croat
more than 60 percent Muslim
more than 60 percent Serb
ethnically mixed area
Bosnian–Croat Federation, 1995
Bosnian Serb Republic, 1995
Croatian territory under Serbian control, 1995
⊙   UN-designated "safe havens"

TIMELINE		1990	1992	1994	1996
	Eastern Europe	**1989** Fall of the Communist regimes in Poland, Hungary, Czechoslovakia, Bulgaria, East Germany, and Romania	**1991** A failed Communist coup leads to the breakup of the Soviet Union	**1993** Russia adopts a new constitution, giving the president increased powers	**1995** US president Clinton achieves agreement between the warring parties in Bosnia in Dayton Accord
		1989 Ethnic conflicts begin in Azerbaijan and Armenia	**1992** Bosnia-Herzegovina breaks away from Yugoslavia	**1994** Chechen nationalists are crushed by the Russian army at Grozny, southern Russia	**1996** Elections in Russia confirm Yeltsin's position
		1990 Slovenia breaks away from Yugoslavia	**1992** Siege of Sarajevo by the Bosnian Serbs begins	**1995** Croatia launches offensive against Serbs in Krajina and eastern Slavonia	
		1990 Croat-held Dubrovnik is shelled by Serb forces	**1993** Czechoslovakia splits into the Czech Republic and Slovakia		
	Western Europe	**1990** The European Bank for Reconstruction and Development is founded	**1992** The EU single market comes into force	**1994** Norway rejects membership of the EU	**1996** Intergovernmental Conference (IGC) is held to explore the future of Europe
		1991 EU heads of government define a strategy for closer political and financial union at Maastricht	**1992** France and Germany found a joint army (Euro-corps) to strengthen the Western European Union	**1995** Austria, Sweden and Finland join the EU	**1997** Plans for common European currency are confirmed
				1995 Schengen agreement allows some open frontiers	
		1990	1992	1994	1996

communism. The country split into its constituent republics but – unlike in Czechoslovakia where a similar divorce occurred – this took no account of the ethnic complexity on the ground.

With the Serbs in the grip of a militant nationalist spirit, and with Bosnia's population divided culturally and religiously between Bosnians, Croats and Serbs, the conflict focused on Bosnia– Herzegovina and its capital Sarajevo, which had provided the stage for the outbreak of European war in 1914. The states of the former Yugoslavia – especially Bosnia and Croatia – experienced four years of bloody civil war, where atrocities and policies of "ethnic cleansing" forced hundreds of thousands of civilians to flee their homes. The war revealed the political and military impotence of the rest of Europe, which was unable to agree a common policy on the problem, preferring to leave the task of peace-keeping to the United Nations. Behind this failure lay a fear of the war spreading. For this reason, western Europe's economic and military ties with the east, particularly Russia, continued to grow in importance: foreign

policy cooperation agreements were signed while the EU assisted with trade and communication links.

The relationship between Europe and the United States was uncertain. The Western European Union (WEU), an alliance excluding the United States, was promoted as a alternative to the US-dominated NATO. In 1995, however, the United States succeeded where Europe had failed, and brokered a settlement in Bosnia. And in 1997 NATO and Russia signed an agreement that allowed for NATO's expansion and ended what remained of the Cold War.

1 Berlin, symbol of the divided Europe from 1945, was quickly reunited and became capital of the new Germany in 1991.

2 In 1991 at Maastricht the EU agreed to move to common economic and social conditions. Britain rejected Europe-wide provisions on social issues.

3 In 1996, Venice was the focus of a movement, promoted by the separatist Northern League, for an independent "Padania", based on the Po valley.

4 Prague, like many cities of eastern Europe, saw a boom in the early 1990s, with tourists and industrialists attracted by new opportunities and low costs.

5 The mainly Muslim inhabitants of Sarajevo, capital of Bosnia, were besieged by Bosnian Serb forces from 1992 to 1995.

6 Grozny, capital of the Chechens in their attempt to break away from the Russian Federation, was destroyed by the Russians in December 1994; elections in 1997 confirmed the desire for independence.

7 A ceasefire from October 1994 to February 1996 interrupted 25 years of "troubles" in Northern Ireland, involving conflict between the Protestant majority, Catholic nationalists and the British government.

8 Moscow and much of Russia suffered inflation, shortages, gangsterism and unemployment in the early 1990s in the rush to build a market economy.

See also 6.10 (Cold War Europe); 6.16 (decline of the Soviet Union); 6.26 (Middle East)

6.12 The Americas • 1914 – 1945 •

World War I involved many of the American states, despite an original intention to stay out of the conflict. The Caribbean islands and Canada owed direct allegiance to Britain, but most other countries had divided loyalties and were anxious to preserve their own interests; US president Woodrow Wilson advised neutrality. By 1918 Brazil and several Central American states had joined the Allies; the United States itself stayed out until German U-boat (submarine) attacks drove Wilson to declare war in 1917. The nation was put on a war footing: the government took over the railroads and strikers were threatened with the draft. Factories and shipyards converted to warwork, and thousands of African–Americans moved north to the munitions factories.

By the end of the war, there was little enthusiasm for any US involvement in Europe's postwar territorial arrangements. The Treaty of Versailles and the League of Nations, Wilson's brainchild, were both rejected by Congress as Americans sought "normalcy". The "jazz age" of the 1920s brought a quest for consumer goods and material comfort, despite a moral backlash in the form of the Volstead Act which brought Prohibition in 1920, with intoxicating liquor banned across the country. The result was a rise in political corruption and gangsterism.

In 1929, the Wall St stock market crash threw the country into the Great Depression, which had global resonance as US loans and investments had propped up the world's trade. The shadow of the depression was felt throughout the Western Hemisphere. In the United States itself, the crisis was exacerbated by drought and storms that devastated parts of Texas and the Mid-West, and created a dustbowl on the Great Plains. Some 12 million Americans lost their jobs, and shanty-towns (Hoovervilles) sprang up around the main cities. In 1933, Democrat Franklin D. Roosevelt became president, offering a New Deal to alleviate the depression through unprecedented government spending, giving work to millions on infrastructure projects such as dams and airports. The New Deal could not, however, cure all the economic ills of the country: agriculture and heavy industry recovered only after 1940, mainly due to US contributions to Britain's war effort, followed by

the outbreak of war with Japan in December 1941.

Canada had suffered in the Great War, and lost 60,000 men by 1918. This experience, followed by the prosperity of the 1920s, encouraged a new spirit of independence; but the country was hit hard by the depression, as it was heavily reliant on the export of wheat and lumber. The great drought of 1934 also wrought havoc on the farmers of the prairies. New political groupings suggested nationalization and the redistribution of income as a cure to national ills, while separatists won a large following in Quebec. The rise in world prices after 1937 and closer economic ties with the United States caused both proposals to be shelved for several decades.

The United States claimed the Caribbean and Central America as its "backyard", intervening to maintain its investments (including the Panama Canal and the oil reserves of Mexico and Venezuela) and building a military base at Guantanamo Bay on Cuba. The region was badly hit by the recession, and strikes and demonstrations were common, especially in the British West Indies. Several countries turned to dictatorships: some, such as Lázaro Cárdenas, ruler of Mexico from 1934–40, tried honestly to improve the condition of their people. Cárdenas restored communal lands to the peasants, and nationalized railroads and oil companies. Venezuela was ruled by Juan Vicente Gómez from 1908–35; he took over the Lake Maracaibo oil reserves but failed to address the weakness of so many Latin American states: the reliance on a single export commodity.

Colombia became the world's second producer of coffee but, like its main rival Brazil (ruled after 1930 by Getúlio Vargas), tried to reduce the economy's dependence on the fragile coffee trade in the 1930s by industrial diversification and import substitution. Argentina, which had flourished since the 19th century on grain and meat exports, now had to endure austerity measures. Chile too suffered with the fall in copper prices, while its nitrate exports were hit by the discovery of new chemical methods of production. Several South American states engaged in border disputes: Chile and Peru clashed over nitrate resources; the Chaco War between Bolivia and Paraguay in the 1930s was the most

violent conflict to take place in the world between 1918 and 1939; and Ecuador lost the Amazonian region to Peru in 1942.

World War II brought full employment and high wages to North America: by 1943 the USA was outproducing all the enemy nations combined. Millions moved to the cities; African–Americans flooded to California, Detroit and New York. Convoys took troops and supplies to all main theaters of war, and aid to Britain and the USSR. To counter enemy submarines operating down the Atlantic seaboard and in the Gulf of Mexico, air patrols were maintained far out to sea. For the Latin American countries the war years were eased by Roosevelt's "good neighbor" policy. The Coffee Accords of 1940 guaranteed US markets; in return Roosevelt gained bases and promises of military support.

TIMELINE

	1920		1930		1940	
North America	**1914** Canada enters the war against Germany	**1923** Chinese settlement in Canada is stopped	**1929** Wall St Crash leads to financial chaos in the United States		**1937** Automobile workers strike in Detroit	**1945** First atomic explosion takes places in New Mexico
	1917 The United States declares war on Germany			**1932** F.D. Roosevelt wins the US election, and introduces New Deal policies (1933)	**1939** Canada declares war on Germany	
	1919 The US Senate rejects the Treaty of Versailles				**1941** The Lend-Lease Act stimulates US industry in support of Allied war effort	
	1919 The United States outlaws intoxicating liquor (1920–33)			**1933** Newfoundland gives up its status as a dominion, but remains within the British empire	**1941** The Pearl Harbor attack leads the USA to enter the war	
Central and South	**1917** A new Mexican constitution embodies the principle of land reform	**1925** The United States intervenes in Nicaragua following a civil war	**1930** Getúlio Vargas leads a revolution in Brazil		**1939** Unions and the military clash in Argentina	
		1921 Guatemala, Honduras and El Salvador form the Republic of Central America		**1934** Cárdenas begins his reform program in Mexico	**1940** War begins between Ecuador and Peru over the Amazonia region (to 1942)	
			1929 The United States arbitrates over a border dispute between Chile and Peru	**1935** End of the Chaco War between Paraguay and Bolivia (since 1932)	**1940** "Destroyers-for-bases" deal between the United States and Britain leads to new US bases in Caribbean	
	1920		1930		1940	

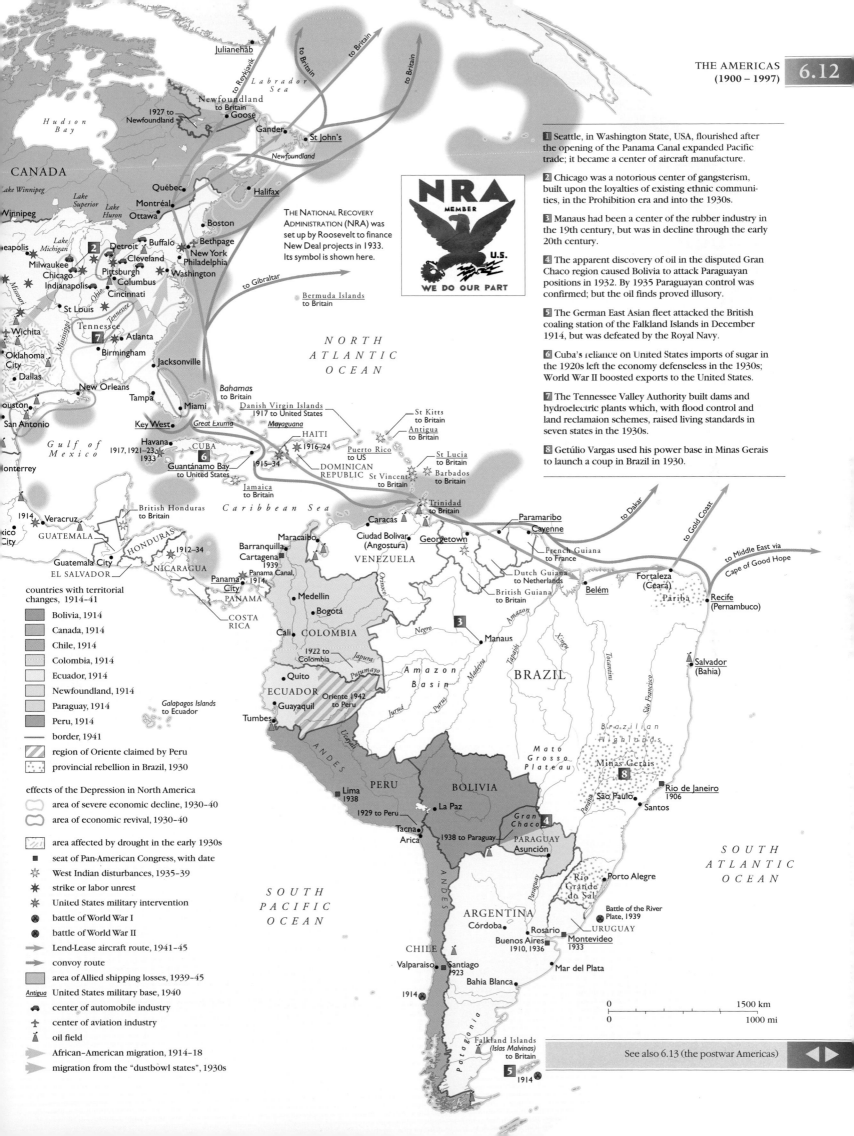

THE NATIONAL RECOVERY ADMINISTRATION (NRA) was set up by Roosevelt to finance New Deal projects in 1933. Its symbol is shown here.

NRA MEMBER U.S. WE DO OUR PART

1 Seattle, in Washington State, USA, flourished after the opening of the Panama Canal expanded Pacific trade; it became a center of aircraft manufacture.

2 Chicago was a notorious center of gangsterism, built upon the loyalties of existing ethnic communities, in the Prohibition era and into the 1930s.

3 Manaus had been a center of the rubber industry in the 19th century, but was in decline through the early 20th century.

4 The apparent discovery of oil in the disputed Gran Chaco region caused Bolivia to attack Paraguayan positions in 1932. By 1935 Paraguayan control was confirmed; but the oil finds proved illusory.

5 The German East Asian fleet attacked the British coaling station of the Falkland Islands in December 1914, but was defeated by the Royal Navy.

6 Cuba's reliance on United States imports of sugar in the 1920s left the economy defenseless in the 1930s; World War II boosted exports to the United States.

7 The Tennessee Valley Authority built dams and hydroelectric plants which, with flood control and land reclamaion schemes, raised living standards in seven states in the 1930s.

8 Getúlio Vargas used his power base in Minas Gerais to launch a coup in Brazil in 1930.

countries with territorial changes, 1914-41

- Bolivia, 1914
- Canada, 1914
- Chile, 1914
- Colombia, 1914
- Ecuador, 1914
- Newfoundland, 1914
- Paraguay, 1914
- Peru, 1914
- border, 1941
- region of Oriente claimed by Peru
- provincial rebellion in Brazil, 1930

effects of the Depression in North America

- area of severe economic decline, 1930-40
- area of economic revival, 1930-40
- area affected by drought in the early 1930s
- ■ seat of Pan-American Congress, with date
- ✳ West Indian disturbances, 1935-39
- ✴ strike or labor unrest
- ✴ United States military intervention
- ⊗ battle of World War I
- ⊗ battle of World War II
- → Lend-Lease aircraft route, 1941-45
- → convoy route
- area of Allied shipping losses, 1939-45
- *Antigua* United States military base, 1940
- center of automobile industry
- center of aviation industry
- oil field
- → African-American migration, 1914-18
- → migration from the "dustbowl states", 1930s

See also 6.13 (the postwar Americas)

0   1500 km
0   1000 mi

6.13 The Americas • 1945 – 1997 •

The United States was the undoubted victor of World War II. It suffered only sporadic attacks on its territory, while its armed forces played a decisive role in theaters of war from east Asia to western Europe. Its economy was stimulated by the war; and with its unique access to the atomic bomb, the United States looked forward to dominating the postwar world, and to a spell of prosperity at home.

In many ways the domestic dream was realized. American families formed the largest property-owning democracy in the world; they moved in large numbers away from the drudgery of field and factory into the rewarding aerospace, automobile, information technology and service industries. Their ambitions led to continuous resettlement in the United States itself, a pattern imitated by hopeful immigrants including Hispanics, Filipinos and east Asians. By 1960 almost 40 percent of American families were in the professional or skilled worker classes and prosperity grew faster than in any other industrialized country. Federal aid supported business, commerce and defense; consumer spending rose and strikes never obstructed production. Yet the United States failed to abolish the poverty that still touched a fifth of the population, to improve health care or to provide real educational opportunity for all. Poverty, especially among the blacks, was a major issue in the Civil Rights campaigns of the 1960s, and resurfaced in the 1980s and 1990s. Though sympathetic, the federal government tried to balance the undoubted needs of the poor with the demands of the United States' role as a superpower.

Nor was it unchallenged in that role, at least until the 1990s. With the start of the Cold War in the late 1940s, a nuclear arms race ensued that developed into the space race of the 1960s, culminating in putting men on the Moon in 1969. Meanwhile, the United States was drawn into costly conflicts across the globe. The Cold War affected Americans at home, too, with the McCarthy "witchhunts" against suspected Communists and sympathizers from 1950.

Latin America was a battleground of the Cold War; nowhere more so than Cuba, a virtual US client since 1898 but one overtaken by socialist–nationalist revolution in 1959. Soviet support for the new Castro regime led to a crisis in 1962, when the Soviet Union threatened to use the island as a base for nuclear missiles. The United States reasserted its dominance, though at the cost of increasing complaints at its heavy-handed involvement in the affairs of others.

The United States dominated even its northern neighbor, Canada, where economic and cultural life was increasingly dictated by the United States (most of the population lived within a few hundred kilometers of the border), even though Canada sought to build an independent Pacific role in the later 20th century. At the same time, Quebec's demands for independence grew louder.

South America too was a source of important United States commercial and political involvement, as the governments of the region – which ranged from the more or less democratic to out-and-out military dictatorships – wrestled with the problem of having such a rich and powerful neighbor. In Chile in 1973, an elected Marxist government was replaced, with United States connivance, by a right-wing dictatorship, whose practice of military rule characterized by brutal suppression of opposition was followed in many countries. Occasionally dictatorial methods were put to more constructive ends, notably in Brazil in the 1940s and 1950s. In the 1940s the charismatic Juan and Eva Perón were popular in Argentina until unemployment, strikes and inflation destroyed their appeal and brought the army to power. Argentina's military regime sought to revive its flagging popular appeal by invading the British Falkland Islands in 1982. Failure resulted in the civilian "Peronist" government of Carlos Menem, who sought to reduce inflation, privatize industry and introduce healthcare for workers.

The vested interests of the well-off, combined with the policies of the international banks to whom most countries were in debt, argued against drastic social change. As a result the environmental and social problems associated with a rapidly expanding population worsened (especially in Brazil, where São Paulo and Rio de Janiero were among the world's largest, fastest-growing cities). Indigenous peoples, like the rainforests that they inhabited, were treated as expendable in the face of land hunger and mineral-prospecting. Several countries, including Peru, endured long and violent revolutionary conflicts; others, such as Colombia, had their economies increasingly dominated by illegal drug trafficking.

Many countries entered into economic organizations: Venezuela and Ecuador were founder members of the Organization of Petroleum Exporting Countries (OPEC) in 1960; the Mercosur or Southern Cone Common Market (1991), Latin American Integration Association (1980) and Andean Pact (1969) were all attempts at economic cooperation. In 1992, to the dismay of many in the United States and Canada who feared the competition of Third World wages, the North American Free Trade Agreement was extended to include Mexico.

TIMELINE

North America

1945 The United States develops the first atom bomb at Los Alamos, New Mexico

1949 Newfoundland becomes a province of the Canadian Federation

1961 US president Kennedy launches the manned space program

1963 John F. Kennedy is assassinated in Dallas, Texas

1968 Martin Luther King is assassinated in Memphis Tennessee; youth and antiwar protests across North America

1974 US president Nixon resigns following revelations in the Watergate affair

1982 Britain gives up its last constitutional rights in Canada

1988 The North American Free Trade Agreement is signed by the United States and Canada

1992 A Canadian referendum rejects limited autonomy for Quebec

1995 A terrorist bomb explodes in Oklahoma, USA

Latin America

1946 Juan Perón is elected president of Argentina

1954 The pro-American Alfredo Stroessner becomes president of Paraguay (to 1989)

1959 Castro's Marxist revolutionaries take over in Cuba

1967 Bolivian military capture and kill Che Guevara, former associate of Castro

1967 A free-market economic boom in Brazil leads to violent opposition in the early 1970s

1973 Chile's Marxist president Allende is killed in a US-backed coup

1976–82 The "dirty war" is fought between the Argentinian military and guerrilla forces

1982 An Argentinian invasion launches the Falklands War, in which the British confirm their control over the islands

1989 Carlos Menem comes to power in Argentina, introducing economic and political reform

1990 Democracy is restored in Chile under Patricio Aylwin

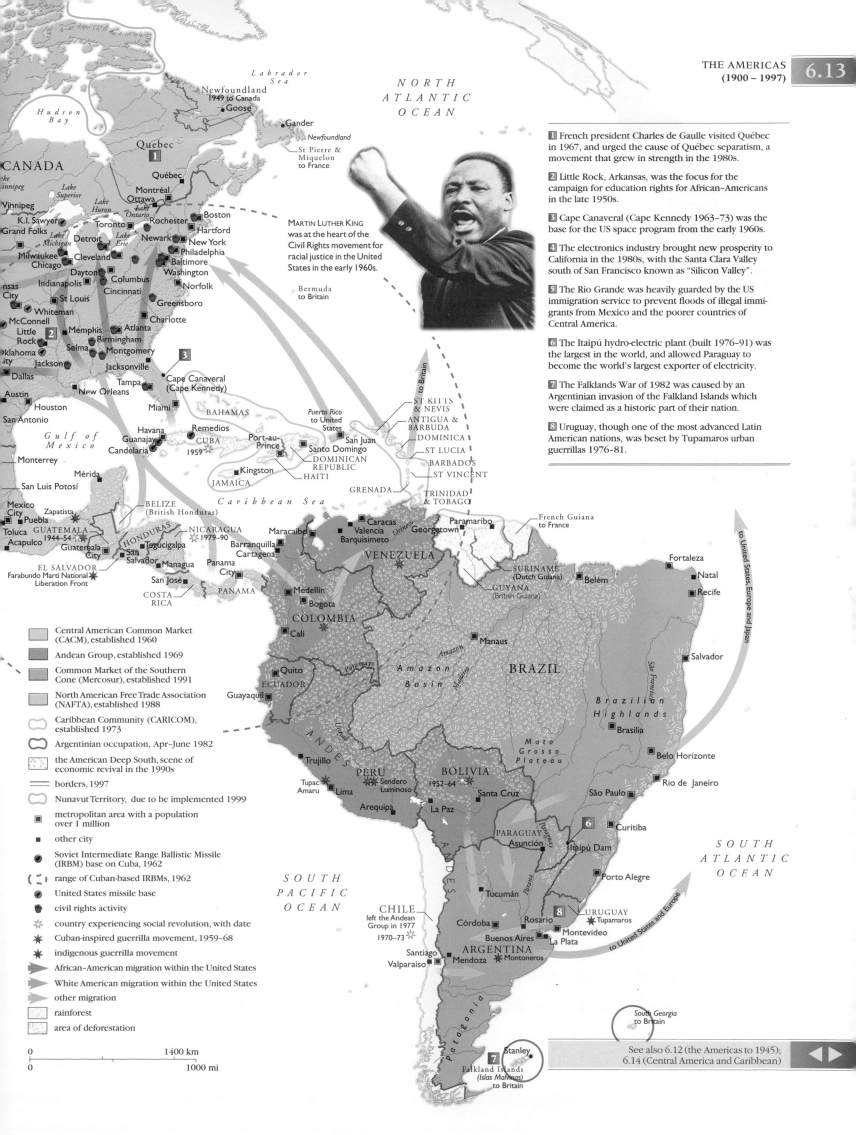

1 French president Charles de Gaulle visited Québec in 1967, and urged the cause of Québec separatism, a movement that grew in strength in the 1980s.

2 Little Rock, Arkansas, was the focus for the campaign for education rights for African–Americans in the late 1950s.

3 Cape Canaveral (Cape Kennedy 1963–73) was the base for the US space program from the early 1960s.

4 The electronics industry brought new prosperity to California in the 1980s, with the Santa Clara Valley south of San Francisco known as "Silicon Valley".

5 The Rio Grande was heavily guarded by the US immigration service to prevent floods of illegal immigrants from Mexico and the poorer countries of Central America.

6 The Itaipú hydro-electric plant (built 1976–91) was the largest in the world, and allowed Paraguay to become the world's largest exporter of electricity.

7 The Falklands War of 1982 was caused by an Argentinian invasion of the Falkland Islands which were claimed as a historic part of their nation.

8 Uruguay, though one of the most advanced Latin American nations, was beset by Tupamaros urban guerrillas 1976–81.

MARTIN LUTHER KING was at the heart of the Civil Rights movement for racial justice in the United States in the early 1960s.

Central American Common Market (CACM), established 1960

Andean Group, established 1969

Common Market of the Southern Cone (Mercosur), established 1991

North American Free Trade Association (NAFTA), established 1988

Caribbean Community (CARICOM), established 1973

Argentinian occupation, Apr–June 1982

the American Deep South, scene of economic revival in the 1990s

borders, 1997

Nunavut Territory, due to be implemented 1999

metropolitan area with a population over 1 million

other city

Soviet Intermediate Range Ballistic Missile (IRBM) base on Cuba, 1962

range of Cuban-based IRBMs, 1962

United States missile base

civil rights activity

country experiencing social revolution, with date

Cuban-inspired guerrilla movement, 1959–68

indigenous guerrilla movement

African-American migration within the United States

White American migration within the United States

other migration

rainforest

area of deforestation

0   1400 km
0   1000 mi

See also 6.12 (the Americas to 1945);
6.14 (Central America and Caribbean)

All the eight states of Central America, together with several islands of the Caribbean, have suffered from similar problems in the later 20th century. All had subsistence agriculture, unfair land distribution and a deprived native peasant class. Tax evasion by the wealthy was endemic, and labor-intensive industries were lacking. The states were too poor to fund welfare sufficiently to prevent political revolt, so political violence and state repression were commonplace. Aid (overwhelmingly from the United States) tended to prop up military leaders committed to anti-Communist policies despite frequent corruption and human rights abuses.

Before its revolution, Cuba was dominated by United States interests, with US marines stationed at their Guantánamo Bay base. Cubans who demanded political independence were treated as rebels, and any government that supported US interests was guaranteed a supply of dollars. Fidel Castro's successful revolution led to hostility from the United States and the International Monetary Fund (IMF). The Soviet Union gave Castro support, especially after the American-supported but abortive counter-coup at the Bay of Pigs in 1961. The following year, United States air surveillance revealed that Soviet intermediate range ballistic missiles (IRBMs) had been stationed on the island, and all of eastern and most of the southern United States lay within their 3,200-kilometer (2,000-mile) range. The US president Kennedy imposed a naval blockade on the islands and even considered invasion, a step that seemed inevitably to lead to nuclear war. When Soviet leader Khrushchev removed the missiles, the threat of invasion was lifted, but Castro became an enduring Soviet ally. He grew into the first Caribbean leader to have a marked impact on world affairs, sending trained guerrillas to spread Marxism–Leninism in Africa (including Angola and Ethiopia). The Soviet Union supported Cuba's economy and funded its welfare state, but Cuba went into decline after 1990 and faced severe American sanctions.

The United States believed Cuba to have fostered guerrilla revolts in Nicaragua, El Salvador, Guatemala and Honduras, and feared that these countries would come under Soviet control. Cuban guerrillas were active in El Salvador, training rebels and organizing protests. By 1976 they were fomenting strikes on coffee and cotton plantations. The army responded by taking over the government and thousands of civilian suspects were killed. A similar cycle of events occurred in Guatemala. In Nicaragua, which was ruled by the wealthy Samoza family, Sandinista guerrillas occupied Managua and set up a Marxist–Leninist state in 1979. This was, however, subverted by rightwing Contra guerrillas trained by the United States; and in 1990, with more than three-quarters of the population still below the poverty line, the Sandinista leader Daniel Ortega was voted out of office in a general election.

Mexico, the richest country in the region thanks to its reserves of oil, opposed foreign intervention and defended the Sandinistas as a "stabilizing factor" entitled to transform the people's way of life through

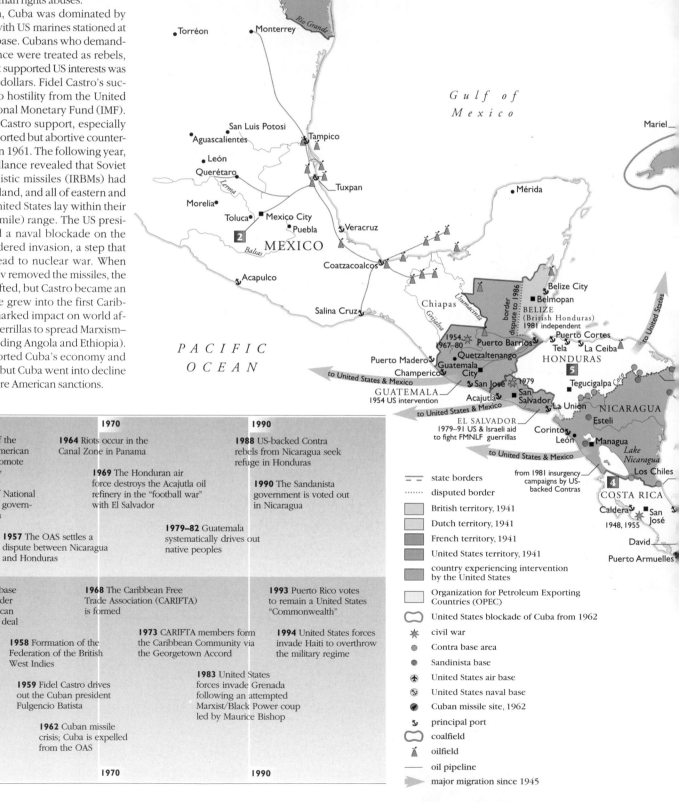

TIMELINE

Central America	**1950**	**1970**	**1990**
	1948 Formation of the Organization of American States (OAS) to promote peace and security	**1964** Riots occur in the Canal Zone in Panama	**1988** US-backed Contra rebels from Nicaragua seek refuge in Honduras
	1948 The Army of National Liberation forms a government in Costa Rica	**1969** The Honduran air force destroys the Acajutla oil refinery in the "football war" with El Salvador	**1990** The Sandinista government is voted out in Nicaragua
		1957 The OAS settles a dispute between Nicaragua and Honduras	**1979–82** Guatemala systematically drives out native peoples	

Caribbean			
	1941 A United States base is built on St Lucia under the 1940 Anglo-American "destroyers for bases" deal	**1968** The Caribbean Free Trade Association (CARIFTA) is formed	**1993** Puerto Rico votes to remain a United States "Commonwealth"
		1973 CARIFTA members form the Caribbean Community via the Georgetown Accord	**1994** United States forces invade Haiti to overthrow the military regime
	1958 Formation of the Federation of the British West Indies		
	1959 Fidel Castro drives out the Cuban president Fulgencio Batista	**1983** United States forces invade Grenada following an attempted Marxist/Black Power coup led by Maurice Bishop	
	1962 Cuban missile crisis; Cuba is expelled from the OAS		

1950 **1970** **1990**

Map legend:

- — — state borders
- .... disputed border
- British territory, 1941
- Dutch territory, 1941
- French territory, 1941
- United States territory, 1941
- country experiencing intervention by the United States
- Organization for Petroleum Exporting Countries (OPEC)
- United States blockade of Cuba from 1962
- ✳ civil war
- ● Contra base area
- ● Sandinista base
- ✈ United States air base
- ⚓ United States naval base
- Cuban missile site, 1962
- ⚓ principal port
- coalfield
- oilfield
- — oil pipeline
- ➤ major migration since 1945

1 In 1977 the United States agreed the Canal Zone, under US control since the beginning of the century, would be handed over to Panama in 2000.

2 The population of Mexico City rose to more than 20 million in the mid-1990s. Many people lived on the streets or in squalid and dangerous conditions.

3 The last Soviet advisors left Cuba in 1993, when a renewed United States blockade of the island took effect. Many Cubans attempted to reach the United States illegally; Miami became a popular destination for Cuban exiles.

4 Costa Rica sought to avoid many of the political conflicts of Central America, and in 1987 its president Arias Sánchez won the Nobel Prize for his attempt to draw up a peace plan for the region.

5 In 1969 war between Honduras and El Salvador broke out following a World Cup soccer match between the two countries.

6 Barbados, which was a British colony until 1966 but which had enjoyed a degree of self-government since 1639, was used as a base for the United States invasion of Grenada in 1983.

CHE GUEVARA, from Argentina, helped Castro in Cuba. He was an icon of revolution through the Americas.

revolution. The country had few law and order problems, although the population quadrupled from 1940 and a recession hit in 1984. A Zapatista revolt in Chiapas province was crushed ten years later.

The United States intervened in the internal affairs of several Caribbean islands, again prompted by fear of Communism. The Dominican Republic was invaded by paratroopers in 1965, Grenada in 1983, and Haiti (the first Caribbean state to gain its independence) in 1994. Another United States intervention was to arrest on charges of drugs smuggling the president of Panama, Manuel Noriega, in 1989.

In 1958-62 an unsuccessful federation of West Indian states was tried, after which most sought independence (achieved peacefully for the most part) or chose to remain as British dependencies. In the 1950s, Britain actively sought immigrants from the West Indies, but curtailed this in 1962. Jamaica faced overpopulation, unemployment and racial tension, but its educational programs and tourist attractions improved job opportunities. Trinidad and Tobago, richly endowed with oil, natural gas and asphalt, suffered from a high birth rate, strikes and sabotage due to Black Power groups and embittered Asians working on the sugar plantations. Belize, a former British colony, was the last Central American country to gain its independence; it remained a firm supporter of United States policies.

See also 6.13 (the Americas from 1945)

World War I imposed unbearable social and economic strain on Russia. The czar, who had assumed personal command of the armed forces in 1915, was held responsible for many of the failures of the war, and abdicated following a revolution in Petrograd in March (February in the Russian calendar) 1917. A provisional government took power but its decision to continue the war combined with fear of counterrevolution led to increasing radicalization. Local *soviets* – committees of workers, soldiers and sailors – sprang up in industrial areas. Many were dominated by the radical socialist parties, among whom the anti-war Bolsheviks (led by Vladimir Ilych Lenin since his return in April from exile in Berne) won growing influence. In November (October) 1917, the Bolsheviks overthrew the government.

The Bolsheviks were heavily outnumbered in the Constituent Assembly by the Socialist Revolutionaries representing the peasantry. Lenin therefore dissolved the Assembly and fought a bloody civil war to secure his position. Non-Bolshevik socialists, liberals, aristocrats, national minorities and the peasantry all opposed the regime, and several foreign powers also intervened. Nevertheless, the "Whites" (anti-Bolshevik forces) were too divided geographically and politically to depose the government. Nineteen independent governments were formed but, although at one point the Whites were within 400 kilometers (250 miles) of Moscow, the Bolsheviks ("Reds") recaptured the Ukraine, Caucasus, central Asia and Siberia. They ceded territory to Poland and recognized the independence of the Baltic states, but in 1923 the Union of Soviet Socialist Republics (USSR) was created, comprising the republics of Russia, Ukraine, Belorussia and Transcaucasia.

During the civil war the Bolsheviks adopted a policy of "war communism" and requisitioned food for the army and cities. This brought an arduous struggle with the peasantry which culminated in widespread revolts in 1920–22 and a famine in the Volga region that killed five million people. With the end of the civil war in 1921 Lenin adopted the "new economic policy" (NEP). This reintroduced limited

TIMELINE

Political change

1920	1930	1940
1917 Ukraine, Finland. Latvia, Lithuania claim independence	**1926** The Soviet Union and Germany sign a neutrality pact	**1939** Stalin signs the Nazi–Soviet pact with Hitler
1920 The Red Army invades Poland	**1934** Start of the "great terror" after the assassination of Leningrad Party secretary Kirov	**1939** The Soviet Union occupies eastern Poland and Finland
1917 (Mar) First revolution; czar abdicates and provisional government is set up	**1920–21** Ukraine, the Caucasus states and Turkestan are reconquered; Mongolia expels the Chinese	**1934** The Soviet Union joins the League of Nations
1917 (Nov) The Bolsheviks seize power	**1922** Treaty of Rapallo: Soviet–German commercial and military agreement	**1936–38** Height of the great purges in the Soviet Union
1918 (Mar) Bolsheviks sign the Treaty of Brest-Litovsk	**1922–23** Formation of the Union of Soviet Socialist Republics (USSR)	**1940** The Soviet Union occupies the Baltic states; Finland sues for peace
1918–21 Civil war between the "Whites" and the "Reds"	**1924** Death of Lenin	**1936** Stalin's constitution is promulgated
1918 The Caucasus states and Estonia declare independence		**1941** Germany invades the Soviet Union
		1938 Purge of the armed forces by Stalin

Economic change

1920	1930	1940
1918 Depopulation of towns and cities in the civil war	**1928** The first Five Year Plan is announced	**1933** The second Five Year Plan is announced	**1939** The third Five Year Plan is announced
1920–22 Peasant revolts occur throughout Russia	**1929** The collectivization of agriculture is announced	
1921 The "new economic policy" is introduced	**1932–33** Famine in the Ukraine and central Asia	

1920   1930   1940

free trade to encourage the peasants to produce more while the Bolsheviks (soon to be called Communists) tried to modernize the country.

Lenin died in 1924 without leaving an obvious successor, but Joseph Stalin used his post as general-secretary of the Communist Party to secure control of the state. The Communists now had to face the contradiction that they were a workers' government in a peasant country. In 1929 Stalin addressed this issue by ordering the collectivization of agriculture.

Private trade was abolished and peasants forced to give up their private holdings and work on collective farms. Many responded by slaughtering their livestock and planting only enough grain to feed themselves. When this was requisitioned famine ensued, and millions were deported to the *gulag* (prison camps), resulting in around 14.5 million deaths.

Collectivization was intended to cow the peasantry and provide sufficient grain to support a massive program of industrialization as the Soviet

Union was built into a modern economic power. Even during the famine, grain was being used to feed the city population and sold abroad to buy western technology. In 1928 Stalin announced the first Five Year Plan, with which he proposed that the Soviet Union should catch up with the west which, he claimed, was "50 to 100 years ahead". Production grew quickly, especially in the heavy and defense industries as old industrial centers were expanded and new ones created in remote regions.

Industrial development was undermined by the purges that Stalin unleashed in 1934. "Subversives" (in the first instance, old Bolsheviks) appeared in show trials, were convicted of fantastic crimes and shot, while millions of others faced deportation to labor camps. Stalin's war with his own population extended across the Soviet Union as he sought scapegoats for the failures of collectivization and industrialization to achieve the targets set out in the Plan. Fear and suspicion led to mass denunciations and the decimation of the upper levels of bureaucracy and Party.

By 1938 a purge of the army and navy began and the country lost most of its officer corps. The following year Stalin agreed the Nazi–Soviet pact with Hitler and subsequently occupied eastern Poland and the Baltic states. Stalin apparently believed that Hitler would not invade Russia until France and Britain were defeated; he also thought that fascism, which he saw as the highest form of capitalism, must presage the Communist revolution in Europe.

In 1941, though, Hitler did invade. The Soviet Union was in a better position to resist than Russia had been in 1914, despite the depredations of the purges. Communism had been established against all the odds in what had been Europe's most backward country. Stalin's policies, which were mainly an extension of those used by Lenin to win the civil war, were pursued at massive human cost and allowed the Communist Party to prevail.

1 Petrograd (renamed Leningrad in 1924) was imperial Russia's capital and largest city. It was the conduit for revolutionary ideas and the center of events in 1917.

2 The Bolsheviks held the central position in the civil war and control of the rail network centered on Moscow (the capital from March 1918), was vital to their cause.

3 A variety of forces opposed the Bolsheviks: the Czech legion, formed to fight for the Allies during World War I, tried to get home via Vladivostok and in 1918 controlled the trans-Siberian railroad.

4 Magnitogorsk was the showpiece of Soviet industrializiation, a huge industrial plant built in the shadow of the Urals.

5 The Soviet "corrective labor camps", known by their acronym (*gulag*), were originally set up by Lenin. They became a key feature of Stalin's economic policy as well as of the eradication of opposition.

6 Tambov was the focus of violent peasant rebellions in 1920–22.

POSTERS publicized the Bolshevik cause. This image shows Lenin in typical pose.

Map labels

New Siberian Islands
Wrangel Island
Nordvik
Dubinka
Norilsk
Igarka
Tiksi
Kolymskaya
Ambarchik
Anadyr
Maklakovo
Krasnoyarsk
Lena
Magadan

UNION OF SOVIET
SOCIALIST REPUBLICS
from 1923

Petropavlovsk
Sea of Okhotsk

Cheremkhovo
Lake Baykal
Irkutsk
Ulan Ude
Chita
Far Eastern Republic
1920–22 independent
Magdagachi
Nikolaevsk
1925 to Russia
Aleksandrovsk
Sakhalin
Komsomolsk
Sovetskaya Gavan
Khabarovsk
Ulan Bator

Kuril Islands

MONGOLIA
1924 Communist state under Russian influence

Gobi Desert
Manchuria
Harbin

Mukden
(Shenyang)
Vladivostok
Beijing
Lushun
(Port Arthur)
Sea of Japan
Yellow
Lanzhou
CHINA
Korea
Chosen from 1910 to Japan
Tokyo
JAPAN
Yellow Sea

NORTH
PACIFIC
OCEAN

Legend

— western frontier of Russian empire, 1914
🚩 principal town where Bolsheviks seized power, Nov–Dec 1917
▨ area controlled by Bolsheviks, Aug 1918
➤ advance of anti-Bolshevik armies, 1918–20
⊃ area controlled by Bolsheviks, Oct 1919
— border of temporarily independent area
➤ Japanese Siberian expedition, 1918–22
▨ Union of Soviet Socialist Republics, 1939
— border, 1939

➤ Russian campaign, 1939
▨ main area of collectivization
⊃ area under *gulag* administration
● new town founded 1925–38
⚒ oilfield
≈ hydroelectric power station
— railroad

0   800 km
0   500 mi

See also 6.16 (postwar Soviet Union)

The German army took full advantage of the depradations wrought by the purges to advance far into Russia. Yet after the defeat of the Germans at Stalingrad and Kursk, the Soviet forces advanced to Berlin by April 1945. At the cost of 20 million lives, the Soviet Union emerged from the war a superpower; it took back the lands it had lost in 1918 and liberated most of east Europe, then incorporated the region into what was effectively an empire. In 1949 it became a nuclear power.

However, the basic problems of the Soviet Union remained: agricultural production was costly and weak, bureaucracy was rampant in state and industry, and order (especially over national minorities) was enforced by terror. The Red Army took several years to put down partisan armies in Ukraine and Poland, while the annexed Baltic states were also hostile to Soviet rule. The western republics had sustained the highest casualty rates of the war, yet Stalin dealt with resurgent nationalism by deporting several subject nationalities for alleged collaboration. An anti-Jewish campaign was begun in 1948 to widespread dismay; many, including members of the ruling Politburo, greeted Stalin's death in 1953 with relief rather than sorrow.

Many political prisoners were freed shortly after and, in another sign of a change of atmosphere, only Lavrenti Beria, head of the security forces, was executed after wrangling over the succession. Eventually Nikita Khrushchev emerged as the new Soviet head and he tried to rectify the problems of the Soviet Union, attacking Stalin in 1956. Khrushchev tried to enthuse, rather than coerce, the Soviet people, launching a "race to Communism" to be completed by 1980. He sought to improve the sluggish economy by producing consumer goods and the bureaucratic administration by decentralizing economic planning. However, he often relied on publicity stunts, especially in foreign policy. Two notable failures were the Cuban missile crisis and the Sino-Soviet split. Planning for the possibility of war

TIMELINE

Political change

1944 The Soviet Union occupies the Baltic states

1945 Following the end of the war in Europe, Stalin deports many subject nationalities

1953 Death of Stalin; Khrushchev is general-secretary

1956 Khrushchev denounces Stalin

1957 The political rift between Moscow and Beijing widens

1961 Khrushchev launces the "race to Communism"

1964 Khrushchev is ousted from power; Brezhnev and Kosygin vie for power

1972 US president Nixon visits the USSR

1977 The "Brezhnev constitution" is introduced; Brezhnev becoomes president

1980 Demonstrations break out in Estonia

1982 Yuri Andropov becomes Soviet general secretary on death of Brezhnev

1985 Mikhail Gorbachev becomes Soviet leader

1989 The USSR withdraws from the war in Afghanistan

1990 Under a more liberal constitution, Gorbachev is elected president

1991 Gorbachev resigns after an attempted coup

1991 Dissolution of the USSR, formation of the CIS

Other change

1949 The USSR explodes its first atomic bomb

1954 Khrushchev launches the "virgin lands" policy

1957 The launch of Sputnik II initiates the space race

1961 Soviet cosmonaut Yuri Gagarin is first man in space

1964 Subsidies are paid to peasant farmers

1968 Censorship is tightened following Czechoslovak attempted liberalization

1974 Peasants are granted limited freedom of movement

1986 Chernobyl nuclear power plant blows up

1988 Nationality disturbances in Nagorno-Karabakh

1989 Miners' strikes in Donbass region threaten the Soviet regime

with NATO and China simultaneously proved a huge drain on Soviet resources. Increasingly, heavy industry and rocket technology (with which the Soviet Union astonished the world by launching the world's first artificial satellite, Sputnik 2, in 1957) absorbed money earmarked for other areas.

Khrushchev could not remedy the problems of agriculture. Artificial fertilizers increased the yield of existing farms and helped cultivate untilled soil – the "virgin lands" campaign. Despite initial successes, the overfarming of land led to poor harvests and soil erosion; in 1963 the USSR was forced to import grain from the United States and Canada. Shortly thereafter, Khrushchev was deposed in a palace coup.

Under his successor Leonid Brezhnev, the Soviet Union atrophied. Brezhnev reversed Khrushchev's administrative policies and gave the bureaucracy the security it craved. Corruption became endemic and growth rates slowed. By his death in 1982, it was evident that decisive action was required. The climate of international détente fostered in the 1970s evaporated with the Soviet invasion of Afghanistan and the election of the hawkish Ronald Reagan as president of the United States in 1980. Arms spending soared and the technological gap became ever more apparent. Grain subsidies, first paid to farmers by Khrushchev and increased by Brezhnev, were now four times larger and exceeded the defense budget. In 1985 Mikhail Gorbachev, the youngest general-secretary of the Party since Stalin, took over.

Gorbachev aimed to reduce spending on arms and introduce reform at home. Glasnost ("openness") and perestroika ("restructuring") became the key notes of his program but they failed to bring a reformed Soviet system as he envisaged. He underestimated the extent to which internal tensions were hidden by the firm hand of the state. The introduction of discussion into public life and the relaxation of censorship allowed grievances – social, economic and national – to surface. Economic difficulties were exacerbated by Gorbachev's reforms, but the crucial area of dispute proved to be the nationalities question. Liberals in the republics fixed onto the idea of independence, the Baltic states and the Caucasus leading the way. At the same time the state was undermined in its heartland by the opposition of the Moscow-based reformist Boris Yeltsin. Elections did not provide a mandate for Gorbachev's reforms but rather took them further than he had envisaged and led to the dissolution of the Soviet Union, despite a last-gasp coup in 1991 by reactionaries to forestall change. The Union was replaced by a loosely-based Commonwealth of Independent States (CIS). These faced drastic reorganization into market economies, and several – including the Russian Federation – faced civil war over nationality issues. Some inherited part of the decaying nuclear arsenal and environmental problems, including outdated nuclear power plants such as that at Chernobyl in Ukraine, which in 1986 had exploded in the world's worst nuclear disaster.

YURI GAGARIN, in 1961 the first man in space, provided a propaganda coup worldwide for Khrushchev's USSR.

1 The murder of Politburo member Andrei Zhdanov in 1948 gave Stalin a chance to purge the Leningrad Communist Party. In 1991 the city rejected its Soviet past and reverted to its former name of St Petersburg.

2 Chernobyl's aging nuclear reactor exploded in 1986, causing much of west and north Europe to be exposed to radiation. The Soviet bureaucracy was blamed for allowing the accident to occur.

3 Demonstrations in Estonia in 1980–81 followed the success of the Solidarity movement in Poland, which was reported on Finnish television.

4 Nagorno-Karabakh, an Armenian enclave in Azerbaijan, became the focus for fierce fighting in 1988.

5 As the granary of the Soviet Union, Ukraine was essential to its existence. It had a tradition of opposition, including partisan resistance from 1945 to the early 1950s, and voted for independence in 1991.

6 Tatarstan declared its independence in 1991, and in 1992 claimed to be a sovereign state; in 1994 it compromised, agreeing to be a state united with Russia.

Map labels:
New Siberian Islands
Wrangel Island
Taimyr (Dolgan–Nenets)
Bilibino
Chukot
RUSSIAN FEDERATION from 1991
Evenki
Koryak
Yenisey
Magadan
Gladkaya
Krasnoyarsk
Kansk
Lena
Sea of Okhotsk
Ust Ordyn Buryat
Irkutsk
Lake Baykal
Chita
Sakhalin
Agin Buryat
Olovyannaya
Svobodnyy
Ulan Bator
Kuril Islands
Birobijan Jewish Autonomous Region
Khabarovsk
MONGOLIA
Gobi Desert
CHINA
Harbin
Vladivostok
Mukden
Yellow
Beijing
NORTH KOREA
Pyongyang
Sea of Japan
Seoul
SOUTH KOREA
JAPAN
Tokyo
NORTH PACIFIC OCEAN

Legend:
— border of USSR, 1945
— border, 1991
CIS member states
autonomous state within Russian Federation
— border of autonomous ethnic area
territory disputed with China
* uprising against Soviet intervention
☆ ethnic unrest
area under Soviet influence at some time between 1945-91
⊘ ICBM base
★ cosmodrome
⌂ nuclear power station
area of "virgin land" policy
wheat production area
1991 date of independence from USSR

A.   Albania
B–H. Bosnia-Herzegovina
C.   Croatia
M.   Macedonia (former Yugoslav Republic of)
S.   Slovenia
Y.   Yugoslavia

0   800 km
0   500 mi

See also 6.08, 6.09 (World War II in Europe);
6.15 (USSR to 1941); 6.11 (Europe since 1991)

The sudden but relatively bloodless revolution of 1911 led to the abdication of the Manchu emperor; the new republic was headed first by Sun Yixian (Sun Yat-sen) and then by Yuan Shikai (from 1912). Yuan used terror to consolidate his power and banned the Guomindang (KMT – Nationalist Party); the disillusioned Sun Yixiang sought refuge in Japan which was allied with Britain and France against Germany. Japanese troops landed on the Shandong peninsula, seized the German base at Qingdao and demanded concessions from Yuan. Yuan, seeing China threatened by Japan and by continuing uncertainty, planned a new dynasty with himself as emperor. After another rebellion, Yuan retreated to Beijing where he died in 1916.

China drifted into a state of chaos. Warlords pillaged the countryside. When floods or famine struck, there was no administration available to alleviate the effects. China sided with the Allies in World War I, but gained nothing at the Versailles peace conference. Japan kept its foothold in Shandong, while foreign governments held concessions along the coast as well as those bordering the Yangtze river. Chinese sovereignty and territorial rights were ignored. Students receptive to the teachings of Marx led nationalist demonstrations and helped form the Chinese Communist Party (CCP) in Shanghai.

The Soviet Union assisted in the formation of the CCP but supported Sun Yixiang's Guomindang and provided military and political guidance to emerging Guomindang leaders such as Jiang Jieshi (Chiang Kai-shek), who succeeded Sun Yixiang, and who built up a powerful base in Guangdong province. Jiang moved against the warlords in the north and devised the "white terror" to eliminate the Communists. The survivors fled into Jiangxi province where they soon came under Guomindang attack.

The Japanese invasion of Manchuria transformed the situation. Jiang was unwilling to commit himself to a major war against Japan, regarding the Japanese as a "disease of the skin" but the Communists as a "disease of the heart". He continued his war of extermination against the Communists and forced them to break out from their Jiangxi soviet. From here they began their Long March to Yan'an in Shaanxi province, during which Mao Zedong emerged as the CCP leader. Their retreat left Jiang master of the rich valley of the lower Yangtze. Here he attempted to force through an industrial and communications revolution, bringing in expertise from Fascist Italy, Nazi Germany and the United States.

In 1937 Japan launched a fullscale invasion of China from Manchuria, and Jiang shifted his capital from Nanjing to Chongqing. Since Jiang could hold out as long as he received supplies from the western Allies, Japan moved into French Indo-China to cut the rail link with Chongqing. Jiang used conscripted armies equipped with American materiel, and cajoled and bribed warlords to fight on his behalf. His supplies arrived via the Burma Road (until the Japanese cut it in 1942), via the Ledo Road during 1945 and by Allied transport aircraft flying over the mountains east of the Brahmaputra. In the north Mao Zedong organized a guerrilla war against the Japanese but the fighting remained local. When the Americans built up a bomber force in west China, the Japanese overran a great deal of China in an attempt to destroy the US bases.

For the Chinese people, World War II was merely an interruption in the protracted civil war. The Japanese surrender gave the Communists and the Nationalists the chance to compete for Manchuria. At this point, however, the US terminated all aid to both sides. Inflation, corruption and food shortages soon wrecked civilian morale and despair transferred to the Nationalist soldiers. In 1948, when US president Truman agreed to restore aid supplies, the Communist People's Liberation Army (PLA) was already moving south. The PLA crossed the Yangtze in 1949 and, as Nationalist armies crumbled, began a triumphal march through the cities of southern China. By September the civil war was virtually over and Mao Zedong announced the final victory over foreign and domestic enemies, and the establishment of the People's Republic of China with himself as chairman of the central government.

☼ strike or demonstration, 1919
→ Nationalist and pro-Nationalist "Northern Expedition", 1926–28
□ area under Nationalist China control, 1937
□ area under Chinese warlord control, 1937
— provincial border, 1937
⬭ area of Communist soviet
➤ Long March, 1934–35
⬭ area of Communist headquarters after 1935
⬛ area occupied by Japan, 1931–33
⬭ Japanese gains, 1934–44
⬭ Japanese gains, 1944–45
➤ Japanese invasion
⊕ US airbase, 1944
▨ Communist occupation by 1946
▨ Communist occupation, 1946–48
▨ Communist occupation, 1948–49
➤ PLA campaign, 1949
— border, 1949
⬭ Nationalist China, 1949
— important supply road
— railroad

Xinjiang

TIBET
1912 independent

Brahmaputra

NEPAL

HIMALAYAS

Lhasa •

1 In May 1919 students at Beijing University protested fruitlessly against the disregard of Chinese interests at the Versailles peace conference.

2 The Communists set up a Peasants' Union in 1922 near Haifeng in eastern Guangdong to mobilize rural hatred of landlords and to build a peasants' army.

3 Nanjing was the capital of Jiang Jieshi's Guomindang government from 1928–37; Jiang presented himself as "China's Hitler or China's Stalin".

4 More than 100,000 Communists under Mao Zedong trekked over 8,000 km (5,000 miles) between October 1934 and October 1935 in order to escape Guomindang encirclement.

5 At Xuzhou in December 1948 to January 1949, the Communists achieved a decisive victory over a larger, better equipped Nationalist army.

6 The Battle of Kaifeng in 1948 (a brief Nationalist victory) was the first "positional" battle between the Nationalists and Communists.

7 Jiang Jieshi planned his final stand against the Communists at Xichang in 1949, but then decided to flee to Taiwan.

TIMELINE

Nationalist China and Japan

1920

1911 The Chinese revolution begins in the Wuhan area

1912 Proclamation of Republic of China; the last Manchu emperor abdicates

1914 Japanese troops land on the Shandong peninsula

1917 Sun Yixiang establishes headquarters in Guangzhou

1923 Jiang Jieshi visits Moscow to study Soviet Red Army tactics

1925 Sun Yixiang dies

1926–28 Northern Expedition against the warlords

1940

1931 Japan invades Manchuria

1937 Japan invades China

1937 Nonaggression Pact with Russia is signed

1937–38 The Burma Road is constructed

1942 Britain and US airlift supplies to Kunming

1944 Japanese offensive to capture US air bases

1949–50 Jiang Jieshi flees to Taiwan and establishes the Republic of Nationalist China government there

Communists

1921 Chinese Communist Party (CCP) holds its first national congress in Shanghai

1927 The CCP's United Front with the Guomindang against the warlords collapses with the start of the "white terror"

1930–31 The CCP survives three Nationalist attacks

1934–35 The CCP undertakes the Long March to Yan'an

1947 Communist leader Mao Zedong leaves Yan'an

1948 Lin Biao forms the People's Liberation Army (PLA) and campaigns successfully in Manchuria

1949 PLA captures Beijing

1949 Mao Zedong proclaims the People's Republic of China

1920

1940

Jiang Jieshi shifted his power base to Chengdu and then abandoned the mainland, transferring "Nationalist China" to the island of Taiwan where he remained as president until his death in 1975. Apart from Taiwan and some offshore islands, mainland China was now under the control of the CCP. The Soviet Union and the Communist bloc recognized the People's Republic, as did Britain in 1950. The United States, though, remained hostile and refused to allow China's admission to the United Nations, insisting until 1971 that Taiwan retain China's seat on the Security Council.

A 1930s WOODCUT by artist Li Hua captures the anger, frustration and restlessness of the Chinese peasantry in an age of warfare.

Lake Baykal

Chita

Nerchinsk

Amur

Blagoveshchensk

Khabarovsk

1931

Manchuria
(Manzhouguo)

Xinqing

Hailar

Nomonhan
1939

Qiqihar

Harbin

1939

1931

Songhua

Ussuri

Changchun

Jilin

1931

Vladivostok

Lake Khanka

Inner Mongolian Plateau

MONGOLIA
1911 independent,
1924 Communist state under
Russian influence

Gobi Desert

Chahar

Jehol
ceded to Japan 1933

Chengde

Shenyang
(Mukden)

Fushun
1948

Anshan

Yalu

1931

Sea of Japan

North Korea
1948 independent

Pyongyang

Lushun
(Port Arthur)

Seoul

SOUTH KOREA
1948 independent

Pusan

Suiyuan

Ghanzou

Ningxia

Baotou

Zhangjiakou

1

Beijing

Tangshan

1937

Datong 1949

Baoding

Tianjin

Dengzhou

Shandong Peninsula

Ordos Desert

Yulin

Yellow

Taiyuan

Zhili

Jinan

Shandong

Qingdao

1914

Yellow Sea

Lake Qinghai

Shanxi

Yan'an

Handan

Anyang

Xinxiang

Yellow

6

Xuzhou
1948–49

Lianyungang

Nagasaki

Qinghai

Lanzhou

QIN MTS

Gangu

Yuncheng

Zhengzhou

Luoyang

Xi'an

Kaifeng
1948

5

Jiangsu

JAPAN

Shaanxi

Henan

Nanyang

Anhui

Taizhou

Yangzhou

Zhenjiang

1932

Ryukyu Islands
to Japan 1879

CHINA

Guangha

Huai

Nanjing

Wuxi

Shanghai

1937

Han

Hubei

Wuhan

3

Hangzhou

Suzhou

East China Sea

Sichuan

Nanchong

Wanxian

Yichang

Ningbo

Chengdu

Lichuan

Yangtze

Zhejiang

Hsikang

Chongqing

Luzhou

Lake Dongting

Nanchang

Lake Pengli

Wenzhou

1942

7

Changsha

Jiangxi

Yalong

Xichang

Zunyi

Hunan

Fuzhou

Matsu
1942

Jinsha

4

Hengyang

Lingling

Suichuan

Juichin

Fujian

Dinjan

Ledo

Burma Road

Kunming

Guizhou

Guilin

Guangdong

Xiamen
(Amoy)

Quemoy
1938

Taipei

Bhamo

Yunnan

Liuzhou

Wuzhou

Shantou
(Swatow)

1939

Taiwan
to Japan until 1945

Lashio

Gejiu

Guangxi

Nanning

Xi

Guangzhou
(Canton)

Haifeng

2

South China Sea

Mandalay

Ledo Road

Irrawaddy

Saluween

BURMA
1948 independent

1942

Vietnam

Lan Son

Hanoi

Beihai

Zhanjiang

Macao
to Portugal

Hong Kong
to Britain

1938

FRENCH INDO–CHINA

Haiphong

Lan-zang

THAILAND
Siam until 1939

Laos

1940

Rangoon

Mekong

1941

Haikou

Hainan
1938–39 to Japan,
1945 to Nationalist China,
1950 to Communist China

1941

0   800 km

0   600 mi

See also 6.19 (World War II);
6.20 China under Mao)

The Russo-Japanese War of 1904–05 gave Japan protectorate authority over Korea and the lease of Chinese territory in south Manchuria. From these bases the army looked to consolidate its influence in Manchuria and north China. By this time, a new and increasingly militant anti-imperialist nationalism was developing among young Chinese intellectuals, merchants and soldiers. This development was echoed elsewhere in the region, for example in the growth of Indian and Vietnamese national movements. In the case of China, resentment after 1905 was clearly focussed on Japan as the other western powers were preoccupied with European politics and hoped merely to hold onto their Asian interests.

Tokyo's decision to enter World War I was driven as much by interests in China – where the Manchu dynasty had finally fallen three years earlier – as by the desire to help its ally Britain. In August 1914 Japan issued an ultimatum to Germany to hand over territories in Shandong province. Japan then took the German outpost of Qingdao; the whole province was eventually occupied.

As one of the victorious nations, Japan was invited to attend the Versailles peace conference in 1919 and retained the former German territory in Shandong. However, this conference marked a turning point in the position of the European powers in east Asia – Britain, France, the Netherlands, and, to a lesser extent, Portugal. All had been weakened by the war, while the revolution of 1917 ended Russia's imperialism. The League of Nations, created in the aftermath of war, adopted a policy generally critical of colonialism. In the interwar years Britain, while publicly supporting its empire, privately explored ways to enable the Asian colonies to achieve self-governing Dominion status (like New Zealand, since 1907) or Commonwealth status (like Australia). The Dutch, too, were beginning to consider ways of passing power to the native populations.

Nationalist movements in the colonies were given impetus by the severe effects of the worldwide depression of the 1930s and the collapse of European prestige wrought by the carnage of World War I. In India, the Indian National Congress, led by Jawaharlal Nehru and Mohandas "Mahatma" Gandhi, organized a mass self-rule movement in the 1920s and 1930s. In Burma, which was separated from India and given a form of responsible government in 1937, nationalist demands were heightened by the depression. The Dutch East Indies experienced a Communist uprising in 1926–27, and French Indo-China also saw Communist-inspired strikes and rural unrest with the overall objective of national independence. Neither the French nor the Dutch made significant concessions, and – except in India – the nationalist movements appeared divided and unable to make a lasting impression. The United States, though, appeared to support the nationalists, and in 1935 promised independence for its own colony in the Philippines within ten years.

The general unrest in east and southeast Asia led Japan into further military expansion from 1931. After establishing the puppet state of Manzhouguo in Manchuria, however, Japan was criticized by the League of Nations and quit this body in protest. The resulting international isolation made Japan turn for new allies to Germany and Italy and, in China, to pursue an even more aggressive and uncompromising policy toward the Nationalist government which was already engaged in civil war with Chinese Communists. In mid-1937 Japan and China engaged unofficially in a war which Japanese generals confidently promised would be over by the end of the year. Japan's bombing of cities and the massacre of civilians as its forces took the Nationalist cities of Shanghai and Nanjing brought the war to the attention of the world, heightening criticism in the west.

In 1939 Japanese forces landed in French Indo-China to cut off supply routes to the Chinese Nationalists. After the fall of France to Hitler in 1940, the Japanese went on to occupy most of the colony, while maintaining a French administration. Politically, the Japanese exploited the anti-European feeling among the nationalist groups, promising a form of independence such as Burma had been given. Economic prosperity was similarly promised in the Japanese-sponsored Greater East Asian Co-Prosperity Sphere. Some – such as the Indian leader

borders, 1914
British territory, 1914
Dutch territory, 1914
French territory, 1914
German territory, 1914
Japanese territory, 1914
Portuguese territory, 1914
United States territory, 1914

territorial gains from Germany by mandate, 1920
  Australian
  Japanese

Japanese territorial expansion in Asia
  temporary occupation, 1915–25
  gains by 1934 (empire of Manzhouguo)
  gains by 1937
  gains by 7 Dec 1941

  under Japanese influence, 1936–40
  Chinese Communist headquarters, 1937
  strong Indian National Congress support
● Allied base
oil strategic resource
☆ area of anti-colonial agitation
— Burma road
➤ Japanese attack

0   1200 km
0   800 mi

TIMELINE

Japan

1904–05 Japan defeats Russia and wins control of Manchuria

1910 Japan annexes Korea

1914 Japan takes the German-leased territory in Shandong province, China

1918–22 Japanese forces invade Siberia as part of an Allied expedition to Russia

1919 Japanese gains in China are confirmed by Treaty of Versailles

1920 Japan is mandated control of the former German Pacific islands by the League of Nations

1932 Japan sets up the puppet state of Manzhouguo in Manchuria

1933 Japan withdraws from the League of Nations

1937 Japanese expansion in China begins

1937 The United States threatens to impose an oil embargo on Japan

1938 Fighting breaks out between Japanese and Soviet forces on Manzhouguo–Soviet border

1940 Japanese control is extended over Indo-China

1941 Japan attacks the United States at Pearl Harbor

Other powers

1915 Australian and New Zealand forces make an important contribution to the Allied attack on Turkey at Gallipoli

1920 Former German territories in the Pacific are mandated to Australia, Britain and Japan by the League of Nations

1920 Mahatma Gandhi takes control of the Indian National Congress

1926 Anticolonial Communist agitation takes place in the Dutch East Indies

1927 Ahmed Sukarno sets up the Indonesian Nationalist Party

1930 Gandhi institutes salt marches to protest against British rule in India

1935 British Government of India Act reforms the Indian administration

1939 The kingdom of Siam is renamed Thailand, celebrating its avoidance of colonial rule

1941 A Communist-nationalist guerrilla organization, the Viet-minh, is set up in Indo-China

1920   1940

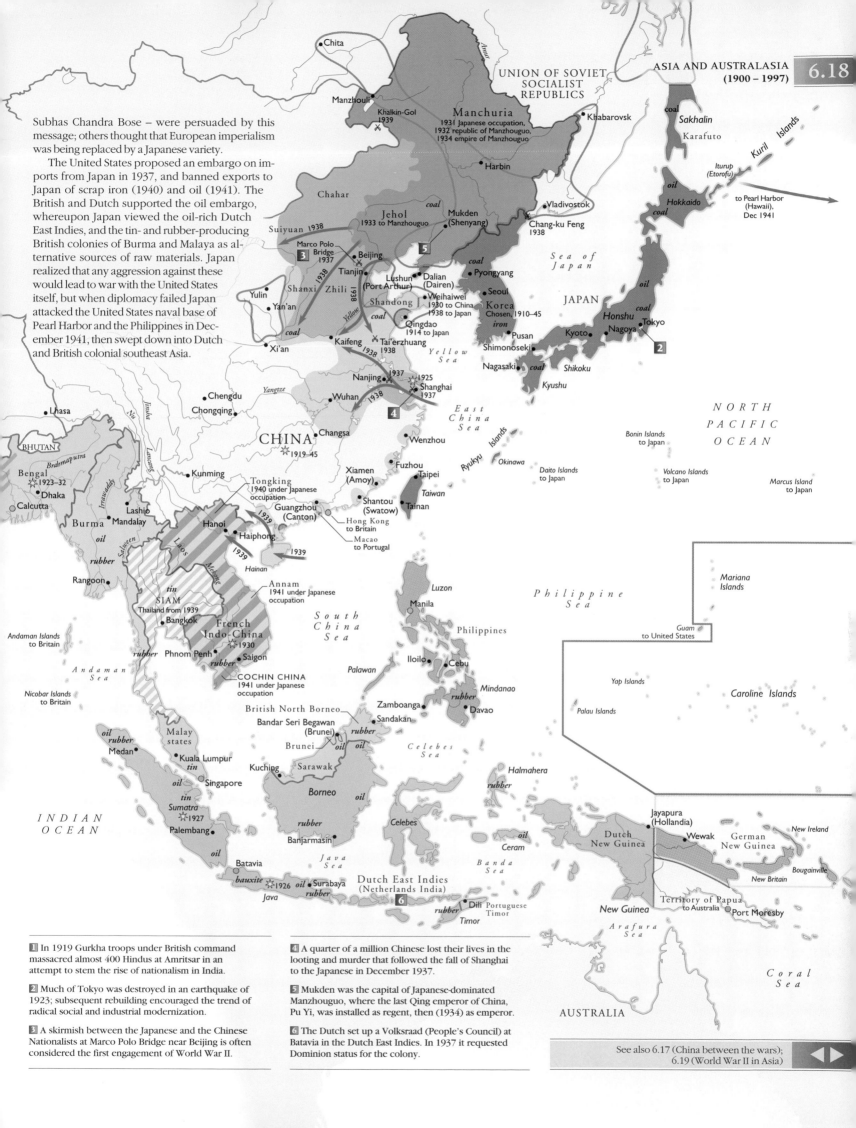

Subhas Chandra Bose – were persuaded by this message; others thought that European imperialism was being replaced by a Japanese variety.

The United States proposed an embargo on imports from Japan in 1937, and banned exports to Japan of scrap iron (1940) and oil (1941). The British and Dutch supported the oil embargo, whereupon Japan viewed the oil-rich Dutch East Indies, and the tin- and rubber-producing British colonies of Burma and Malaya as alternative sources of raw materials. Japan realized that any aggression against these would lead to war with the United States itself, but when diplomacy failed Japan attacked the United States naval base of Pearl Harbor and the Philippines in December 1941, then swept down into Dutch and British colonial southeast Asia.

1 In 1919 Gurkha troops under British command massacred almost 400 Hindus at Amritsar in an attempt to stem the rise of nationalism in India.

2 Much of Tokyo was destroyed in an earthquake of 1923; subsequent rebuilding encouraged the trend of radical social and industrial modernization.

3 A skirmish between the Japanese and the Chinese Nationalists at Marco Polo Bridge near Beijing is often considered the first engagement of World War II.

4 A quarter of a million Chinese lost their lives in the looting and murder that followed the fall of Shanghai to the Japanese in December 1937.

5 Mukden was the capital of Japanese-dominated Manzhouguo, where the last Qing emperor of China, Pu Yi, was installed as regent, then (1934) as emperor.

6 The Dutch set up a Volksraad (People's Council) at Batavia in the Dutch East Indies. In 1937 it requested Dominion status for the colony.

See also 6.17 (China between the wars); 6.19 (World War II in Asia)

In late 1941 the Japanese planned a series of synchronized attacks to secure control in the Pacific and Asia. Prime minister Hideki Tojo and Isoroko Yamamoto, head of the navy and mastermind behind the attack on the United States naval base of Pearl Harbor in Hawaii, sought to create a defense perimeter from the Kurils to the Dutch East Indies and containing all the oil, rubber and rice Japan would need for survival. Yamamoto promised a string of victories in the first six months.

The surprise attack on Pearl Harbor on 7 December 1941 destroyed the US Pacific battlefleet, but all the large aircraft carriers were at sea. Their survival was to be of crucial significance. By the spring of 1942 Japan had taken the Philippines (attacked the same day as Pearl Harbor), ejected the Dutch from the East Indies, driven the British from Hong Kong, Malaya (including the great naval base of Singapore) and most of Burma, and forced the Americans to surrender Guam, Wake Island, Attu and Kiska. At this point, Japan suffered a setback at the Battle of the Coral Sea as the Japanese attempted to take the Allied base at Port Moresby on New Guinea (thus isolating Australia). Further advances across the Pacific were decisively halted when their fleet was defeated by the US Navy at the Battle of Midway.

Allied strategy for the destruction of Japan's new empire depended upon the immense resources and manpower that the United States could bring to bear. The plan required the British, who had suffered during their long retreat in Burma, to block a Japanese invasion of India, undertake offensives in the Arakan and recapture Rangoon. They would have limited US assistance and cooperation from Chinese Nationalist armies from Yunnan. These forces came under a new southeast Asia command headed by Lord Louis Mountbatten. US forces in the south and southwest Pacific under General Douglas MacArthur

and Admiral William Halsey were planned to retake New Guinea and the Solomons. Admiral Nimitz would assemble fresh task forces at Pearl Harbor and attack Japanese-held islands in the central and north Pacific. Key bases would be established on the islands and in China for an air assault upon Japan.

In the north Pacific, US and Canadian troops attacked in the Aleutians and forced the Japanese back. In the central Pacific, US marines assaulted the tiny coral atoll of Tarawa, 5,000 kilometers (3,000 miles) from Japan. They wiped out its Japanese and Korean defenders, but only after three days of bitter fighting. After this experience, the Americans

decided to ignore unimportant islands and by-pass many Japanese bases. They fought and won the Battle of the Philippine Sea and then targeted Kwajalein and Eniwetok in the Marshalls. They went on to occupy Saipan, Guam and Tinian, the bases from which in 1944–45 US B-29 bombers undertook their raids on Japanese cities.

US forces returned to the Philippines and fought the Battle of Leyte Gulf, during which the Japanese navy was effectively destroyed. The Battle of Iwo Jima, the fiercest of the war, provided the Americans with a base for their fighter aircraft capable of escorting the bombers to Japan and back. About 500,000

Map legend

- borders, 7 Dec 1941
- Japanese occupied territory, 7 Dec 1941
- maximum extent of Japanese occupied territory, June 1942
- intended eastern perimeter of Japanese territory
- Japanese occupied territory, 6 Aug 1945
- Japanese occupied territory, Sep 1945
- Allied territory, June 1942
- Nationalist Chinese or warlord territory
- Communist Chinese territory, 1937
- Japanese advance, with date
- Allied advance, with date
- Russian advance, 9 Aug 1945
- Japanese base, June 1942
- Japanese air strike outside occupied territory
- US bombing raids on Japan, 1942–45
- nuclear air strike, Aug 1945
- Japanese victory
- Allied victory
- *oil* strategic resource vital to Japan

Map labels

Yellow
Yan'an 1937–45
Lanzhou
Xi'an 1937–45
CHINA
Chengdu Sept 1944
Chongqing 1937–45
TIBET
June 1942
Lhasa
BHUTAN
NEPAL Thimphu
Kathmandu
Southeast Apr–June 1944 Kohima
Asian Forces
India to Britain
Imphal Mar–June 1944
Yunnan
Kunming 1937–45
Guilin Sept 1944
Calcutta Burma oil
Mandalay
Hanoi Haiphong coal
Vishakhapatnam Apr 1942
Arakan rubber
Haina
Kakinada Apr 1942
Bay of Bengal
Rangoon tin
THAILAND
Bangkok 1941
French Indo-Chi
Andaman Islands
rubber Phnom Penh
Saigo
Trincomalee Apr 1942
Nicobar Islands
rubber
Colombo Apr 1942
Bay of Bengal Apr 1942
oil rubber
Malaya
Kuala Lumpur tin
Kuch
Medan tin
Feb 1942
Sumatra oil Singapore
2
Palembang
Ja Se
Batav
bauxite
Java

0 — 1500 km
0 — 1200 mi

1 The attack on Pearl Harbor was essential to Japan's plans to control the Pacific. Eight battleships were destroyed but dockyard facilities remained intact.

2 Singapore was Britain's foremost and most recently equipped naval base in the region, but it fell to a surprise land attack in February 1942.

3 The Bataan peninsula in the Philippines was the scene of an incident in April 1942, when the Japanese forced 35,000 men to march 100km (60 miles) in six days; more than 10,000 died.

4 The Japanese invasion of the Dutch East Indies was welcomed by Ahmed Sukarno, leader of the Indonesian Nationalist Party (PNI).

5 Darwin and other north Australian towns were bombed, and the east coast was blockaded by submarines in 1943; the country was a key base for US operations in the southwest Pacific.

6 Saipan was a major air base, used by the US Air Force for bombing Japan from November 1944.

7 Hiroshima suffered the world's first atomic bomb attack on 6 August 1945; 80,000 people died instantly.

TIMELINE

	1943	1945	
Japan	1941 Japan and the Soviet Union sign a neutrality pact	1944 (July) Prime minister Tojo resigns	1945 (Aug) Atomic attacks on Hiroshima and Nagasaki
	1942 (Apr) B-25 bombers from USS *Hornet* raid Tokyo		1945 (Sep) Formal Japanese surrender
Pacific war	1941 (Dec) Japan attacks Pearl Harbor and Philippines	1943 (Nov) Tarawa captured by US forces	
	1942 (Feb) Japanese troops win the Battle of Java Sea	1944 (July) US troops land on island of Leyte	
	1942 (May) Battle of the Coral Sea halts Japanese attack on Port Moresby	1944 (Oct) The Battle of Leyte Gulf ends Japanese naval power	
	1942 (June) Japanese carriers are destroyed at Midway		1945 (Feb–Mar) The Battle of Iwo Jima is followed by the invasion of Okinawa
	1942 (Aug) US marines land on Guadalcanal		
Southeast Asia	1941 (Dec) Japan attacks Hong Kong and Malaya	1943 Nationalists stem the Japanese offensives in China	1945 (May) The Burma Road reopened and Rangoon recaptured
	1942 (Feb) British forces in Singapore surrender to Japan	1944 Japanese invasion of India; sieges of Imphal and Kohima (Mar–June)	1945 (Aug) The Soviet Union declares war and attacks in Manchuria and Korea
	1942 (Mar) The Dutch surrender the East Indies	1944 Chinese Communists and Japan stop fighting	
	1942 British retreat from Burma		
	1943	1945	

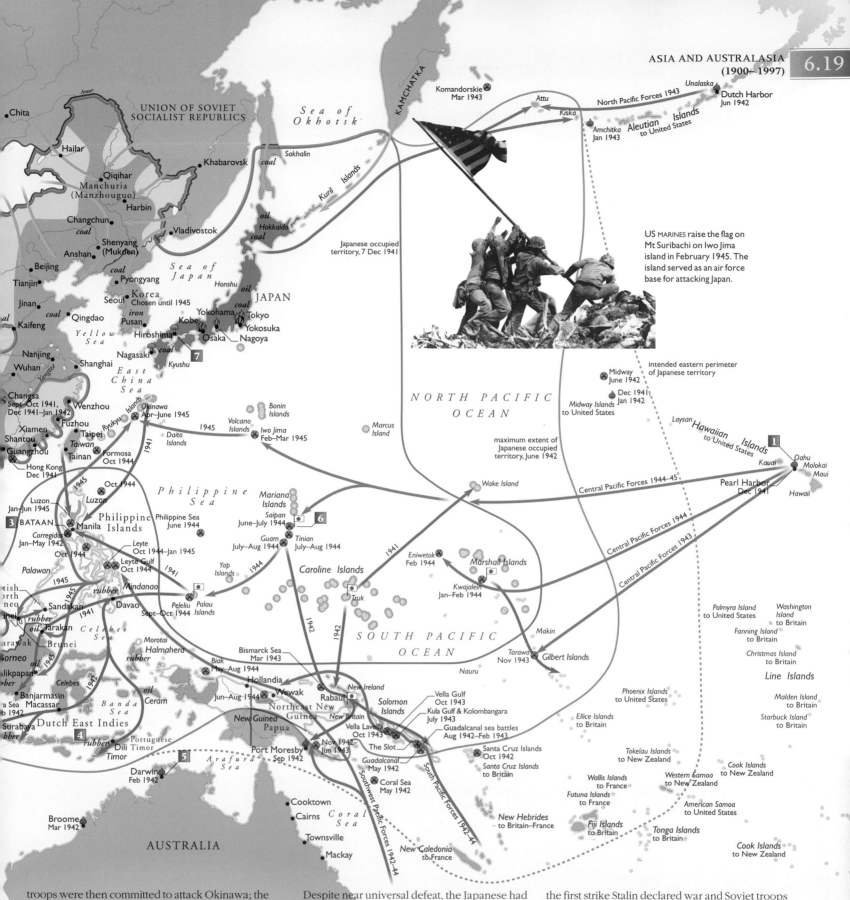

US MARINES raise the flag on Mt Suribachi on Iwo Jima island in February 1945. The island served as an air force base for attacking Japan.

troops were then committed to attack Okinawa; the Japanese defenders employed *kamikaze* aircraft and piloted bombs against American and British ships.

Before and during the Iwo Jima and Okinawa campaigns the Americans subjected Japan to ruthless bombing. Tokyo, Nagoya and Osaka were devastated and the Tokyo firestorm of May 1945 is considered to be the most destructive air raid in history. In the Philippines, the Battle of Luzon was still in progress and in Burma the British, Indian, African, Chinese and US troops, after great battles at Kohima and Imphal, were slowly pushing down the Irrawaddy toward Mandalay and Rangoon.

Despite near universal defeat, the Japanese had no desire to surrender and all sides anticipated a fight to the finish. Allied planning for an amphibious attack on Japan went ahead. Stalin promised that the Soviet Union would enter the war against Japan three months after the total surrender of Nazi Germany. President Truman assessed the likely scale of casualties involved in an invasion (approximately one million fighting men), and compared this with the enemy civilian deaths that would result from the use of the new atomic bomb being tested in New Mexico. He chose the atomic weapon: the bombs fell on Hiroshima and Nagasaki in August 1945. After

the first strike Stalin declared war and Soviet troops invaded Manchuria and Korea. As Japan reeled, carrier aircraft harried Honshu and Kyushu and a giant bombing raid savaged the remains of Tokyo. On 15 August 1945, Emperor Hirohito asked the Japanese people to "endure the unendurable and suffer the insufferable." Japan formally signed the surrender document on the battleship USS *Missouri* on 2 September 1945.

See also 6.07, 6.08 (World War II in Europe);
6.18 (east Asia between the wars);

The end of World War II left the United States dominant but the Soviet Union was also moving strongly into east Asia. The Chinese civil wars were soon to be resolved, while the European colonies had been decisively altered by the experience of Japanese occupation and US liberation.

In September 1945 US forces landed at Inchon on the former Japanese colony of Korea, in response to the presence of Soviet troops in north Korea. No formula could be found for unifying the country and the UN approved an American plan to hold elections in the south. Syngman Rhee's Republic of Korea (South Korea) emerged in 1948, followed shortly by Kim Il Sung's Communist Democratic Republic of Korea (North Korea). The Soviet Union and United States withdrew in 1948 and 1949 respectively, leaving Korea divided.

Many US troops withdrew to Japan, where America was responsible for its military occupation and the repatriation of three million Japanese servicemen. The United States and its Commonwealth Allies met with unexpected cooperation from Japanese police and local officials. Emperor Hirohito remained, though only as titular ruler, and real power was in the hands of General MacArthur, Supreme Commander of Allied Powers. MacArthur introduced a democratic constitution, ensured that the United States shipped in adequate food supplies and generally charmed the Japanese with his dignity and benevolence. The Japanese came to admire Americans and their way of life. By 1949 Japan was willingly drawn inside America's defense perimeter.

By 1950 Mao Zedong had succeeded in unifying China, partly by demonstrating that the PLA was no warlord army. Soldiers, workers, the Party hierarchy (cadres) and the government were united. Mao assured the people that China was no longer isolated: the Sino–Soviet Treaty (1950) guaranteed their membership of a international socialist brotherhood. He promised land reform and development plans, and protection for China's frontiers. His first move was to invade Tibet in the winter of 1950–51 to recover what China considered a historic province.

North Korea invaded South Korea in 1950. This provoked a major United Nations response and an army from sixteen nations, spearheaded by the Americans, was sent to Korea to resist the invaders. UN forces attacked across the 38th Parallel dividing North from South, and a few reached the border with China on the Yalu River. At this point the PLA entered the war and forced a UN retreat. A static war ensued, with both sides digging in. An armistice was agreed at Panmunjom in 1953 and five years later the PLA left Korea, although a UN presence remained. After the war, North Korea remained a Stalinist state, while the South began to rebuild its shattered economy. Heavy industry and infrastructure, as well as electronics and consumer industries, were all constructed from scratch as Korea, like Japan, used the opportunity of war to build a new prosperity.

Chinese armed forces were also involved in 1954 when PLA gunners shelled the two small islands of Quemoy and Matsu that were claimed by the Nationalist government based in Taiwan. PLA forces landed on other Nationalist islands and in 1958 resumed the shelling of Quemoy. America mobilized a massive fleet in the Taiwan Straits in support of Jiang Jieshi, who still claimed to be the legitimate ruler of the whole of mainland China. In 1962 PLA forces attempted to push across the Indian border and were poised to enter Assam. After brief fighting against ill-prepared Indian troops, the Chinese withdrew. Along the Ussuri River Chinese patrols clashed with Soviet troops in 1969.

In the 1950s and 1960s, Mao Zedong attempted to forge a Chinese version of Marxism, based on a drive toward establishing economic modernization (especially in the chaotic "Great Leap Forward" of 1958–60) and the collectivization of agriculture. From the mid-1960s he fomented "permanent revolution" by encouraging the youthful Red Guards to challenge all forms of authority, especially in education, administration, industry and the Party itself, and to send many intellectuals to work on communes. China was almost totally cut off from the outside world until after Mao's death in 1976.

Legend

former colony, c.1939
- British
- Dutch
- French
- United States

- North Korea, 1948
- South Korea, 1948
- People's Republic of China (Communist), 1950
- Republic of China (Nationalist), 1950
- Tibet prior to the Chinese invasion, 1950
- North Vietnam, 1954
- South Vietnam, 1954
- Japan, 1972
- Indonesia, 1949
- United Nations Trust Territory
- **1946** date of independence as a nation-state
- LAOS Communist state by 1976
- insurgency, with date
- clash between Red Guards and the Army or workers, 1965–69
- disruption caused by Red Guards, 1965–69
- urban youth sent to Chinese provinces, 1974–76
- main center from where urban youth were removed
- Chinese troop movements, with date
- Nationalist Chinese attacks, 1954–55
- Nationalist Chinese evacuation to Taiwan, 1950
- borders, 1976
- disputed border, 1976

Korean War, 1950–53
- United Nations airbase
- Chinese and North Korean airbase
- North Korean advance, June–Sep 1950
- United Nations advance, July–Sep 1950
- Chinese and North Korean advance, Nov 1950–Jan 1951
- limit of North Korean advance, Aug–Sep 1950
- limit of United Nations advance, Nov 1950
- limit of Chinese and North Korean advance, Jan 1951

Islamabad

PAKISTAN
West Pakistan until 1971, 1947

TIMELINE

China, Korea and Japan

1950	1960	1970
1945 The United States occupy Japan (to 1952)	**1958–60** Mao's "Great Leap Forward" establishes agrarian and industrial communes	**1966–70** The Cultural Revolution to prevent revisionism causes internal disruption in China	**1971** People's Republic of China is admitted to the United Nations

1948 The states of North and South Korea are established

1958 Agricultural collectivization in North Korea

1968 Japan is the world's second largest economy

1975 Death of Jiang Jieshi

1949–50 Chinese Nationalists evacuate to Taiwan

1962 China challenges India in the Himalayas

1969 China confronts the Soviet Union in east Asia

1976 Death of Mao Zedong

1950 North Korea invades the South

1962 Start of policy of export-led growth in South Korea

1953 Korean armistice is signed in Panmunjom

Indo-China

1946 French forces return to Indo-China

1954 The French surrender at Dien Bien Phu

1964 The US assert that "all measures will be taken to resist aggression" in Vietnam

1970 US troops enter Cambodia

1954 Laos and Cambodia become independent states; Vietnam is divided

1973 US troops leave South Vietnam

1965 US ground troops in action against the Viet Cong

1976 Vietnam is reunited

Southeast Asia

1946 The Philippines become an independent republic

1956 Indonesia's last links with the Dutch crown are severed

1963 Federation of Malaysia set up, including Malaya, North Borneo, Sabah and Sarawak, Singapore (to 1965)

1971 The British military presence in Singapore is ended

1948 Burma is independent

| 1950 | 1960 | 1970 |

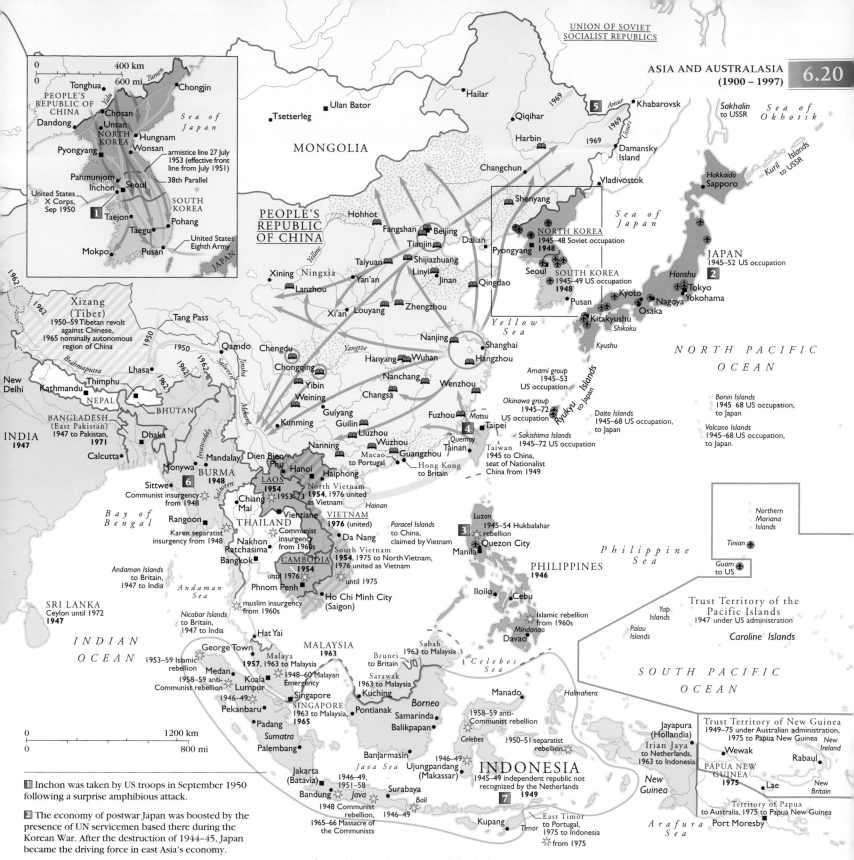

1 Inchon was taken by US troops in September 1950 following a surprise amphibious attack.

2 The economy of postwar Japan was boosted by the presence of UN servicemen based there during the Korean War. After the destruction of 1944–45, Japan became the driving force in east Asia's economy.

3 The Hukbalahar revolt from 1945 in Luzon, a peasant uprising over land ownership, was crushed by the government in 1953–54.

4 In 1958 US president Eisenhower sent "the most powerful fighting force in history" to confront the Communist Chinese in the Taiwan Straits.

5 Tension between the Soviet Union and Maoist China on the Amur River border from 1969 emphasized the rift between these former allies.

6 Burma, which pursued a neutral foreign policy after independence under U Nu, was under a socialist military regime led by Ne Win from 1962.

7 East Timor, a Portuguese colony until the Portuguese revolution of 1975, was invaded by Indonesia the same year, and annexed in 1976.

Independence and unity arrived slowly for many east Asian nations. The Philippines became an independent republic in 1946; Burma in 1948; after the partition of India in 1947, East Pakistan became Bangladesh in 1971. But the former French Indo-Chinese colonies of Laos, Cambodia and Vietnam became embroiled in the longest war of the century. During World War II the French had accepted Japanese domination of the area; only the Communist Vietminh forces led by Ho Chi Minh resisted, and declared independence in 1945. The return of the French led to a long guerrilla war in which the French initially drove the Vietminh from the major cities, but in 1953–54 the Vietminh general Giap won a remarkable and decisive victory over the French at Dien Bien Phu.

Maoist China was the chief supporter of the insurgents in Indo-China, and also of the Communists in Malaya who inspired a long guerrilla campaign against the British; eventually independence was achieved by the anti-Communist, Malay-led nationalists in 1957. Indonesia, which claimed its independence after the war and won Dutch acceptance of the fact in 1949 after a bitter struggle, also suffered Communist, regionalist and Islamist activity. To a lesser extent, the Philippines (where United States' influence was still paramount), Burma and Thailand also saw Communist movements.

See also 6.19 (World War II in Asia); 6.21 (Vietnam War); 6.23 (the Pacific Rim after 1976)

Following the victories of Ho Chi Minh's Viet-minh guerrilla forces in 1943–54, France with-drew from most of Indo-China. The subsequent Geneva Conference ruled that Vietnam would be divided between the North, ruled from Hanoi by the Vietminh, and the non-Communist South, with its capital in Saigon. Two neutral states, Laos and Cam-bodia, would also be formed and within two years the Vietnamese would hold free elections and be united under a government of their own choice.

The elections were never held. Vietnam stayed divided and weak: the North by being cut off from the rich rice-fields of the Mekong delta, and the South by the presence of the Vietminh. Land reform was a key issue in the Mekong delta where two mil-lion peasants were landless, with many more paying high rents to absentee landlords. Saigon was reluc-tant to redistribute the land, whereas the Vietminh soldiers gave land to the peasants and also handed over responsibility for food production and local government. The Communists thus began to win the hearts and minds of the people, who were alienated by the anti-Buddhist president Diem in Saigon. Coercion, too, was rife on the Communist side in intimidating or eliminating anti-Communists.

John Foster Dulles, US secretary of state from 1953, had never endorsed the Geneva agreements. He intended to save all of southeast Asia from Communism and to this end set up the South-East Asia Treaty Organization (SEATO) to prevent sub-version within member states. When guerrilla upris-ings began in Vietnam during 1955–56, the United States sent military advisers to train the ARVN (Army of the Republic of South Vietnam). Gradually the guerrillas, now termed the Viet Cong (Vietnamese Communists or VC), won control of half of Diem's provinces. Disillusioned ARVN officers killed him.

A succession of Saigon governments followed. For the United States, the war against North Vietnam (NVN) became "the great issue" of the 1960s. America's leaders accepted the "domino theory": if South Vietnam (SVN) succumbed to Communism, the same fate would in turn befall Laos, Cambodia, Thailand, Burma and Pakistan. After Kennedy's

assassination in 1963, president Johnson left the conduct of the war in the hands of defense secretary Robert McNamara. More American troops arrived in the South as VCs and their supplies swarmed down the "Ho Chi Minh Trail". In an effort to halt the flow of war materiel from China and Russia via Hanoi, the US provoked the Tongking crisis in 1964: an attack by patrol boats on US destroyers became an excuse for bombing North Vietnam 1965–70.

Air attack failed to reduce VC activity. US soldiers (and others from Australasia and South Korea) were sent to fight an elusive enemy hiding in the hamlets, jungles and paddy fields. They had enormous fire-power; but the fundamental issue – how to defeat well-armed, well-supplied nationalists operating in an agrarian economy – was never resolved. The Central Intelligence Agency (CIA) did not penetrate the VC high command; it did not warn of the Tet offensive of 1968 when Viet Cong battle-squads entered Saigon, Hue and other towns, and failed to reveal the buildup around the US base at Khe Sanh.

With antiwar sentiment growing in the United States, president Johnson authorized negotiations with North Vietnam in Paris. His successor Richard Nixon pledged to scale down US troop involvement and to "vietnamize" the war by boosting the ARVN military contribution. Even as US troops were quit-ting Vietnam, he backed the invasions of Cambodia and Laos plus Operation Linebacker II, a resumption of the air war designed to destroy the transportation systems of North Vietnam. US air power now proved irresistible, destroying bridges, truck factories and harbor installations. Linebacker II encouraged Le Duc Tho, the NVN delegation leader, to sign the Paris peace agreement with Henry Kissinger (US national security adviser). South Vietnam's president Thieu reluctantly agreed to the ceasefire, and the last American combat troops left Vietnam in 1973.

Nixon's subsequent resignation and the decline of US aid encouraged Le Duan (Ho Chi Minh's suc-cessor) to attempt the reunification of Vietnam. The Ho Chi Minh Trail now provided unhindered access to the south, and China and the Soviet Union had re-equipped the regular NVN Army so that it could put

infantry divisions, armored brigades and artillery regiments into the field. These advanced from the north and the west, fighting the kind of war that the Americans had always wanted them to fight. In 1975 SVN's president Thieu fled to Taiwan; American heli-copters ferried their remaining personnel from the capital as NVN tanks entered Saigon. At the same time Laos and Cambodia, both destabilized by Viet Cong activity and by constant US air attack, also fell to the Communists: Pathet Lao guerrillas set up a People's Democratic Republic in Laos, while the Khmer Rouge captured Cambodia's capital, Phnom Penh. Vietnam was reunited as the Socialist Republic of Vietnam under the leadership of Le Duan.

Legend

- border, 1954
- Communist control within Indo-China, 1954
- under Vietnamese Communist control, 1970
- Vietnamese Communist gains by Jan 1975
- Vietnamese Communist gains by Apr 1975
- Khmer Rouge control, 1975
- Pathet Lao control, 1975
- Communist guerrilla activity in Thailand, 1975
- US carrier fleet on permanent station
- US air base in South Vietnam and Thailand
- North Vietnamese air base
- Tet Offensive assault, Jan–Feb 1968
- major combat area
- interdiction by US Air Force
- **VIA** zoned target area (Route Packages) of the US Air Force within North Vietnam
- border of zoned target area
- forbidden target for US air strikes until Operation Linebacker II, 1972
- <u>Vinh</u> harbor mined by the US Navy
- Viet Cong supply route
- US and South Vietnamese offensive, 1970
- Vietnamese Communist advance, Jan–Apr 1975
- Vietnamese invasion of Cambodia, 1978–79
- Chinese invasion of Vietnam, 1979
- US evacuation, with date
- railroad

TIMELINE

Vietnam War

1960	1965	1970	1975
1954 Geneva agreements temporarily divide Vietnam	**1962** First Australian troops arrive in South Vietnam	**1966** US orders a bombfree zone around Hanoi	**1972** North Vietnamese troops cross the demilitarized zone (DMZ)	**1975** US Congress rejects president Ford's request for further aid to South Vietnam
1955 Ngo Dinh Diem, new president of South Vietnam rejects reunification	**1963** 15,000 US military advisers in South Vietnam	**1968** Tet offensive	**1972** The largest force of bombers takes part in Linebacker II	**1975** North Vietnamese troops capture Saigon
1959 Infiltration of South Vietnam begins via the Ho Chi Minh Trail	**1963** China promises more military aid to the North	**1968** VC besieges US marines at Khe Sanh, for 77 days	**1973** The Paris Agreement is signed	
1960 Hanoi forms a National Liberation Front (NLF) to operate in South Vietnam	**1964** The Tongking Gulf crisis: USS *Maddox* is attacked	**1968** US troops strength in Vietnam tops 540,000		
	1965 First US combat troops land at Da Nang	**1969** Death of Ho Chi Minh, succeeded by Le Duan	**1973** The last American troops leave Vietnam	

Other countries

1960	1965	1970	1975
1956 Prince Sihanouk of Cambodia adopts neutrality		**1968** Sihanouk permits US troops to pursue Viet Cong units within Cambodia	**1973** US Congress ends bombing of Cambodia
1958 Laos adopts anti-Communism with US support			**1973** Anti-government demonstrations in Thailand
1959 Hanoi sends weapons to guerrilla groups in Laos		**1970** South Vietnamese troops enter Cambodia, later supported by US troops	**1975** Pathet Lao form government in Laos; Khmer Rouge in Cambodia
1960 Khmer Rouge guerrillas active in Cambodia		**1971** South Vietnam troops enter Laos, but fail to cut Ho Chi Minh Trail	

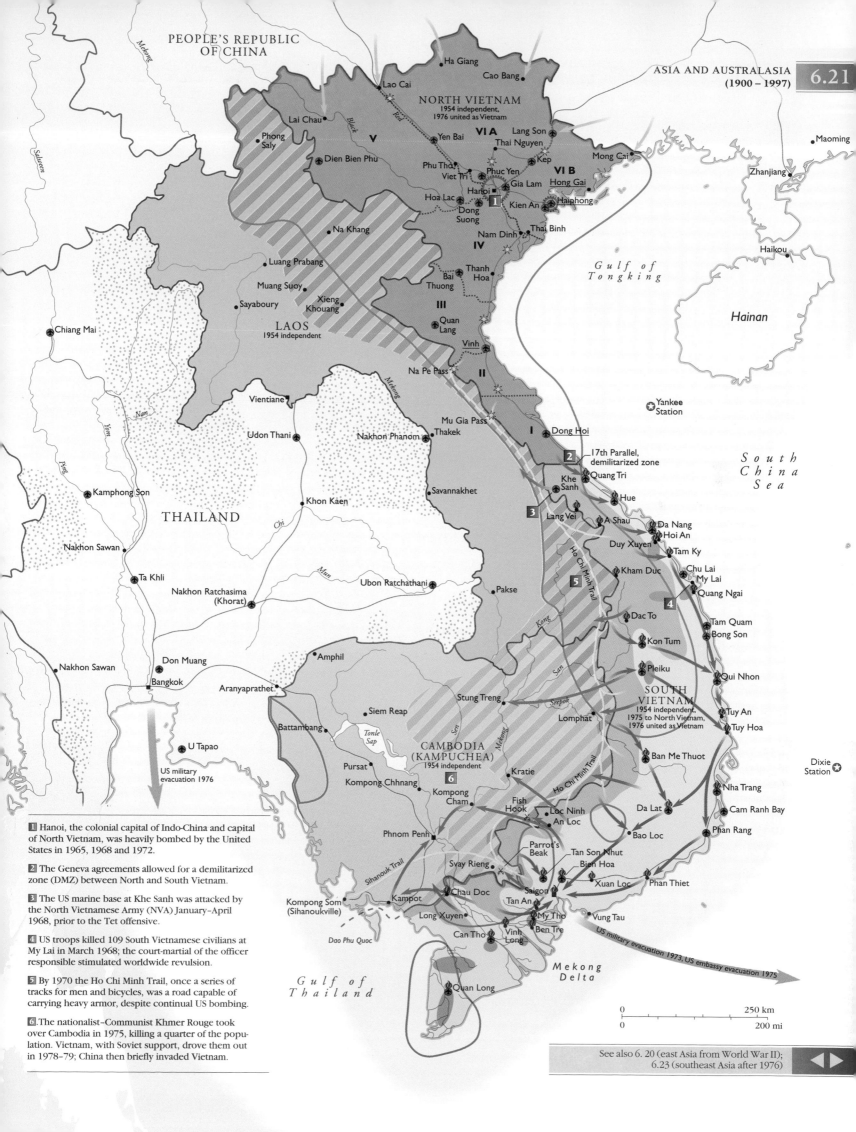

PEOPLE'S REPUBLIC
OF CHINA

Maoming

Zhanjiang

Mekong

Saluwen

NORTH VIETNAM
1954 independent,
1976 united as Vietnam

Ha Giang

Cao Bang

Lao Cai

Lai Chau

Phong
Saly

Dien Bien Phu

Yen Bai

Lang Son
Thai Nguyen

Mong Cai

VI A

V

Phu Tho

Viet Tri

Phuc Yen

Kep

VI B

Gia Lam

Hong Gai

Na Khang

Hoa Lac

Hanoi

Kien An

Haiphong

Luang Prabang

Dong
Suong

Nam Dinh

Thai Binh

Muang Suoy

Bai
Thuong

Thanh Hoa

Sayaboury

Xieng
Khouang

III

Hainan

Haikou

Gulf of
Tongking

LAOS
1954 independent

IV

Chiang Mai

Quan
Lang

Vinh

Na Pe Pass

II

Vientiane

Nan

Mu Gia Pass
Thakek

I

Dong Hoi

Yankee
Station

South
China
Sea

Udon Thani

Nakhon Phanom

17th Parallel,
demilitarized zone

Khe
Sanh

Quang Tri

THAILAND

Savannakhet

Hue

Kamphong Son

Khon Kaen

Lang Vei

A Shau

Da Nang
Hoi An

Duy Xuyen

Tam Ky

Nakhon Sawan

Kham Duc

Chu Lai
My Lai

Ta Khli

Ubon Ratchathani

Pakse

Quang Ngai

Dac To

Nakhon Ratchasima
(Khorat)

Kon Tum

Tam Quam
Bong Son

Pleiku

Qui Nhon

Amphil

SOUTH
VIETNAM
1954 independent,
1975 to North Vietnam,
1976 united as Vietnam

Tuy An

Nakhon Sawan

Don Muang

Stung Treng

Lomphat

Tuy Hoa

Bangkok

Siem Reap

Ban Me Thuot

Aranyaprathet

Battambang

Tonle
Sap

Nha Trang

Da Lat

Cam Ranh Bay

U Tapao

Pursat

CAMBODIA
(KAMPUCHEA)
1954 independent

Kratie

Bao Loc

Phan Rang

Dixie
Station

US military
evacuation 1976

Kompong Chhnang

Kompong
Cham

Fish
Hook

Loc Ninh
An Loc

Phnom Penh

Parrot's
Beak

Tan Son Nhut
Bien Hoa

Xuan Loc

Phan Thiet

Svay Rieng

Kompong Som
(Sihanoukville)

Sihanouk Trail

Chau Doc

Saigon

Tan An

Vung Tau

Long Xuyen

My Tho
Ben Tre

Dao Phu Quoc

Can Tho

Vinh
Long

Gulf of
Thailand

Mekong
Delta

US military evacuation 1973, US embassy evacuation 1975

Quan Long

Ho Chi Minh Trail

Kong

San

Srepok

Mekong

Se

Chi

Mun

Ping

Yom

Black

Red

1 Hanoi, the colonial capital of Indo-China and capital
of North Vietnam, was heavily bombed by the United
States in 1965, 1968 and 1972.

2 The Geneva agreements allowed for a demilitarized
zone (DMZ) between North and South Vietnam.

3 The US marine base at Khe Sanh was attacked by
the North Vietnamese Army (NVA) January–April
1968, prior to the Tet offensive.

4 US troops killed 109 South Vietnamese civilians at
My Lai in March 1968; the court-martial of the officer
responsible stimulated worldwide revulsion.

5 By 1970 the Ho Chi Minh Trail, once a series of
tracks for men and bicycles, was a road capable of
carrying heavy armor, despite continual US bombing.

6 The nationalist–Communist Khmer Rouge took
over Cambodia in 1975, killing a quarter of the population. Vietnam, with Soviet support, drove them out
in 1978–79; China then briefly invaded Vietnam.

0   250 km

0   200 mi

See also 6. 20 (east Asia from World War II);
6.23 (southeast Asia after 1976)

India played an important part in the Allied war effort in 1939–45, and expectations of political change were high. However, the main parties, the Congress Party (led by Mahatma Gandhi and Jawaharlal Nehru) and Mohammed Jinnah's Muslim League, were hostile to one another. By 1945 enmity between Muslims and Hindus caused rioting in Calcutta and Delhi, and the British decided on a rapid withdrawal. Lord Louis Mountbatten was charged with this task as violence spread across the entire Ganges valley. Consequently, two independent republics – a divided, predominantly Muslim Pakistan as well as India itself – were carved out of the subcontinent in 1947. Partition brought renewed civil conflict plus mass migration as millions of Muslims moved from India to East and West Pakistan and Hindus and Sikhs made their way to India. Appalled by the suffering, Mahatma Gandhi began a religious fast, only to be assassinated by a Hindu.

The two republics continued to dispute Kashmir, and a war in 1948–49 led to a UN truce line across Kashmir. The truce lasted until 1965 when troops from both sides crossed the ceasefire line. Hostilities flared again in 1971, after Bangla Desh guerrillas in East Pakistan clashed with troops sent in from West Pakistan by president Yahya Khan. Ten million refugees crossed from East Pakistan into India, imposing enormous strain on West Bengal. In December 1971, India invaded East Pakistan in support of the guerrillas, defeated the Pakistani army and the region gained its independence as Bangladesh.

As a secular state India tried to change long-established customs through parliamentary legislation. The minimum age for women to marry was raised and the right of divorce was granted; discrimination against *harijans* (untouchables) was outlawed. When Congress Party leader Indira Gandhi became prime minister in 1966, her watchword was *Garibi Hatao* ("reduce poverty"). She invested heavily in industry, food-grain production and family planning, including compulsory sterilization. She made many enemies and was assassinated in 1984 by her own Sikh bodyguard.

By this time India was an industrial and military power, one which had fought China in the Himalayas, acquired nuclear military technology in 1974 and launched a satellite into orbit. India had built up an aerospace industry and a navy that included a potent carrier fleet. During the 1990s India's economy was steadily liberalized and measures of positive discrimination were taken in favor of people of lower castes and minorities. Prime minister Rajiv Gandhi was assassinated in 1991 and riots continued to blight cities such as Bombay, as Hindu fundamentalism began to challenge the constitutional assumptions of the state.

In Pakistan in the 1960s, Zulfikar Ali Bhutto tried to initiate a program of nationalization (or "Islamic socialism") but his ruthless approach led to his execution by President Zia ul-Haq who later died in an air crash. Bhutto's daughter, Benazir, then began a stormy political career and was prime minister in the early 1990s. From independence Pakistan had powerful military forces and in the 1990s it was suspected to have nuclear weapons comparable with India's Prithvi missiles. It was threatened by endemic corruption and Islamized state and society, especially after the Soviet invasion of Afghanistan in 1979 caused a huge influx of refugees.

Bangladesh, one of the poorest countries in the world, is subject to cyclones that flood huge regions and cause widespread death and destruction. The country's first prime minister Sheikh Mujibur, who nationalized the jute, tea and textile industries, was assassinated, as was president Zia Rahman. Neighboring Burma (now the Union of Myanmar) experienced little of the democracy promised after General Aung San led it to independence in 1948. His daughter, Aung San Suu Kyi, opposed military rule but languished under house arrest through much of the 1990s. Burma enjoyed Chinese support in return for bases at Coco Island and Victoria Point. Sri Lanka, also independent in 1948, was racked by civil war between the minority Tamils and the Sinhalese from 1983. The Tamil Tigers attempted to establish an independent state in the north of the island and captured Jaffna in 1991. The government retook the city in 1996 as Tamil bomb squads resorted to terrorism.

communal rioting in British India, 1946–47

independent state formed by the partition of British Indian territory, 1947

India

Pakistan

cession of princely state or protectorate between 1947 and 1950

to India

to Pakistan

refugee movement, 1947–50

Hindu

Muslim

other migration

other former British territory gaining independence in 1948

People's Republic of China, 1950

Tibet, 1950

Union of Soviet Socialist Republics, 1950

Soviet occupation

Mujihadeen activity, 1979–88

territory disputed between China and India from 1947 until 1993

Chinese offensive

Pakistani offensive

Indian offensive

Soviet advance

Indian airfield bombed by Pakistan, 1971

city captured by Taliban militia, 1996

separatist movement

Burmese road linking China with Bay of Bengal

Chinese military base

United Nations truce line, 1949

borders, 1997

disputed border

Aral Sea

UZBEKISTAN
to Soviet Union
1991 independent

TURKMENISTAN
to Soviet Union
1991 independent

Ashkhabad

1979

Herat

Shindand
Farah

IRAN

Gwadar
to Muscat,
1958 to Pakistan

Muscat

0   400 km
0   300 mi

Tibet, occupied by the People's Republic of China in 1950, experienced military rule after the failure of the Lhasa rebellion and the flight of the Dalai Lama to India in 1959. The Chinese declared the Dalai Lama a traitor and when his successor, the Panchen Lama, died in 1989, installed a puppet ruler; mass immigration of Han Chinese to the region threatened to swamp the indigenous population.

Afghanistan tried to retain its independence during the Cold War, but in 1973 its constitutional monarchy was ousted and the Communists became increasingly strong. In 1979 the government sought Soviet assistance against the Muslim *Mujihadeen* guerrillas. Soviet occupation forces suffered heavy losses against guerrillas operating from mountain bases and finally withdrew after the peace settlement negotiated with Afghan president Najibullah in 1988. The Soviet withdrawal paved the way for a bitter civil war, and in 1996 the Taliban militia, an extreme fundamentalist grouping, captured Kabul.

Dramatic changes in central Asia followed the breakup of the Soviet Union in 1991, as eight Soviet republics in the Caucasus and along the Iranian and Chinese frontiers declared themselves independent.

1 The affiliations of some of the Indian princely states were not clear on independence; the nizam of Muslim Hyderabad had to be forced to join India in 1949.

2 India and Pakistan clashed in 1965 over the border in the marshy Rann of Kutch.

3 Dharamsala became the center for the Dalai Lama and the Tibetan government in exile after fleeing from the Chinese in 1959.

4 Bangladesh and India engaged in a long dispute over water resources after India built the Farakka dam over the Ganges in 1989.

5 An explosion at the chemical factory in Bhopal in 1984 killed about 2,500 people, revealing the dangers of poor administration and planning at this high-technology site.

6 Hindus destroyed a mosque at Ayodhya in 1992 at the supposed birthplace of the Hindu god Rama.

7 Sikh extremists occupied the Golden Temple in Amritsar and made it an operation base in the early 1980s; the Indian army drove them out in 1984.

INDIRA GANDHI was Indian prime minister (1966–77; 1980–84). She built India's international standing but was more controversial in her domestic policies.

See also 6.18 (India between the wars); 6.20 (east Asia after 1945)

The balance of world power was dramatically altered by the rise of the Asian economies in the last quarter of the 20th century; these were expected to be responsible for no less than half the world's growth by the year 2000. The region had plentiful supplies of cheap labor able to take on work of a highly technical nature. Infrastructural projects, heavy industry, textiles and high technology were developed in parallel to allow these countries – many of them, such as South Korea and China, devastated by political turmoil in mid-century – to emerge from poverty to compete on the world stage within a few decades.

The economic power driving this development was that of Japan, which trebled its investments in many of the east and southeast Asian countries after 1985 when a revaluation of the Yen made home-produced goods uncompetitive. By the late 1990s, the east and southeast Asian countries had overtaken the United States as Japan's main trading partner, with Malaysia, Hong Kong, Taiwan and, increasingly, China, as the main beneficiaries.

As the region developed, new countries opened up for development. Japan and Korea competed for a position in the Vietnam economy, especially after relations between Vietnam and the United States were normalized in 1995. Vietnam's transport and energy infrastructure was particularly weak following the destruction from the war that ended in 1975.

The tiger, or dragon, economies of Asia – South Korea, Hong Kong, Taiwan and Singapore – grew up alongside Japan. These newly industrializing economies (NIEs) had a number of characteristics in common. None had significant raw materials, so all had to export in order to grow. From the 1950s all nurtured their industries by government protection, and turned to export-oriented small light industries in the 1960s and 1970s. Like Japan, they had lost the advantage of low labor costs by the mid 1990s, and moved to invest in their neighbors with reserves of cheap labor, notably China.

By the 1980s South Korea had shifted its manufacturing base toward high technology, transport and heavy industry, and growth continued at a high rate. South Korean firms slowly opened trading links with the Communist regime in North Korea, but relationships between the two countries remained tense even after the death in 1994 of Kim Il Sung, ruler of North Korea since its foundation.

The foundations for Taiwan's economy were laid by Jiang Ching-kuo, the son of Chinese Nationalist leader Jiang Jieshi, from the late 1970s. He developed shipbuilding, petrochemicals and electronic industries, especially computers. By the mid-1990s this small island, remarkably, had the eighth largest trading power in the world. Mainland China, however, regarded Taiwan as a part of the People's Republic; Taiwan's democratic elections in 1987, and the election in 1996 of a leader more committed to an independent Taiwanese future, exacerbated tensions between the two. Hong Kong, China's small offshore island leased to Britain until 1997, moved toward trade and banking but retained its textile and other labor-intensive industries. Singapore, by contrast, pursued high-technology manufacture in conjunction with finance and business services.

In 1975, China had little or no foreign investment, no foreign loans and little direct trade with non-Communist states other than Japan. In 1978, vice-premier Deng Xiaoping embarked on economic

and educational reforms, aiming to replace Mao Zedong's class struggle with the goal of economic modernization. Political reform, however, was not pursued and a prodemocracy movement that arose in the wake of economic reform was crushed in 1989. Despite worldwide condemnation of China's human rights record, China actively sought investment, trade and technology from overseas. South Korea located plant and machinery in China's special economic zones; but the tiger economies that did most in China were those with the strongest political or ethnic ties with the country – notably Singapore and Taiwan (even though trade between Taiwan and mainland China was officially illegal). From 1984 Hong Kong, many of whose inhabitants came from Guangdong province, increasingly shifted its production to nearby Chinese provinces to take advantage of lower labor costs. The return of Hong Kong to China in 1997 was a step toward further integration of the two economies.

Japan retained its status as economic superpower thanks to its technological superiority, even though its growth was slowing in the 1990s, and other Asian countries beside China were industrializing fast. Thailand, Malaysia and Indonesia – which has large reserves of oil and gas to finance the growth of heavy industries such as petrochemicals, shipbuilding and steel – were growing. The Philippines, too, opted in the mid-1990s for policies modeled on the successes of other economies of the region.

A few countries did not form part of the "Asian miracle": notably Cambodia and Myanmar (formerly Burma), where oppressive regimes deterred foreign

Map legend

— border, 1997
■ original newly industrializing economies
■ emergent newly industrializing economies
■ Chinese special economic zone
■ little industrialization
■ Organization for Economic Cooperation and Development
⌒ ASEAN member state (Association of Southeast Asian Nations), 1967
➤ Japanese investment flow
■ population over 1,000,000
⚓ port
Manila industrial center
✳ Chinese prodemocracy demonstration
✺ separatist movement
— fiber-optic cable, 1996

source of major resource
◇ gold
◆ copper
◆ nickel
◆ tin
◇ other metal

⚑ oilfield

BHUTAN
NEPAL
BANGLADESH
INDIA

0 — 1200 km
0 — 800 mi

TIMELINE

East Asia

1975 In Taiwan, Jiang Ching-kuo plans for rapid growth

1978 In China, Deng Xiaoping advocates economic reforms; China and Japan sign a trade agreement

1979 China and the United States normalize relations

1984 The NIEs begin to invest in China

1984 Revaluation of the Yen leads Japanese countries to invest in southeast Asia

1987 Democratic elections are held in Taiwan, and martial law is lifted for the first time since 1949

1989 Japan becomes the world's largest foreign aid donor and supplier of capital

1989 In China, the prodemocracy movement led by students is crushed at Tiananmen Square, Beijing

1993 Japan's Liberal Democratic Party loses power for the first time since 1955

1994 Kim Il Sung, Stalinist president of North Korea, dies

1997 Death of Deng Xiaoping; Hong Kong returns to Chinese rule

Southeast Asia

1975 The Khmer Rouge take over Cambodia, leading to mass killings

1975 Collapse of South Vietnam and creation of a single Vietnamese state

1976 Indonesia annexes Portuguese East Timor

1977 The Communist regime in Laos signs a friendship treaty with Vietnam

1978–79 Vietnam invades Cambodia to crush Khmer Rouge regime; China invades northern Vietnam

1986 Prodemocracy candidate Corazon Aquino takes over from Ferdinand Marcos after the Philippines presidential elections

1986 Laos signs an economic development agreement with Thailand

1987 Democratic elections are held in South Korea

1988 A military junta seizes power in Burma

1989 Australia initiates the Asia Pacific Economic Cooperation Forum

1991 Burmese prodemocracy leader Aung San Suu Kyi is imprisoned by the military government

1992 Vietnam opens a free-trade zone, funded by Taiwan

1980　1990

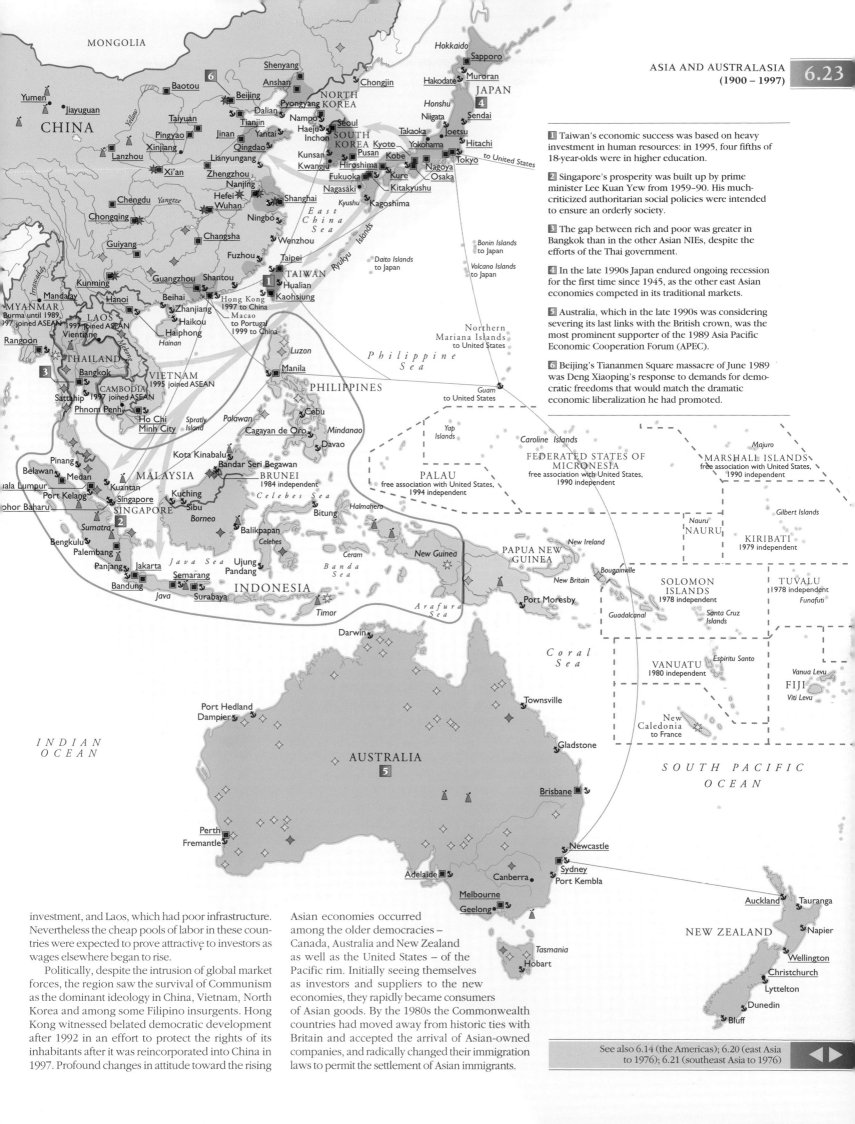

MONGOLIA

CHINA

Yumen △ ◆ Jiayuguan

Baotou □ ⑥ Shenyang □
Anshan □
Beijing □ ⚒ Chongjin ⚓

Taiyuan □ Pyongyang NORTH KOREA
Pingyao □ Tianjin □ Nampo
Xinjiang □ Jinan □ Yantai ⚓
Lanzhou □ Lianyungang ⚓ SOUTH KOREA
Xi'an ⚒ Zhengzhou □ Seoul □ Inchon ⚓
Nanjing □ Kunsan ⚓
Chengdu □ Yangtze Hefei ⚒ Kwangju
Chongqing □ Wuhan □ Shanghai ⚒
Changsha □ Ningbo ⚓

Guiyang □ Wenzhou ⚓

Fuzhou ⚓ Taipei □
Kunming □ Guangzhou ⚒ Shantou ⚓ TAIWAN ①
Mandalay Beihai ⚓ Hualian
MYANMAR Zhanjiang ⚓ Kaohsiung ⚓
Burma until 1989, Haikou ⚓ Hong Kong
1997 joined ASEAN LAOS Haiphong 1997 to China
Rangoon 1997 joined ASEAN Vientiane Hainan Macao
to Portugal
1999 to China
THAILAND
③ Bangkok □ VIETNAM
1995 joined ASEAN
Sattahip CAMBODIA 1997 joined ASEAN
Phnom Penh □ Ho Chi Spratly
Minh City Island

Shenyang... (China cities)

Hokkaido Sapporo □ ⚓
Hakodate Muroran ⚓
JAPAN ④
Honshu Niigata Sendai ⚓
Takaoka Joetsu ⚓ Hitachi ⚓
Kyoto Yokohama ⚓
Pusan ⚓ Kobe Nagoya ⚓ Tokyo
Hiroshima ⚒ Osaka to United States
Fukuoka ⚓ Kitakyushu ⚓
Nagasaki ⚓ Kyushu Kagoshima ⚓
Kure

East China Sea
Ryukyu Islands

Bonin Islands
to Japan

Daito Islands
to Japan

Volcano Islands
to Japan

Northern
Mariana Islands
to United States

Philippine Sea

Luzon

Manila ⚓
PHILIPPINES

Guam
to United States

Cebu ⚓
Palawan Mindanao
Cagayan de Oro ⚓
Davao ⚓

Kota Kinabalu ⚓
Bandar Seri Begawan
Pinang ⚓ MALAYSIA BRUNEI
Belawan ⚓ Medan 1984 independent
Kuala Lumpur Kuantan ⚓ Celebes Sea
Port Kelang ⚓ Kuching ⚓
Johor Baharu Singapore ② Sibu Halmahera
SINGAPORE Borneo Bitung ⚓
Sumatra Balikpapan ⚓
Bengkulu Celebes Ceram
Palembang □ Banda Sea
Panjang Jakarta □ Ujung Java Sea Pandang
Semarang □ INDONESIA
Bandung □ Java Surabaya □ Timor

Yap Islands

Caroline Islands

PALAU
free association with United States,
1994 independent

FEDERATED STATES OF
MICRONESIA
free association with United States,
1990 independent

Majuro

MARSHALL ISLANDS
free association with United States,
1990 independent

Gilbert Islands

Nauru
NAURU KIRIBATI
1979 independent

New Ireland
New Britain
Bougainville
SOLOMON
ISLANDS
1978 independent
Guadalcanal Santa Cruz
Islands

TUVALU
1978 independent
Funafuti

PAPUA NEW
GUINEA
New Guinea
Port Moresby ⚓

Arafura Sea

VANUATU
1980 independent
Espiritu Santo

Vanua Levu

FIJI
Viti Levu

New
Caledonia
to France

Coral Sea

INDIAN
OCEAN

Darwin ⚓

Port Hedland ⚓
Dampier ⚓

AUSTRALIA
⑤

Townsville ◆

Brisbane □ ⚓

SOUTH PACIFIC
OCEAN

Perth □ Fremantle ⚓

Newcastle ⚓
Sydney
Port Kembla
Adelaide ⚓ Canberra
Melbourne ⚓
Geelong ⚓

Tasmania
Hobart ⚓

Auckland ⚓ Tauranga
Napier ⚓
NEW ZEALAND Wellington ⚓
Christchurch ⚓
Lyttelton
Dunedin ⚓
Bluff ⚓

① Taiwan's economic success was based on heavy investment in human resources: in 1995, four fifths of 18-year-olds were in higher education.

② Singapore's prosperity was built up by prime minister Lee Kuan Yew from 1959–90. His much-criticized authoritarian social policies were intended to ensure an orderly society.

③ The gap between rich and poor was greater in Bangkok than in the other Asian NIEs, despite the efforts of the Thai government.

④ In the late 1990s Japan endured ongoing recession for the first time since 1945, as the other east Asian economies competed in its traditional markets.

⑤ Australia, which in the late 1990s was considering severing its last links with the British crown, was the most prominent supporter of the 1989 Asia Pacific Economic Cooperation Forum (APEC).

⑥ Beijing's Tiananmen Square massacre of June 1989 was Deng Xiaoping's response to demands for democratic freedoms that would match the dramatic economic liberalization he had promoted.

investment, and Laos, which had poor infrastructure. Nevertheless the cheap pools of labor in these countries were expected to prove attractive to investors as wages elsewhere began to rise.

Politically, despite the intrusion of global market forces, the region saw the survival of Communism as the dominant ideology in China, Vietnam, North Korea and among some Filipino insurgents. Hong Kong witnessed belated democratic development after 1992 in an effort to protect the rights of its inhabitants after it was reincorporated into China in 1997. Profound changes in attitude toward the rising

Asian economies occurred among the older democracies – Canada, Australia and New Zealand as well as the United States – of the Pacific rim. Initially seeing themselves as investors and suppliers to the new economies, they rapidly became consumers of Asian goods. By the 1980s the Commonwealth countries had moved away from historic ties with Britain and accepted the arrival of Asian-owned companies, and radically changed their immigration laws to permit the settlement of Asian immigrants.

See also 6.14 (the Americas); 6.20 (east Asia to 1976); 6.21 (southeast Asia to 1976)

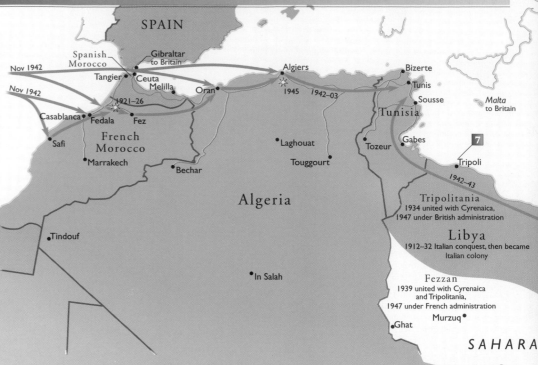

In 1914 the Allies decided to carry the war into every German colony in Africa. Military operations in Togoland, Cameroon and South-West Africa were completed by 1916; the campaigns in German East Africa (later Tanganyika) continued until 1918, a week after the armistice was signed on the Western Front. Turkey's alliance with Germany led to assaults on the Suez Canal and Basra, both repelled by Allied forces. The British supported the Arab revolts against the Turks: they took Jerusalem in 1917, and a more general assault on Turkish control of the Middle East followed as the British raced to occupy the Mesopotamian oilfields. Britain ensured its hold over the oilfields of southern Persia, too, claiming a *de facto* protectorate in 1918.

The Covenant of the League of Nations required the peacemakers to help underdeveloped peoples to cope with the "strenuous conditions of the modern world". The colonies of the defunct German and Turkish empires were administered under the mandate system. Some ex-colonies were scheduled for rapid independence: on this understanding Britain was awarded a mandate over Palestine, Iraq (formerly Mesopotamia) and Transjordan; France gained Syria and Lebanon. Less advanced areas could not expect independence in the near future; these included the Cameroons and Togoland, shared between Britain and France; Britain acquired Tanganyika, Belgium was awarded Ruanda-Urundi.

This redistribution of territory meant that the British and French colonial empires grew substantially; the indigenous peoples were not consulted about their aspirations for independence. The notable exception was in Palestine where, the British government declared in 1917, it favored the establishment of a national home for the Jews. This conflicted with an earlier promise to the Arabs that their

new lands would include Palestine, where the population was 90 percent Muslim. Jewish immigration to the area was limited through the 1920s, but grew substantially in the 1930s, when the British first proposed the division of Palestine into separate Jewish and Arab states. After World War II, with the world horrified by the Holocaust and the Jews and Arabs in Palestine engaged in civil war, the United Nations supported partition and approved the state of Israel which came into being in 1948.

Britain, by 1918 the dominant power in the region, held back from interfering in central Arabia, permitting the Saudi kingdom to emerge in 1932.

Britain's mandate in Iraq ended in 1932 but the right to protect oil and military interests was retained, notably by means of two airforce bases. A native Pahlavi dynasty seized control of Persia in 1925, renaming it Iran in 1935. By the outbreak of war, Iran produced more oil than the rest of the Middle East, and the shah's ties with Nazi Germany led the Allies to occupy the country again in 1941; the shah was forced to abdicate and his son Mohammed Reza Pahlavi installed in his place. The market for Middle Eastern oil grew in the interwar years, but the oilfields were not fully developed until the 1950s. French rule in Syria and Lebanon was benevolent, but was compromised by the fall of France in 1940; both countries were occupied during the war by Free French and British troops, and their independent status was recognized in 1946.

North and east Africa, too, were caught up in the conflicts of the European powers. The British confirmed Egyptian independence in 1922 but maintained the right to use Egypt's facilities in time of war, to defend the Suez Canal and maintain the Anglo-Egyptian condominium in the Sudan. The British in Egypt and Italians in Libya began a conflict in 1940 which drew in the German army the following year; by 1943 the entire North Africa littoral was involved. Meanwhile indigenous independence movements were beginning to emerge, though most did not bear fruit until after World War II.

Ethiopia had retained its independence from colonial rule since defeating the Italians in 1896, and from 1935 was ruled by Haile Selassie (formerly Ras Tafari), who faced an invasion from Italy's Fascist dictator Mussolini. After using mustard gas on the Ethiopians, the Italians took Addis Ababa in 1936; a resistance movement continued to harry the Italians until World War II, when the British invaded and drove the Italians out once more, restoring Haile Selassie in 1941 and making Ethiopia the first African country to be liberated. Britain now took over the adminstration of the former Italian colonies of Eritrea and Somaliland.

French colonization of north Africa had failed to create a settler class comparable with the traditional peasantry of France. Settlers tended to be large farmers engaged in speculative agriculture for

TIMELINE

Middle East

1920	1940
1916 Arab revolt in the Hejaz against Ottoman rule	**1930** Standard Oil and Texas Oil form Bahrain Petroleum Company	**1946** Transjordan wins independence, annexes the West Bank and becomes kingdom of Jordan
1917 "Balfour Declaration" promises a national homeland for the Jews in Palestine	**1932** The British mandate in Iraq ends	**1948** Proclamation of the state of Israel
1918 Iraq is brought under British rule	**1933** Ibn Saud permits Standard Oil to prospect in Saudi Arabia	
1922 The League of Nations approves Palestinian mandate		**1941** Britain and Soviet Union invade Iran
1924 Britain insists on control of Transjordan's affairs		

North Africa

1914 Egypt is proclaimed a British protectorate	**1928** Muslim Brotherhood founded in Egypt	**1941** Germans conquer north Libya and invade Egypt
1921-26 A nationalist revolt against French and Spanish rule in Morocco	**1934** Formation of Moroccan nationalist party	**1943** Allied forces defeat the Germans in Tunisia
1922 Egypt gains independence under King Fuad I	**1936** Britain is granted use of Egyptian facilities in wartime	

Sub-Saharan Africa

1914 African, French and British forces take Togoland and German East Africa	**1935-36** Italian invasion of Ethiopia	
1920 Old German colonies mandated to Britain, Belgium, France and South Africa		**1941** Italy surrenders Ethiopia, Eritrea, and Somaliland
1920	1940

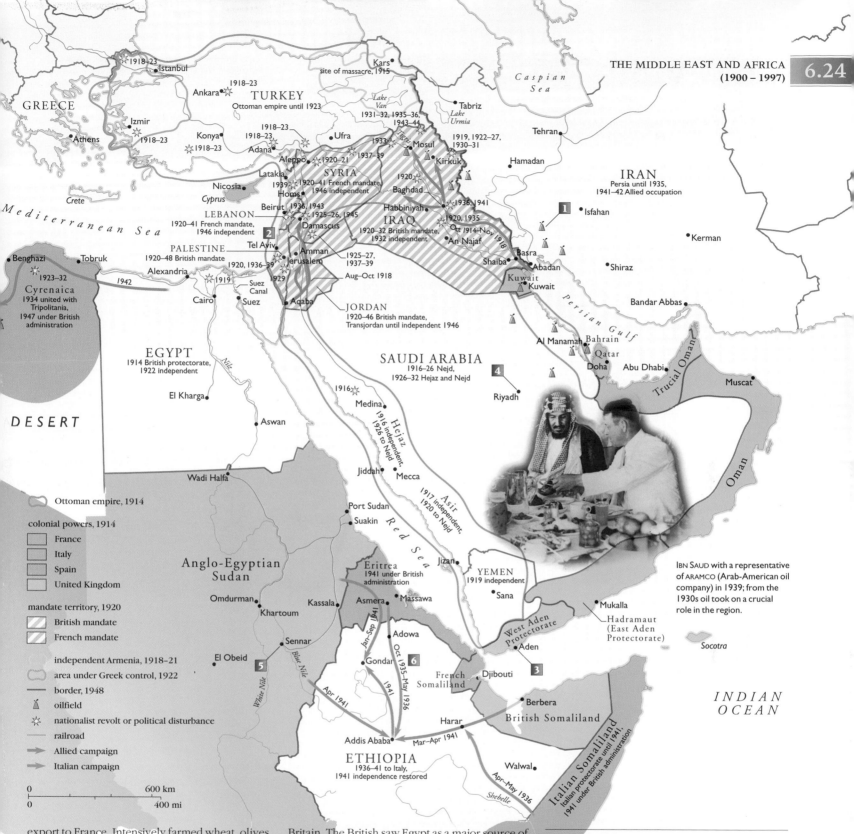

GREECE

Caspian Sea

TURKEY
Ottoman empire until 1923

Istanbul ✲1918–23
Ankara ✲1918–23
Izmir •1918–23
Konya ✲1918–23
Adana 1918–23
Athens •
Crete

Kars
site of massacre, 1915
Lake Van
1931–32, 1935–36, 1943–44

Tabriz •
Tehran •
Ufra •
Mosul ⛽ 1919, 1922–27, 1930–31
1933
1937–39
Kirkuk ⛽
Aleppo ✲1920–21
Latakia ✲ SYRIA 1920–41 French mandate, 1946 independent
Nicosia •
Cyprus
Homs ✲ 1939
Beirut ✲1936, 1943
LEBANON 1920–41 French mandate, 1946 independent
Damascus ✲
1925–26, 1945
Habbiniyah ⛽ 1936, 1941
Baghdad •
1920
IRAQ 1920–32 British mandate, 1932 independent
Oct 1914–Nov 1918
An Najaf ✲

Mediterranean Sea

Benghazi •
Tobruk •
Cyrenaica 1923–32
1934 united with Tripolitania, 1947 under British administration
1942
Alexandria •
PALESTINE 1920–48 British mandate
Tel Aviv 2
Jerusalem ✲ 1920, 1936–39
Amman •
1929
Suez Canal
Cairo •
Suez •
Aqaba •
1919
Aug–Oct 1918
JORDAN 1920–46 British mandate, Transjordan until independent 1946
1925–27, 1937–39

IRAN
Persia until 1935, 1941–42 Allied occupation
Isfahan • 1
Kerman •
Shiraz •
Hamadan •
⛽
Basra •
Shaiba ✲
⛽
Abadan •
Kuwait ⛽
Kuwait •
Bandar Abbas •
Persian Gulf
Al Manamah ⛽ Bahrain
Qatar
Doha • Abu Dhabi •
Trucial Oman
Muscat •

EGYPT 1914 British protectorate, 1922 independent
El Kharga •
Aswan •

DESERT

Wadi Halfa •

SAUDI ARABIA
1916–26 Nejd,
1926–32 Hejaz and Nejd
4
Riyadh •
1916 ✲
Medina •
Hejaz 1916 independent, 1926 to Nejd
Jiddah •
Mecca •
Asir 1917 independent, 1920 to Nejd

Red Sea

YEMEN 1919 independent
Sana •
Mukalla •
Hadramaut (East Aden Protectorate)
West Aden Protectorate
Aden • 3
Socotra

Oman

INDIAN OCEAN

Port Sudan •
Suakin •

Anglo-Egyptian Sudan

Omdurman •
Khartoum •
Kassala •
Sennar •
El Obeid • 5

Eritrea 1941 under British administration
Asmera • Massawa •
Adowa •
Gondar • 6
Oct 1935–May 1936
Apr 1941
1941
Blue Nile
White Nile
Addis Ababa •
Mar–Apr 1941
ETHIOPIA 1936–41 to Italy, 1941 independence restored
Walwal •
Apr–May 1936
Shebelle

Jizan •
Jan–Sep 1941

French Somaliland
Djibouti •
Berbera •
Harar •
British Somaliland

Italian Somaliland, Italian protectorate until 1941, 1941 under British administration

IBN SAUD with a representative of ARAMCO (Arab-American oil company) in 1939; from the 1930s oil took on a crucial role in the region.

Legend:

Ottoman empire, 1914

colonial powers, 1914
- France
- Italy
- Spain
- United Kingdom

mandate territory, 1920
- British mandate
- French mandate

independent Armenia, 1918–21
area under Greek control, 1922
— border, 1948
⛽ oilfield
✲ nationalist revolt or political disturbance
— railroad
→ Allied campaign
→ Italian campaign

0 ———— 600 km
0 ———— 400 mi

---

export to France. Intensively farmed wheat, olives and vines required capital investment but between 1914 and 1935 these produced spectacular yields, strong exports and brought about the development of the north African workforce. In the same way control of mineral resources by French managers meant that virtually all the production of iron ore and phosphates, and the zinc, lead and cobalt deposits, went to France. The depression of the 1930s led to the collapse of much of this activity, and a rise in unemployment.

Libyan resistance to Italian colonization persisted until 1932. Italy's Fascist government encouraged large estates worked by Italian settlers, but there was little investment in infrastructure and barely 90,000 Italians had settled in Libya by 1939.

British policy toward Egypt and the Sudan was very different, with little or no settlement from

Britain. The British saw Egypt as a major source of cotton, and encouraged Egyptian financial institutions to support local industry and cotton-related projects in the Sudan. By 1939 Egypt was approaching self-sufficiency in a range of manufactured goods; production rose further during the war years.

1 Masjed-Suleyman was the site of the first oil find in the Middle East, in 1908. Oil was found in Libya in the 1920s, and in Kuwait in 1932.

2 Tel Aviv was founded in 1909 by Zionist idealists as a suburb of the ancient city of Jaffa; the Turks cleared the settlement in 1916–17, but it became the focus for Jewish immigration in the 1920s and 1930s.

3 Aden, an important British coaling station on the route to India, was ruled from India until 1937 when it became a crown colony.

4 Abdul Aziz Ibn Saud (r.1901-53) took Riyadh in 1901, consolidated his hold over Nejd by 1906 and Hejaz (1926) and set up the kingdom of Saudi Arabia in 1932. Oil reserves were found there in 1938.

5 The Sennar Dam was completed in 1925, marking the beginning of a plan to irrigate the Sudan and develop the cotton industry for export.

6 Italy's invasion of Ethiopia in October 1935 began with a land and air attack on Adowa, the scene of an Italian defeat in 1896.

7 Tripoli was the center of Mussolini's Libyan industrial program: more than 700 factories were in operation there by 1939.

See also 6.25 (postwar Middle East); 6.26 (Africa)

◀ ▶

Only a few hours after the proclamation of the independent state of Israel on 14 May 1948, the armies of Syria, Jordan, Egypt and Iraq invaded, expecting to crush the Jewish state and establish an Arab Palestine. The Jews drew on reserves of experienced soldiers from around the world, defeated the Arabs and conquered territory as far as West Jerusalem. When East Jerusalem and the West Bank of the Jordan became part of the territory of Jordan the following year, Palestine ceased to exist. No Arab state would recognize the permanence of the new frontiers, though they received *de facto* acceptance at armistice talks in 1949. Israel's victory meant that the new state attracted thousands of Jewish immigrants to a new homeland, while more than a million Palestinians became refugees in their own land – a potentially explosive force in the politics of the region and of Jordan in particular.

Defeat led to a nationalist revolt in Egypt in 1952, when the British-sponsored ruling family was expelled and a republic instituted by a group of army officers. Colonel Nasser, president from 1954, relied on American dollars to subsidize the massive Aswan Dam project, regarded as essential for Egypt's economic and industrial development. When the United States withdrew in response to Nasser's increasingly anti-western foreign policy, he nationalized the Suez Canal, long seen as a strategic key to the east by Britain and France. These two old colonial powers decided to invade. Israel's support was secretly secured and Israeli forces invaded Sinai in October 1956, with Anglo-French troops arriving a week later. American pressure brought about a withdrawal and a United Nations force was sent in, while Nasser blocked the canal with sunken ships.

Widespread condemnation of Britain and France was followed by increased superpower involvement in the region: Arab states turned to the Soviet Union for weaponry while the United States became Israel's arsenal. Nasser was convinced that Egypt, allied with Syria (the two were united as the United Arab Republic in 1958–61), would defeat Israel. He assembled an alliance of Arab states and provoked a crisis by closing the Gulf of Aqaba. Israel, however, launched the most effective pre-emptive strike in history, attacking all of Egypt's air bases in June 1967. Most Egyptian combat aircraft were destroyed; Syria and Jordan suffered similar devastation.

When a ceasefire was agreed six days later, Israeli forces had occupied Gaza and the entire Sinai east of Suez, Jordan surrendered East Jerusalem, Bethlehem and Hebron, and Syria lost the Golan Heights, an area dominating the north of Israel.

The United Nations, however, passed resolutions requiring Israel to evacuate the occupied territories, deploring the loss of Palestinian civil rights, and confirming the Palestinian right to selfdetermination. These pointed to the deep divisions within Israel, where the Palestinians were treated as second-class citizens, many of them – particularly in the areas recently occupied by Israel – condemned to a life in refugee camps. The Palestinian Liberation Organization (PLO) was founded in 1964, and by the early 1970s had won, through a combination of terrorist tactics and moral pressure, a powerful and independent voice in the politics of the region. Seeming to endanger the fragile stability of Jordan, the PLO was evicted from the kingdom in 1970 and settled in Lebanon. The growing numbers of refugees there, most with little to lose, proved destabilizing to that country as well and contributed to the outbreak of civil war in Beirut in 1975.

In October 1973 Egypt's new president Anwar Sadat broke through into Israeli-held territory without warning on the Jewish Day of Atonement (Yom Kippur). The Israelis concentrated on holding the Golan Heights against Syrian tanks, but three weeks later Israel had defeated both attacks comprehensively while the two superpowers refused to intervene actively to support the protagonists.

In response to the United States' supply of military materiel to the Israelis, Saudi Arabia (where oil

1 Jerusalem, a holy city to Jews, Muslims and Christians, was divided after the failure of the Arab attack of 1948; the Israelis took the whole city in 1967, but disputes continued into the 1990s.

2 In 1953 the CIA (US intelligence agency) backed a coup against Iranian prime minister Mohammed Moussadeq, who had tried to nationalize the oil industry in 1951. The exiled shah returned to power.

3 Sharm el-Sheikh, a cove on the Sinai peninsula controlling entry to the Straits of Tiran, was captured by the Israelis in 1956 and controlled by the United Nations Emergency Force 1957-67.

4 This neutral zone between Kuwait and Saudi Arabia was partitioned between the two countries in 1966.

5 Israel bombed Palestinian bases in Jordan in 1968 and its troops defeated the Al Fatah (PLO military wing) guerrillas at the Battle of Karama.

6 Jordan expelled the Al Fatah guerrillas in 1970; many established new bases in southern Lebanon.

7 After ethnic conflict in Cyprus through the 1950s and UN intervention from 1964, a Turkish invasion in 1974 divided the island into Greek and Turkish zones.

Mediterranean Sea

Derna

Tobruk

LIBYA
1951 independent
✴ 1969

Matrûh

0   300 km
0   200 mi

revenues had grown dramatically since 1945 and which was the leading member of the Organization of Petroleum Exporting Countries, OPEC) imposed oil sanctions on the west, restricting OPEC exports and causing a sharp price rise. Despite this, the governments of Saudi Arabia and the Gulf states, including Iran (where the Allied occupation in World War II had left a legacy of popular bitterness toward "imperialists"), remained close to the United States and rejected the growing influence of the Soviet Union in the region. The main oil-producing states were reluctant to give military support to the anti-Israeli effort, and tensions developed between Saudi Arabia and Egypt over Egyptian policy in the southern Arabian peninsula. Syria and Iraq, however, were both under the control of the "anti-imperialist" and Arab nationalist Ba'ath Party, from 1963 and 1968 respectively. Libya too, another important oil producer, was in the control of a strongly anti-American regime inspired by the success of Nasser and led by Muammar Qadhafi from 1969.

Following the Yom Kippur War, Menachem Begin became prime minister of Israel, and realized that, like himself, Sadat was now interested in reducing Arab–Israeli tensions. Begin invited Sadat to Jerusalem, and a peace process was initiated which was formalized in the United States in 1979.

TIMELINE

Arab–Israeli Wars

1955	1965	1975
1948 Israel's foundation is followed by an Arab attack	**1964** Palestinian Liberation Organization (PLO) is founded in Jerusalem	**1973** Sadat launches the fourth war against Israel
1949 One million Palestinians flee Israel		**1977** Egypt's president Sadat offers Israel peace in return for a Palestinian state
	1967 Six-Day War ends with Israeli control over Sinai	
1956 Nasser's nationalization of the Suez Canal leads to British, French and Israeli invasions of Egypt	**1969** Yassir Arafat becomes PLO chairman	
	1970 The PLO are driven out of Jordan and settle in Lebanon; terrorist hijacking of civilian aircraft begins	
1958 Nationalist revolution in Iraq overthrows the monarchy		

Other developments

1951 Moussadeq becomes Iranian prime minister and nationalizes the oil industry	**1965** Iran exiles Islamic leader Ayatollah Khomeini	**1975** Civil war breaks out in Beirut
1952 The Egyptian monarchy is overthrown	**1968** Ba'ath leader Saddam Hussein takes power in Iraq	
1953 The CIA sponsor a coup in Iran and reinstate Reza Khan Pahlavi as shah	**1970** General Asad seizes power in Syria	
		1973 OPEC countries raise the price of oil to exert political influence on the west
1961 Kuwait gains its independence, though it is claimed by Iraq		

1955	1965	1975

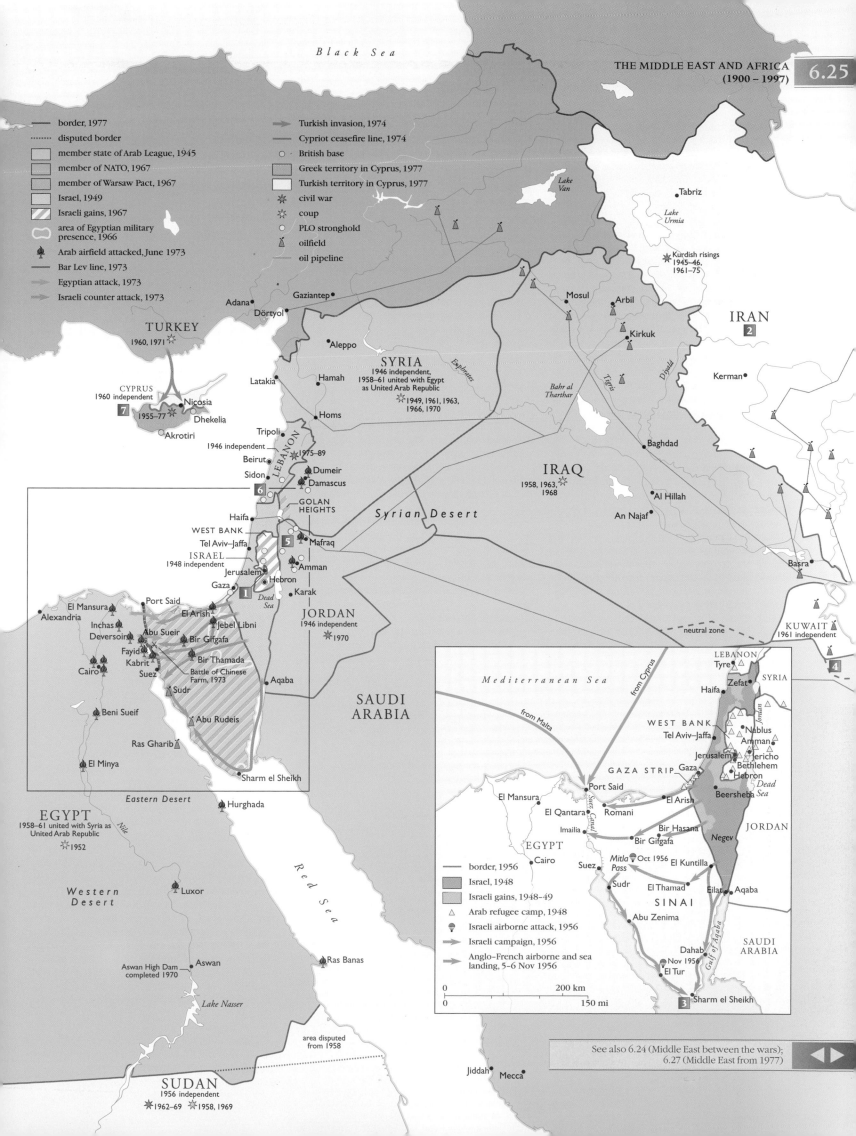

Black Sea

Legend

- border, 1977
- disputed border
- member state of Arab League, 1945
- member of NATO, 1967
- member of Warsaw Pact, 1967
- Israel, 1949
- Israeli gains, 1967
- area of Egyptian military presence, 1966
- Arab airfield attacked, June 1973
- Bar Lev line, 1973
- Egyptian attack, 1973
- Israeli counter attack, 1973
- Turkish invasion, 1974
- Cypriot ceasefire line, 1974
- British base
- Greek territory in Cyprus, 1977
- Turkish territory in Cyprus, 1977
- civil war
- coup
- PLO stronghold
- oilfield
- oil pipeline

Tabriz

Lake Van

Lake Urmia

Kurdish risings
1945–46,
1961–75

Mosul

Arbil

Kerman

TURKEY
1960, 1971

Adana   Gaziantep

Aleppo

Kirkuk

IRAN
2

CYPRUS
1960 independent
7
1955–77

Nicosia

Dhekelia

Akrotiri

Latakia

SYRIA
1946 independent,
1958–61 united with Egypt
as United Arab Republic
1949, 1961, 1963,
1966, 1970

Hamah

Homs

Euphrates

*Bahr al
Tharthar*

Tigris

Diyala

Baghdad

IRAQ
1958, 1963,
1968

Al Hillah

An Najaf

Basra

Tripoli

Beirut   1975–89

LEBANON
1946 independent

Sidon

Dumeir

Damascus

6

GOLAN
HEIGHTS

Haifa

WEST BANK

Tel Aviv–Jaffa

ISRAEL
1948 independent

Jerusalem

Gaza

Mafraq

5

Syrian Desert

*Dead
Sea*

Amman

Hebron

Karak

JORDAN
1946 independent
1970

neutral zone

KUWAIT
1961 independent

4

El Mansura

Alexandria

Port Said

El Arish

Jebel Libni

Inchas
Deversoir

Abu Sueir

Bir Gifgafa

Fayid

Kabrit

Bir Thamada

Cairo

Suez

Battle of Chinese
Farm, 1973

Aqaba

SAUDI
ARABIA

Beni Sueif

Sudr

Abu Rudeis

Ras Gharib

El Minya

Eastern Desert

Hurghada

EGYPT
1958–61 united with Syria as
United Arab Republic
1952

Sharm el Sheikh

*Western
Desert*

Luxor

Red Sea

Nile

Aswan High Dam
completed 1970

Aswan

Ras Banas

Lake Nasser

area disputed
from 1958

SUDAN
1956 independent
1962–69   1958, 1969

Jiddah   Mecca

Inset map (lower right):

Mediterranean Sea

from Cyprus

from Malta

LEBANON

Tyre

Zefat

SYRIA

Haifa

WEST BANK

Tel Aviv–Jaffa

Nablus

Amman

Jerusalem   Jericho

GAZA STRIP

Bethlehem

Gaza

Hebron

*Dead
Sea*

Port Said

El Qantara

Romani

El Arish

Beersheba

JORDAN

Imailia

Bir Hasana

Negev

EGYPT

Cairo

Suez

Bir Gifgafa

*Mitla
Pass* Oct 1956

El Kuntilla

Sudr

El Thamad

Eilat   Aqaba

SINAI

- border, 1956
- Israel, 1948
- Israeli gains, 1948–49
- Arab refugee camp, 1948
- Israeli airborne attack, 1956
- Israeli campaign, 1956
- Anglo-French airborne and sea landing, 5–6 Nov 1956

Abu Zenima

Dahab
Nov 1956

El Tur

SAUDI
ARABIA

Gulf of Aqaba

0   200 km
0   150 mi

3   Sharm el Sheikh

See also 6.24 (Middle East between the wars);
6.27 (Middle East from 1977)

After Egypt's president Sadat visited Jerusalem in 1977, US president Carter arranged meetings between Sadat and Israeli prime minister Begin at Camp David which led to a treaty in 1979 between Israel and Egypt (the first Arab state to take such a step). This recognized the state of Israel, promised autonomy to the Palestinians in Gaza and the West Bank, and returned the Sinai to Egypt.

The Palestine Liberation Organization (PLO) now took on the main task of fighting Israel, through terrorist activities in Europe and from its Al Fatah bases in Lebanon, where civil war was raging between Christian Phalangist and Islamic forces and where, since 1976, Syria had provided the main authority. In 1978 Israel invaded and UN forces struggled to keep apart the armies of Israel, Syria and the Christian militia. Sadat was assassinated by Islamic activists in 1981 but his successor Hosni Mubarak continued his policies. Trying to restore stability to the region, the United States brokered an agreement that the PLO leave Beirut for Tunis, but Lebanon's civil war continued until Syria restored peace in the early 1990s; but Hizbollah fighters funded by Iran, still used Lebanese bases for raids on Israel.

The political force of Islam had been dramatically seen in Iran, where the pro-western shah was overthrown in 1979 by street demonstrations in support of the Ayatollah Khomeini. As president of the new theocratic republic, Khomeini severed diplomatic relations with Israel, welcomed PLO leader Yassir Arafat to Tehran and defined the United States as the "main enemy of mankind". US embassy staff were taken hostage; 52 stayed in captivity for more than a year despite a trade embargo and an abortive rescue mission that summed up the US failure to deal with this new force in regional politics.

Khomeini's resurgent Shiite Islam and apparent intentions of dominating the Middle East, led Saddam Hussein, Ba'athist leader of predominantly Sunni Iraq, to invade Iran in 1980. War between the two states continued for eight years, mainly in the oil-producing region around Abadan. Neither won a clear victory despite almost a million casualties and great damage to oil installations on both sides. After the ceasefire in 1988, Saddam revived an old Iraqi claim on the rich, pro-western emirate of Kuwait, and invaded in 1990. To his surprise, the United Nations condemned the move and imposed sanctions on Iraq. Saudi Arabia, fearing further Iraqi expansion, permitted its territory to be used as a base for an attack on Iraq. Despite Soviet support for Iraq, the United Nations agreed the use of force, and war broke out in January 1991. Iraq tried to draw the entire region into the conflict by goading Israel with missile attacks, but the American-led UN coalition (including Egypt and Syria) succeeded in limiting the scope of the conflict and won a quick victory by bombing followed by a devastating ground attack.

The postwar settlement proved less than straightforward. The coalition had no mandate to topple Saddam and did not wish to take power in Baghdad.

Legend:

- border of Soviet Union to 1991
- member of OPEC
- member of NATO
- Egypt, 1983
- Israel, 1983
- territory restored to Egypt, May 1979–Apr 1982
- area occupied by Israel
- territory captured by Iraq, Sep–Dec 1980
- territory captured by Iran, Oct 1984
- Qom center of Islamic revolution in Iran, 1970s
- PLO diaspora, 1982
- Iran-Iraq war air strike, 1980–88
- area of Shiite population, 1983
- area claimed by Kurds as national homeland

- Anti-Iraq coalition state, 1990–91
- Coalition air base, 1990–91
- Coalition offensive, 1991
- UN-imposed Iraqi "no-fly" zone
- UN peace-keeping force
- movement of refugees
- migrant labor
- border, 1997
- oilfield
- oil pipeline
- desert

The attack ceased once Kuwait was liberated. Civil war broke out in Iraq as Shiites in the south and the Kurds in the north both sought to secede. Saddam remained in power, destroying the Shiite powerbase and forcing two million Kurds to seek asylum in Iran and Turkey, before the UN stepped in to enforce no-fly zones and safe havens from Iraqi attack. Devastating sanctions were imposed, but Saddam rebuilt his military base, including chemical weapons (forbidden by the postwar agreement); he also gradually restored his authority over the Kurdish areas.

Meanwhile, the Camp David agreements on Palestinian rights failed to materialize: Jewish settlers moved into the West Bank and built virtual fortresses there. In 1987 the Gaza and West Bank Palestinians began the *intifada* (uprising) against Israeli intransigence. Eventually a peace process was agreed, with phased Israeli withdrawals and recognition of a Palestinian National Authority under Arafat, initially only in Jericho but later intended to include Gaza and other areas. However, Israel faced a rightwing backlash and prime minister Rabin was murdered in 1995. Thereafter moves toward Palestinian selfrule advanced slowly amid mutual suspicion.

TIMELINE

Arab–Israeli conflict

1978 First Israeli invasion of Lebanon

1978 The Camp David agreements are signed

1981 Assassination of president Sadat of Egypt

1982 Second Israeli invasion of Lebanon: PLO withdraws from Beirut; Christians massacre Palestinian refugees

1983 A suicide bombing in Beirut kills over 300 US and French troops

1985 Israel agrees to withdraw from Lebanon

1987 *Intifada* by Palestinians in occupied territories begins

1989 Israeli premier Yitzhak Shamir opposes the creation of a Palestinian state

1992 Lebanese elections mark the end of the civil war

1993 In the Oslo Declaration, Israel and PLO agree on the formation of a Palestinian state

1995 Israel agrees to begin withdrawal from West Bank towns; premier Yitzhak Rabin is assassinated

1996 Israel attacks Hizbollah strongholds in south Lebanon

The Gulf

1979 Islamic forces in Iran oust the shah; Khomeini comes to power

1980 Iraq invades Iran; Iraqi oil terminals are damaged by Iranian attacks

1981 Israel bombs an Iraqi nuclear installation

1983 Iranian forces invade northern Iraq

1988 Iraq uses chemical weapons on the Kurds of northern Iraq

1988 The UN arranges a cease-fire between Iran and Iraq

1990 Iraq invades and annexes Kuwait

1991 An American-led UN coalition defeats Iraq and liberates Kuwait

1996 The United States launches missile attacks on Iraq to enforce the no-fly zones

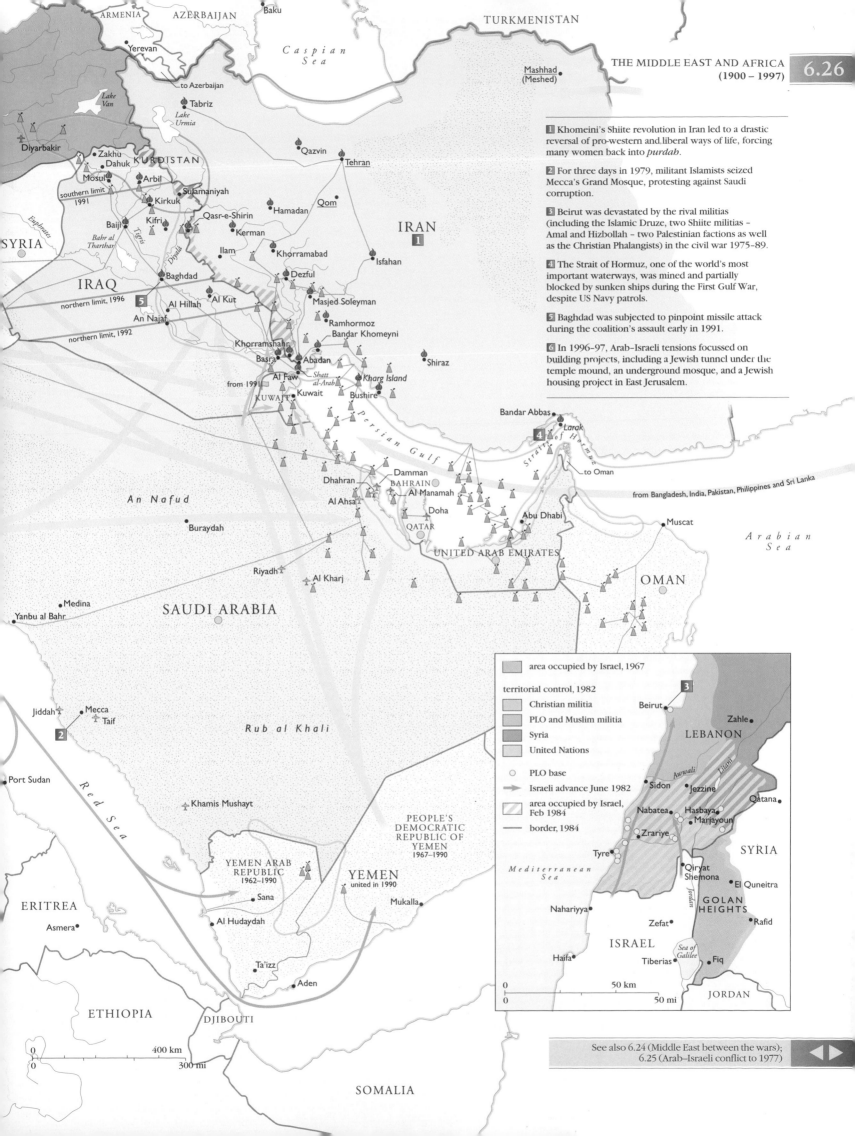

1 Khomeini's Shiite revolution in Iran led to a drastic reversal of pro-western and liberal ways of life, forcing many women back into *purdah*.

2 For three days in 1979, militant Islamists seized Mecca's Grand Mosque, protesting against Saudi corruption.

3 Beirut was devastated by the rival militias (including the Islamic Druze, two Shiite militias – Amal and Hizbollah – two Palestinian factions as well as the Christian Phalangists) in the civil war 1975–89.

4 The Strait of Hormuz, one of the world's most important waterways, was mined and partially blocked by sunken ships during the First Gulf War, despite US Navy patrols.

5 Baghdad was subjected to pinpoint missile attack during the coalition's assault early in 1991.

6 In 1996–97, Arab–Israeli tensions focussed on building projects, including a Jewish tunnel under the temple mound, an underground mosque, and a Jewish housing project in East Jerusalem.

Legend (inset map):
- area occupied by Israel, 1967
- territorial control, 1982
  - Christian militia
  - PLO and Muslim militia
  - Syria
  - United Nations
- ○ PLO base
- → Israeli advance June 1982
- area occupied by Israel, Feb 1984
- border, 1984

See also 6.24 (Middle East between the wars); 6.25 (Arab–Israeli conflict to 1977)

Africans played an active part in World War II, fighting on behalf of the Allies, and building roads, railroads, naval yards and fuel depots. They met whites of a type quite different from the traditional colonial administrators, discovered that imperial powers were not invincible, and identified with democratic freedom for which the Allies were fighting. The war meant that African independence could not long be denied.

No entrenched white community gave up without a fight. In British west Africa, though, where the white population was minimal, the transfer of power was relatively swift and peaceful. In the Gold Coast, the Convention People's Party leader Kwame Nkrumah worked closely with the British governor, and the idea of a unitary independent state was tested in an election in 1956. The Gold Coast became independent as Ghana, with Nkrumah as prime minister. Britain gave independence equally readily to Nigeria, Sierra Leone and the Gambia by 1965.

France had recruited a large number of Africans to its armies in both World Wars, and in French West Africa "colonies" were replaced by "overseas territories" with all Africans made citizens of the French republic itself. While many Africans accepted French control provided that they could keep economic links with France, Algeria began its fight for independence on the day that World War II ended in Europe. In 1958 the nationalist freedom fighters were confronted by settlers, causing a crisis that brought Charles de Gaulle back to the French presidency. He abandoned the policy of direct rule from Paris, and by 1960 most French colonies had been given their independence. In Algeria, though, de Gaulle committed half the army to maintain French rule, but this too was abandoned in 1962 after the loss of more than 10,000 French troops.

In Kenya, where white settlers controlled all the best farming regions, the Mau Mau movement terrorized and murdered 20,000 people, mostly Kikuyu sympathetic to their white masters. The British army and air force were sent in before independence was granted with Mau Mau leader Jomo Kenyatta as prime minister. In contrast, the independence movements in Uganda, Tanganyika, Nyasaland and Northern Rhodesia were relatively peaceful.

The ends of both the Belgian and Portuguese empires were violent. Belgium made no attempt to prepare the Congo for changes in government, and on independence the Congolese army mutinied and thousands of Belgian citizens became refugees. Belgian paratroopers went to their aid, and the copper-rich province of Katanga declared its own independence. Eventually, the Congolese general Mobutu crushed the Katangans and their mercenary supporters, creating a unified state which he renamed Zaire. Portugal was the last colonial power to leave Africa, and bitterly opposed the nationalists in Guinea, Angola and Mozambique. By 1975, though, when Portugal underwent its own political convulsions, the colonies became sovereign states.

Few African states found that independence brought stability or prosperity. Many faced ethnic conflict, a legacy of colonial borders that had little relevance to physical, social or economic realities. Most had impoverished, poorly educated and rapidly growing populations, and their economies proved vulnerable to multinational companies offering desperately needed investment to exploit the region's natural resources. Institutions of government were fragile, and arms manufacturers proved willing to supply weapons profligately. As a result, much of the continent experienced civil war, dictatorship and corruption, interrupted by humanitarian crises for which the world's aid agencies offered relief though they could never tackle the underlying problems.

The experience of Nigeria was typical: a civil war in the late 1960s brought on by a secessionist Igbo revolt led to widespread famine, and resulted in a cycle of weak civilian governments replaced by military strong men. Marxist forces, some with the support of the Soviet Union or Cuba, fought tenaciously in many countries including Mozambique and Angola, and won control of Ethiopia in 1974. Elsewhere, dictators such as Jean-Bédel Bokassa in the Central African Republic and Idi Amin in Uganda ruled by terror with few aims beyond personal aggrandizement. Environmental degradation, as the Sahara moved southward and the continent faced shortages of wood and fresh water, was matched in the 1980s by a demographic crisis as the AIDS virus swept through central and east Africa. Attempts to address such issues were made via the Organization of African Unity (OAU) and other regional groups,

but these often foundered through lack of leadership and political will, and in the face of the overwhelming economic problems. The problems of Rwanda in the 1990s, where old ethnic rivalries overflowed into genocide in 1994, creating a flood of refugees (including many responsible for mass murder) into Zaire – itself suffering from civil war as insurgents attempted to throw off the long-standing Mobutu regime that finally fell in 1997 – seemed to sum up the intractable problems of the continent.

1 Western Sahara was claimed by Morocco but was contested by Polisario guerrillas seeking to establish a Sahara Arab democratic republic.

2 Eritrea was annexed by Ethiopia in 1952, but won its independence in 1993 following a bitter civil war.

3 Zambia was ruled by Kenneth Kaunda from independence in 1964 until 1991; he became a leading figure in the Organization of African Unity.

4 A 20,000-strong United Nations force intervened in the Congo in 1960 to assist in expelling the Belgians.

5 Liberia was the only African country never to experience colonialism; but civil war broke out in 1985.

6 Italian and British Somaliland were united as Somalia in 1960, but civil war broke out in the 1980s over the disputed Ogaden region.

TIMELINE

North & east Africa

1944 French leader de Gaulle promises representative government to French colonies

1946 Houphouet-Boigny of Liberia founds African Democratic Federation

1949 Mau Mau movement founded in Kenya

1954 Algerian National Liberation Front (FLN) declares war on French

1962 End of war in Algeria against French rule

1963 State of emergency ends in Kenya with independence

1974 Marxists oust emperor Haile Selassie in Ethiopia

1977–88 Somali forces clash with Ethiopia in a claim over the Ogaden area

1984–85 Civil war in Eritrea leads to widespread famine in Ethiopia

1992 Civil war in Algeria between Islamic fundamentalists and government

West & central Africa

1954 Gold Coast's National Liberation Movement begins

1956 Representative government promised to Nigeria

1958 French colonies hold referenda on independence

1961 Wars of liberation begin in Portuguese colonies

1965 Southern Rhodesia's whites declare unilateral independence (UDI)

1967–70 Biafran war brings famine to eastern Nigeria

1975 Civil war breaks out in Angola immediately after independence

1994 Ethnic conflict in Rwanda results in mass slaughter and a refugee crisis

1950   1970   1990

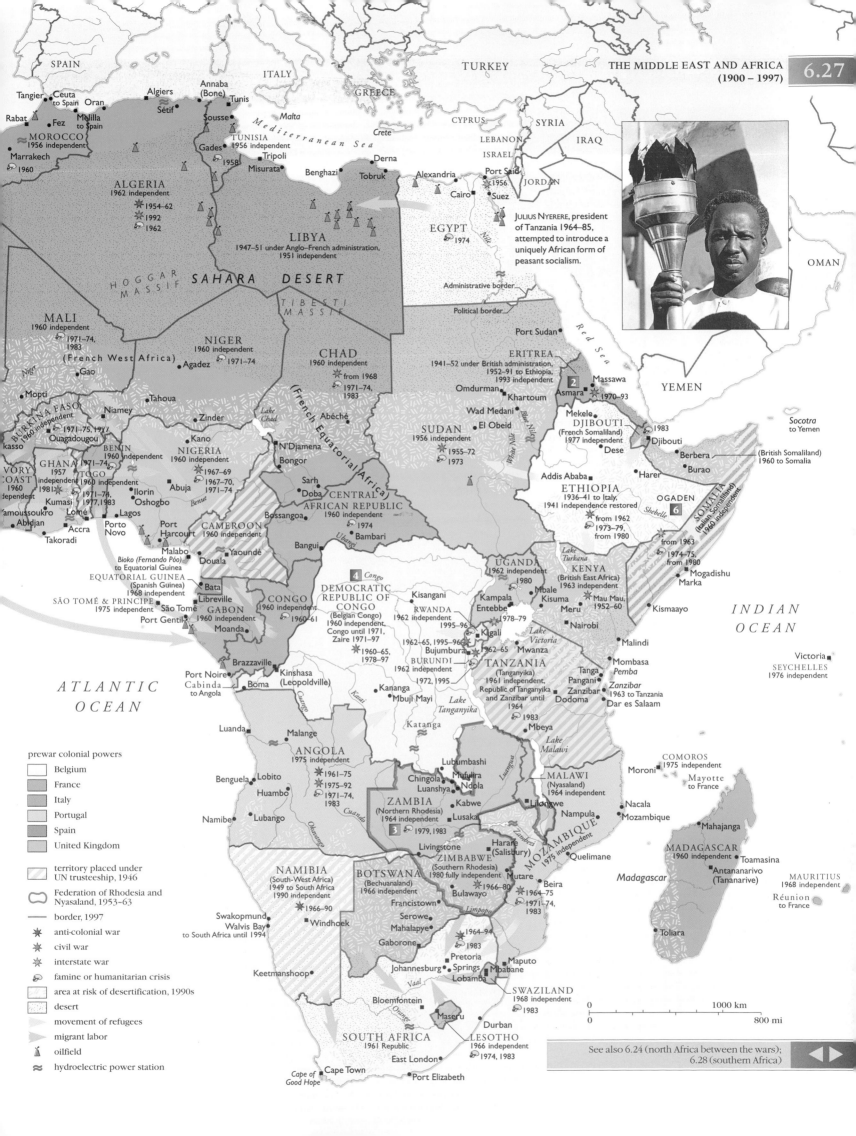

JULIUS NYERERE, president of Tanzania 1964–85, attempted to introduce a uniquely African form of peasant socialism.

See also 6.24 (north Africa between the wars); 6.28 (southern Africa)

In 1910 the Union of South Africa was set up, with Louis Botha as premier. Tension between Afrikaners and British continued, but attempts to unify the two were made during the 1930s in response to the world depression. Elsewhere, the colonial authorities continued to develop southern Africa for their own benefit, although South Africa's mining companies dominated the region economically, attracting laborers on short-term contracts from across the region. South-West Africa was mandated to South Africa in 1920 following South Africa's defeat of German forces there in 1914–15.

The denial of African hopes of self-determination was accompanied by land expropriation, racial legislation and enforced urbanization. Opposition was slow to form politically, and strikes or rebellions were often brutally crushed. The African National Congress (ANC; founded 1912), though, fought against racial segregation. Both the Afrikaner-dominated National Party, led by James Hertzog, and Jan Smuts' South Africa Party were unmoved.

In 1945 every other country south of the Zambezi was still an externally governed colony. South Africa sought to institutionalize white control by creating the system of *apartheid* or separate development. In 1948 the National Party came to power in the wake of white anxiety at the number of blacks moving into white areas. Under prime ministers D.F. Malan and Hendrik Verwoerd, restrictions were imposed on black residence and mobility. The vision was one where blacks and whites would eventually live in different states. To this end people were removed *en masse* to the socalled black "homelands" – nominally independent countries, often with no territorial integrity, natural resources or employment possibilities beyond those offered by white South Africa.

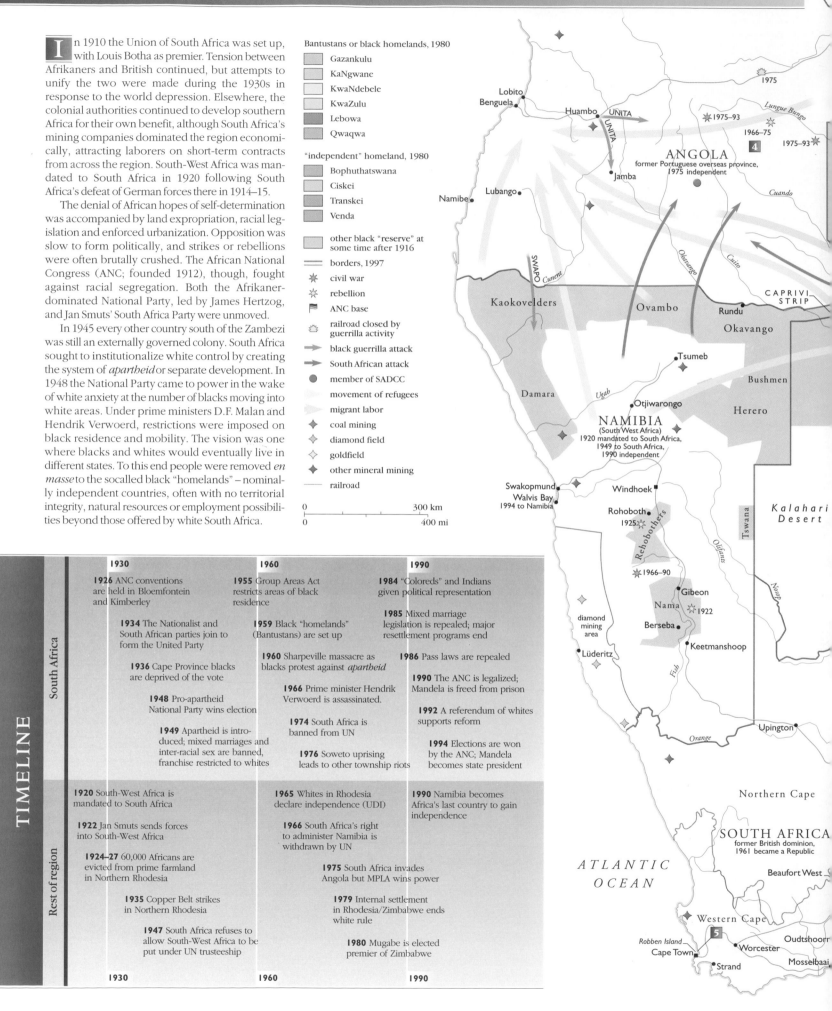

Bantustans or black homelands, 1980
- Gazankulu
- KaNgwane
- KwaNdebele
- KwaZulu
- Lebowa
- Qwaqwa

"independent" homeland, 1980
- Bophuthatswana
- Ciskei
- Transkei
- Venda

- other black "reserve" at some time after 1916
- borders, 1997
- ✳ civil war
- ✿ rebellion
- ⚑ ANC base
- railroad closed by guerrilla activity
- → black guerrilla attack
- → South African attack
- ● member of SADCC
- movement of refugees
- migrant labor
- ◆ coal mining
- ◆ diamond field
- ◇ goldfield
- ◆ other mineral mining
- railroad

0 _____ 300 km
0 _____ 400 mi

TIMELINE

South Africa

1930

1926 ANC conventions are held in Bloemfontein and Kimberley

1934 The Nationalist and South African parties join to form the United Party

1936 Cape Province blacks are deprived of the vote

1948 Pro-apartheid National Party wins election

1949 Apartheid is introduced; mixed marriages and inter-racial sex are banned, franchise restricted to whites

1960

1955 Group Areas Act restricts areas of black residence

1959 Black "homelands" (Bantustans) are set up

1960 Sharpeville massacre as blacks protest against *apartheid*

1966 Prime minister Hendrik Verwoerd is assassinated.

1974 South Africa is banned from UN

1976 Soweto uprising leads to other township riots

1990

1984 "Coloreds" and Indians given political representation

1985 Mixed marriage legislation is repealed; major resettlement programs end

1986 Pass laws are repealed

1990 The ANC is legalized; Mandela is freed from prison

1992 A referendum of whites supports reform

1994 Elections are won by the ANC; Mandela becomes state president

Rest of region

1920 South-West Africa is mandated to South Africa

1922 Jan Smuts sends forces into South-West Africa

1924–27 60,000 Africans are evicted from prime farmland in Northern Rhodesia

1935 Copper Belt strikes in Northern Rhodesia

1947 South Africa refuses to allow South-West Africa to be put under UN trusteeship

1965 Whites in Rhodesia declare independence (UDI)

1966 South Africa's right to administer Namibia is withdrawn by UN

1975 South Africa invades Angola but MPLA wins power

1979 Internal settlement in Rhodesia/Zimbabwe ends white rule

1980 Mugabe is elected premier of Zimbabwe

1990 Namibia becomes Africa's last country to gain independence

1930   1960   1990

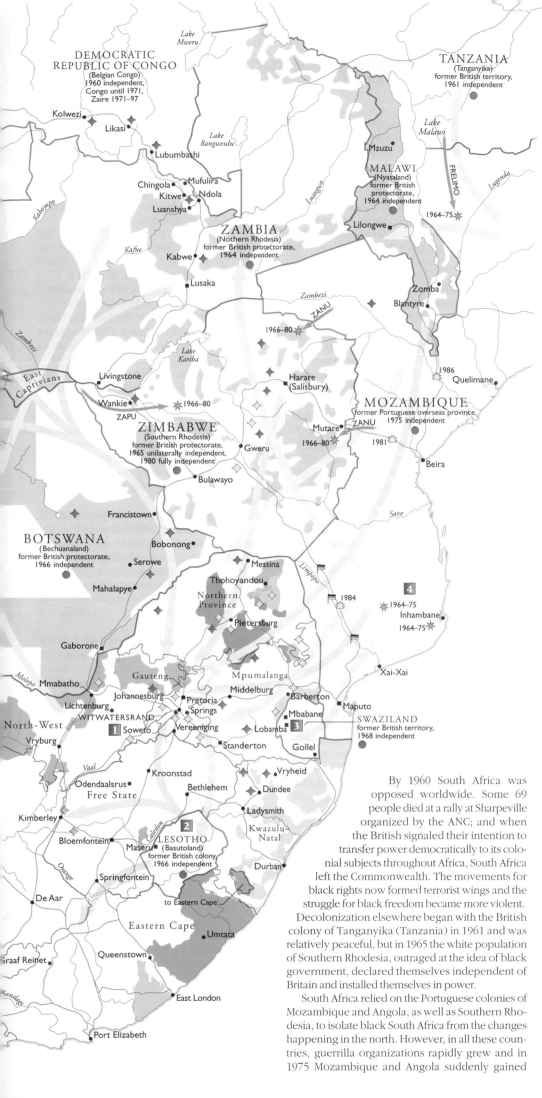

By 1960 South Africa was opposed worldwide. Some 69 people died at a rally at Sharpeville organized by the ANC; and when the British signaled their intention to transfer power democratically to its colonial subjects throughout Africa, South Africa left the Commonwealth. The movements for black rights now formed terrorist wings and the struggle for black freedom became more violent. Decolonization elsewhere began with the British colony of Tanganyika (Tanzania) in 1961 and was relatively peaceful, but in 1965 the white population of Southern Rhodesia, outraged at the idea of black government, declared themselves independent of Britain and installed themselves in power.

South Africa relied on the Portuguese colonies of Mozambique and Angola, as well as Southern Rhodesia, to isolate black South Africa from the changes happening in the north. However, in all these countries, guerrilla organizations rapidly grew and in 1975 Mozambique and Angola suddenly gained their independence following the fall of the right-wing government in Portugal. Civil war erupted between rival factions, while these events gave fresh impetus to liberation movements elsewhere.

South Africa now pursued a strategy of undermining the new black states. In Angola, though forced back from outright confrontation with the Marxists by Cuban intervention, the South Africans fomented civil war by maintaining bases in the south of the country and funding the UNITA resistance group; in Mozambique they supported the anti-government MNR. They controlled investment and the exploitation of the mineral wealth of the region; they supplied the transport infrastructure and drew the neighboring countries into their economic orbit.

White rule ended in Rhodesia in 1980, by negotiations brokered by the British followed by elections. The same year the "front-line states" of black African countries of southern Africa formed an association for development coordination (SADCC) to reduce their dependence on South Africa. South Africa responded with a series of raids allegedly targeting ANC bases within their neighbors' borders, and Mozambique and Swaziland were forced to sign non-aggression treaties. The costs of *apartheid* grew, however, as economic confidence had been shaken by the instability of the region; from 1984 sanctions were widely imposed (the main exception was Britain) and multinational companies pulled out. Proposals for limited electoral reform met with mass protests in the mid-1980s.

As the Cold War ended, United States support for South African activity in Angola evaporated; South Africa pulled out of its expensive involvement in Namibia. In 1990 National Party president F.W. de Klerk announced negotiations for a new democratic constitution. Despite opposition from the Zulus and white extremists, the transition to multiparty democracy was made in April 1994 with the election as state president of ANC leader Nelson Mandela. The first years of the new "rainbow nation" proved optimistic as Mandela fostered reconciliation and restored the prestige of the state overseas. But the task of raising the living standards of the historically disadvantaged groups remained a daunting one, and the changes in South Africa had little immediate impact on prospects for the rest of the region.

1 Soweto (South Western Township) was the largest squatter township for blacks near Johannesburg and the focus of unrest after the Sharpeville and Soweto massacres (1960 and 1976).

2 Poor in agricultural and industrial resources, Basutoland continued to provide huge numbers of migrant workers for South Africa even after its national independence in 1966 as Lesotho.

3 With its greater natural wealth, Swaziland managed to retain a degree of autonomy within South Africa's powerful economic orbit.

4 South Africa fomented civil war in its neighbors to destabilize them. As a result, millions of refugees were forced to flee war and famine, especially from Mozambique and Angola.

5 ANC leader Nelson Mandela was imprisoned in 1964 on terrorist charges, and spent many years in the prison on Robben Island.

See also 6.27 (decolonization in Africa)

the removal of the British monarch as head of state. Aboriginal citizenship was granted in 1967 but disputes over Aboriginal land rights continue. ▷ 6.23

AUSTRIA
Modern European state originating in the Middle Ages. It was created from the crown lands of Austria-Hungary in 1918. Political extremism flourished in Austria in the interwar period. Chancellor ENGELBERT DOLLFUSS abandoned parliamentary government in 1932, and the 1938 ANSCHLUSS incorporated Austria into Germany. Occupied by the Allies (1945–55), Austria was a founder member of the EUROPEAN FREE TRADE ASSOCIATION before joining the EUROPEAN UNION in 1995. ▷ 6.07, 6.10, 6.11

AUTHORITARIANISM
System of government in which traditional pillars of national life are rigidly enforced or supported. FRANCISCO FRANCO's authoritarian regime in Spain supported the Catholic church; elsewhere, especially in interwar Europe, the powers of the monarch or conservative elites were bolstered. ▷ 6.07

AXIS POWERS
Germany, Italy and Japan, in their alliance to fight World War II under the Tripartite Pact of 1940. (Germany and Italy were already joined by the Pact of Steel of 1939 and Germany and Japan by the Anti-Comintern Pact of 1936.) Hungary, Romania and SLOVAKIA joined the Tripartite Pact in November 1940, Bulgaria and YUGOSLAVIA (later CROATIA) in March 1941. In Europe and north Africa Germany was the senior partner in the Axis. There was almost no cooperation between Japan and other Axis members, particularly as Japan refused to attack the SOVIET UNION. ▷ 6.02, 6.03, 6.08, 6.09

AYUB KHAN
(1907–74) Pakistani soldier and politician. He became president of PAKISTAN in 1958. He fought India in the Second INDO-PAKISTAN WAR (1965) and accepted the peace agreement brokered by Soviet premier ALEXEI KOSYGIN at Tashkent 1965. Faced by widespread opposition, he resigned in 1969. ▷ 6.22

AZERBAIJAN
Muslim state in the Caucasus conquered by Russia and TURKEY in the eighteenth and nineteenth centuries. Declaring independence 1918, Azerbaijan was conquered by the BOLSHEVIKS in 1920 and became part of the SOVIET UNION in 1922. In 1988–89, serious clashes with ARMENIAN Christians living in the enclave of Ngorno-Karabakh began, continuing after Azerbaijan became independent of the Soviet Union on 23 August 1991. A cease-fire was agreed (1994–95) but negotiations did not resolve the dispute. ▷ 6.11, 6.15, 6.16

BA'ATH PARTY
("Renaissance") A pan-Arabic socialist party founded in SYRIA by Michel Aflag and Salah al-Din al-Bitar. It held its first congress in Damascus in 1947 and united with the Arab Socialist Party in 1953. The party has been in power in IRAQ since 1958, when King Feisal II was assassinated. ▷ 6.25, 6.26

BAADER-MEINHOF GANG
Communist terror group led by Andreas Baader (1943–77) and Ulrike Meinhof (1943–76). During the 1970s it attacked targets in the FEDERAL REPUBLIC OF GERMANY, which it considered had not properly confronted its NAZI past. ▷ 6.10

BABI YAR
Ravine on the outskirts of Kiev, Ukraine, where on 27–28 September 1941, 33,000 Jews were shot during the NAZI advance through the SOVIET UNION in World War II. ▷ 6.08

BALFOUR DECLARATION
Expression of the British government's support for the idea of a Jewish homeland in Palestine, to be established with respect for Arab rights, made in a letter from Foreign Secretary Arthur Balfour to British Zionist leader Lord Rothschild, 2 November 1917. Subsequently the basis for the British mandate in Palestine (1920–48). ▷ 6.01, 6.24

BALKAN PACT
Pact concluded between YUGOSLAVIA, Romania, Greece and TURKEY in February 1934 guaranteeing the status quo in the Balkans. Weakened by Bulgaria's refusal to join because of its claims to MACEDONIAN territory, it developed into the Balkan Entente, with a permanent administration. This became defunct in 1940 as its members met the NAZI threat in different ways. A second Balkan Pact between Greece, TURKEY and YUGOSLAVIA in 1954 was quickly nullified by Greek-Turkish rivalry over CYPRUS. ▷ 6.07, 6.10

BANDUNG CONFERENCE
The first Afro-Asian international conference. Held in INDONESIA in 1955, it brought together delegates from 29 countries in the hope of forming a "third force" in international politics. It discussed the nuclear arms race, Soviet imperialism in the THIRD WORLD and the ARAB-ISRAELI CONFLICT. ▷ 6.20

BANGLADESH
South Asian state. Originally East Bengal, it was the eastern wing of the state of PAKISTAN, created in 1947. SHEIKH MUJIBUR RAHMAN's secessionist Awami League won the 1970 East Pakistan elections and proclaimed the independent state of Bangladesh on March 26 1971. After the ensuing war with Pakistan, which was won largely thanks to Indian intervention, independence was confirmed and Mujibur became prime minister (January 1972). ▷ 6.22

BANTUSTANS
Ten "racially homogeneous states" or homelands devised by the South Africa in 1959 to permit Africans to develop "separateness". The government later granted independence to selected Bantustans: TRANSKEI (1976), Bophuthatswana (1977), Venda (1979). They received no international recognition. ▷ 6.28

BAR LEV LINE
A series of about 30 isolated strongpoints east of the Suez Canal, devised by and named for Chaim Bar Lev, ISRAELI chief of staff, to block attacks from Egypt by President GAMAL ABDEL NASSER after 1967. President ANWAR AL-SADAT's troops overran them in the YOM KIPPUR WAR but the Israelis quickly regained the initiative. ▷ 6.25

BARBAROSSA
Codename for the German invasion of the SOVIET UNION in World War II, launched on 22 June 1941. A BLITZKRIEG campaign failed because of the size of the country and the onset of winter, difficulties compounded by earlier German intervention in Greece and YUGOSLAVIA and ADOLF HITLER's decision to attack on a broad front rather than concentrating on Moscow. In consequence, Germany had to fight on two fronts against the Soviet Union in the east and Britain (and soon the USA) in the west. ▷ 6.08

BASQUES
Ancient people inhabiting the foothills of the Pyrenees. The Basques speak a non-Indo-European language and are regarded as descendants of Europe's earliest inhabitants. Briefly attaining statehood (1936–37) during the Spanish Civil War, their capital GUERNICA was destroyed by bombing. Basque identity was repressed under FRANCISCO FRANCO. Since 1974 the Basque Separatists have mounted an unsuccessful terror campaign in support of independence. ▷ 6.10

BATISTA, FULGENCIO
(1901–73) Dictator of CUBA. He seized power in 1933, stood down in 1944, and regained power in 1952–59. He exiled or executed his enemies and misused American dollar aid; he suppressed a revolt led by FIDEL CASTRO in July 1953. A second revolt led by Castro (1957–58) overthrew Batista who fled the country. ▷ 6.14

BAY OF PIGS INVASION
(17–19 April 1961) An invasion of CUBA by 1,500 Cuban exiles attempting to overthrow FIDEL CASTRO. Planned with the involvement of the CENTRAL INTELLIGENCE AGENCY, who provided support, the invasion failed. Most of the exiles were captured and the USA was humiliated. ▷ 6.14

BEGIN, MENACHEM
(1913–92) ISRAELI politician who headed the Irgun Zvai Leumi group in Palestine after

1942. As prime minister of Israel (1977–83) he invaded LEBANON (14 March 1978) to attack AL FATAH bases there. With President ANWAR AL-SADAT of Egypt, he signed the CAMP DAVID AGREEMENTS in 1978. ▷ 6.25, 6.26

BELARUS
Russian territory that declared independence in July 1917 before being reconquered by the BOLSHEVIKS during the RUSSIAN CIVIL WAR and partitioned in 1921 after the RUSSO-POLISH WAR. It was occupied by the Germans during World War II, when 2 million people (more than 25 percent of Belarus's population) were killed. Independent of the SOVIET UNION on 26 August 1991, in 1996 it formed a close alliance with Russia with a view to eventual union. ▷ 6.11, 6.15, 6.16

BEN-GURION, DAVID
(1886–1973) Polish-born statesman and creator of ISRAEL; prime minister of Israel (1948–53, 1955–63). He was dedicated to Israel's security and was a driving force behind the excellence of its armed forces. He is regarded as the greatest Jewish leader since Moses. ▷ 6.25, 6.26

BENELUX
Customs union formed by Belgium, the Netherlands and Luxembourg, in force from 1 January 1948. Precursor of later European economic cooperation. ▷ 6.10

BENEŠ, EDUARD
(1884–1948) Czechoslovakian foreign minister (1918–35) and president (1935–38) at the time of the MUNICH AGREEMENT partitioning CZECHOSLOVAKIA. Forced by ADOLF HITLER to resign, he became head of the Czechoslovak government in exile during World War II. Re-elected president after World War II, he resigned (6 May 1948) after the communist takeover. ▷ 6.06, 6.10

BERIA, LAVRENTI
(1899–1953) A Georgian Communist Party official appointed Commissar for Internal Affairs (head of the NKVD, later KGB) in December 1938, and responsible for JOSEPH STALIN's later PURGES and deportations. The only top-ranking communist executed following Stalin's death, by colleagues who feared his potential power. ▷ 6.15, 6.16

BERLIN, TREATY OF
US-German treaty signed 25 August 1921 concluding hostilities from World War I. The US Senate had previously refused to ratify the TREATY OF VERSAILLES and American membership of the LEAGUE OF NATIONS. ▷ 6.01

BERLIN BLOCKADE
(24 June 1948–24 May 1949) Soviet blockade of West Berlin. After World War II Germany was occupied by the ALLIES, Britain, the USA, the SOVIET UNION and France each administering a part. Berlin was similarly divided

but lay 200 miles within the Russian zone. As relations deteriorated, the Soviet Union cut off road and rail access to British, American and French-administered West Berlin. In response, the western Allies supplied the city by air, winning an important COLD WAR trial of strength and ensuring West Berlin became part of the FEDERAL REPUBLIC OF GERMANY when the division of Germany was finalized later in 1949. ▷ 6.10

BERLIN WALL
Wall constructed on 13 August 1961 by the East German communist authorities to stop the exodus of refugees to the FEDERAL REPUBLIC OF GERMANY. It remained a symbol of the division of Germany and Europe until its fall on 9 November 1989. ▷ 6.10

BEVERIDGE, SIR WILLIAM
(1879–1963) Oxford academic whose report, published 1 December 1942, established the basis for the postwar welfare state, proposing a comprehensive system of medical care, unemployment benefits and old age pensions "from the cradle to the grave".

BHUTTO, BENAZIR
Daughter of ZULFIKAR ALI BHUTTO, born 1953, she leads the PAKISTAN People's Party and became prime minister of Pakistan 1989. Dismissed in 1990, she became prime minister and minister of finance in 1993–96. ▷ 6.22

BHUTTO, ZULFIKAR ALI
(1928–79) PAKISTANI politician who as head of government (1971–78) was ruthless in his quest to maintain the power of the People's Party. Popular with his people, he was arrested by General ZIA UL-HAQ on a charge of conspiracy and executed. ▷ 6.22

BIAFRAN WAR
(1967–70) Civil war in Nigeria. Ethnic tensions led the Ibo of eastern Nigeria to declare the independent state of Biafra (30 May 1967). Led by General Emeka Ojukwu, they resisted federal forces under General Olusegun Obasanjo for over two years but were forced to surrender on 12 January 1970. ▷ 6.27

BISHOP, MAURICE
Grenadan leader of the New Jewel Movement (Joint Endeavor for Welfare, Education and Liberation), a Black Power organization composed of Grenadians, Rastafarians and Cuban revolutionaries. In 1979 he overthrew the government and became prime minister of the People's Revolutionary Government. He was assassinated in 1983. ▷ 6.14

BLITZKRIEG
Literally "lightning war", a tactic adopted by German forces in World War II to compensate for Germany's shortage of raw materials with which to fight a long war. Tanks and dive bombers overwhelmed enemy strongpoints, leaving ground troops to mop up survivors.

Successful against POLAND, France and the Low Countries, blitzkrieg failed to knock the SOVIET UNION out of the war during the BARBAROSSA campaign. ▷ 6.08, 6.09

BLUM, LÉON
(1872–1950) French statesman and leader of the French Socialist Party from 1925. Blum was prime minister in two Popular Front governments (June 1936–June 1937 and 1938). Failing to prepare France for war with Germany, he introduced a 40-hour week and other reforms. Imprisoned by the VICHY authorities (1940–42) and incarcerated in Buchenwald and Sachsenhausen CONCENTRATION CAMPS (1943–45), he became prime minister again (1946–47), helping to create the Fourth Republic. ▷ 6.07, 6.10

BOKASSA, JEAN-BÉDEL
(1921–) African soldier and politician who became army commander-in-chief of the newly independent (1960) Central African Republic. He overthrew President Dacko and established himself as life president then as emperor (1976). Exiled in 1979, he returned to be sentenced to life imprisonment. ▷ 6.27

BOLSHEVIKS
Radical wing of the Russian Social Democratic Party, committed to insurrection and led by professional activists, such as VLADIMIR ILYICH LENIN. Splitting from the MENSHEVIKS in 1903, they took power in the OCTOBER REVOLUTION of 1917. They adopted the name "All-Russian Communist Party (Bolsheviks)" in March 1918 and subsequently were known as "the Communists". The term "Bolshevik" was officially dropped in 1952. ▷ 6.15, 6.16.

BOPHUTHATSWANA
Former BANTUSTAN within South Africa, never recognized internationally. It was reabsorbed by South Africa in 1994. ▷ 6.28

BOSE, SUBHAS CHANDRA
(1897–1945) Indian nationalist. He opposed the concept of India as a dominion of the BRITISH EMPIRE and, with JAWAHARLAL NEHRU, formed the Independence League in 1928. He actively supported the AXIS POWERS in World War II, went to NAZI Germany and then formed the Indian National Army and assisted the Japanese to invade BURMA. ▷ 6.18

BOSNIAN CIVIL WAR
Most serious European war since 1945. Bosnia-Herzegovina's declaration of independence from YUGOSLAVIA (3 March 1992) was opposed militarily by Bosnian Serbs and the Serbian federal government of YUGOSLAVIA. The ensuing war was brutal, civilians being killed or expelled from their homes to create ethnically homogeneous areas ("ethnic cleansing"). An international arms embargo kept Bosnia weak, and UNITED NATIONS and the NORTH ATLANTIC TREATY ORGANIZATION action against the Serbs was

ineffective. Only when the federal government (and CROATIA, which also participated in the conflict) had secured the territory it wanted was firm action taken. It involved American-led airstrikes against Bosnian Serbs and setting up the DAYTON AGREEMENT ending the war. ▷ 6.05, 6.11

BOTSWANA
Southern African state, formerly the British protectorate of Bechuanaland. Seretse Khama (1921–80), leader of the Democratic Party, won the 1965 elections and became president and head of state at independence on 30 September 1966. ▷ 6.27, 6.28

BRANDT, WILLY
(1913–92) West German Social Democratic Party politician, chancellor in coalition with the Free Democrats (1968–74). He was formerly mayor of West Berlin (1949–57) and foreign minister (1966–69). His OSTPOLITIK encouraged rapprochement between east and west. Treaties with POLAND and the SOVIET UNION (1972) acknowledged the GERMAN DEMOCRATIC REPUBLIC's sovereignty and its border with POLAND. ▷ 6.10

BREST-LITOVSK, TREATY OF
Treaty signed 3 March 1918, ending fighting between Russia and Germany in World War I. Negotiations began soon after the OCTOBER REVOLUTION, but failure to agree terms led Germany to occupy large parts of Russia. Under the treaty, Russia lost half its European territory, (its Baltic lands, the UKRAINE, BELARUS and the Caucasus). After German defeat by the western ALLIES, the BOLSHEVIKS recaptured the UKRAINE and the Caucasus during the RUSSIAN CIVIL WAR. ▷ 6.06, 6.15

BRETTON-WOODS CONFERENCE
International conference on the organization of postwar finance, held in New Hampshire, USA, in July 1944, where 28 countries agreed to create a world bank and an INTERNATIONAL MONETARY FUND and make their currencies convertible at stable exchange rates linked to the dollar. The USA withdrew from the Bretton-Woods system in 1971, and attempts to preserve stable exchange rates were abandoned in 1976.

BREZHNEV, LEONID
(1906–82) SOVIET leader. Born in the UKRAINE, he was a political commissar in the Red Army in World War II. He entered the Politburo in 1957 and became titular head of state in 1960, succeeding NIKITA KHRUSCHEV as first secretary in 1964. Under him the economy and administration of the Soviet Union stagnated. Brezhnev pursued DÉTENTE, but also ordered the invasions of CZECHOSLOVAKIA (1968) and AFGANISTAN (1979). ▷ 6.05, 6.16

BRITAIN, BATTLE OF
(10 July–31 October 1940) World War II aerial battle fought over the Channel and southeast England. English Hurricanes and Spitfires, guided by information from radar stations, prevented the German Luftwaffe gaining the air superiority necessary for a seaborne invasion of Britain. ▷ 6.08

BRITISH EMPIRE
Britain's overseas possessions, at its peak the largest empire in world history. Obtaining territory in the West and East Indies in the 17th and 18th centuries, Britain established the basis of its empire in the Seven Years War with France 1756–63, winning control of Canada and North America and gaining the upper hand in India. However, the American colonies threw off British rule in the American Revolution (1775–83). AUSTRALIA was claimed by Cook in 1770, and African territory was seized during the 19th century. Canada received autonomy as a dominion in 1867; Australia, New Zealand, South Africa in 1907, although Britain retained control of foreign policy until 1931. The acquisition of LEAGUE OF NATIONS mandates after World War I swelled the empire to its largest extent. It encompassed a quarter of the world's people. DECOLONIZATION occurred after World War II, with independence for INDIA and PAKISTAN from 1947, for the African colonies from the 1950s and for most Caribbean colonies in the 1970s. ▷ 6.01, 6.20, 6.22, 6.24, 6.27

BURMA
Asian republic. A province of British India, then a Crown Colony from 1937, it was occupied by Japan in 1942 and recaptured by the ALLIES in 1944–45. Independent on 4 January 1948, it was controlled by the military under general NE WIN (1964–88) and thereafter by the State Law and Order Restoration Council. Its name was changed to the Union of MYANMAR in 1989. ▷ 6.18, 6.19, 6.20, 6.21, 6.22, 6.23

BURMA ROAD
Road, 1096 kilometers (681 miles) long, linking the Lashio railhead in BURMA and Kunming, Yunnan province, China. It was built by the Chinese in 1938 to transport supplies for their war against Japan. Cut by Japanese troops in 1942, it was reopened in 1945 via the Stilwell Road. It has since been abandoned. ▷ 6.17, 6.18, 6.19

BUSH, GEORGE
(1924–) The 41st president of the USA (1988–92). A pilot in World War II, he was successful in the Texan oil industry before becoming a REPUBLICAN congressman (1966–70) and then head of the CENTRAL INTELLIGENCE AGENCY. He was RONALD REAGAN's vice-president. As president, he moderated Reagan's economic policies and led the UNITED NATIONS coalition against IRAQ in the GULF WAR. ▷ 6.13, 6.26

CAIRO CONFERENCES
Two ALLIED conferences of World War II. In November 1943 WINSTON CHURCHILL, FRANKLIN D. ROOSEVELT and JIANG JIESHI met to determine strategy for the defeat of Japan and to discuss the appointment of a supreme commander. In December 1943 Churchill, Roosevelt and Ismet Inonou, president of TURKEY, met to assess the possibility of a Turkish contribution towards the defeat of Germany. ▷ 6.09

CAMBRAI, BATTLE OF
World War I battle in which massed tanks were first used. British tanks assaulted the HINDENBURG LINE on 20 November 1917, but sufficient reserves were not available to exploit the breakthroughs they made. ▷ 6.06

CAMP DAVID AGREEMENTS
(1978) Agreements brokered by President JIMMY CARTER at CAMP DAVID, Maryland, between Egypt's president, ANWAR AL-SADAT, and ISRAEL's prime minister, MENACHEM BEGIN. They formed a "framework for peace" between Egypt and Israel: self-government for Gaza and the WEST BANK and the withdrawal of Israeli troops from Sinai. ▷ 6.26

CAPE MATAPAN, BATTLE OF
(28 March 1941) Sea battle off the southernmost point of the Greek mainland between an Italian fleet commanded by Admiral Iachino and a British fleet under Admiral Cunningham who sank the heavy cruiser *Pola* and its escorts. Thereafter, most Italian naval units remained in port at La Spezia. ▷ 6.08

CAPORETTO, BATTLE OF
(24 October–12 November 1917) World War I battle in which a surprise Austro-German attack broke the deadlock on the Italian front and nearly forced Italy's surrender. The Italians lost 10,000 men killed in a rapid Austro-German advance, before stabilizing their front on the River Piave. ▷ 6.06

CÁRDENAS, LÁZARO
(1895–1970) Mexican soldier and president (1934–40), a social reformer who helped modernize the country. During his presidency the state oil company, PEMEX (Petróleos Mexicanos), was formed (1938). ▷ 6.12

CARTER, JIMMY
(1924–) The 39th president of the USA (1977–81). DEMOCRATIC senator and governor of Georgia, his presidential successes in international affairs (CAMP DAVID AGREEMENTS and STRATEGIC ARMS LIMITATION TREATIES) were overshadowed by the Soviet invasion of AFGHANISTAN, the disastrous attempted helicopter rescue of hostages held in the US embassy in Teheran, and the impact of the world recession on the American economy. He was defeated in the 1980 presidential election by RONALD REAGAN. ▷ 6.13, 6.26

CASABLANCA CONFERENCE
(14–24 January 1943) World War II meeting between WINSTON CHURCHILL and FRANKLIN

Delano Roosevelt held in French Morocco. Agreement was reached for an invasion of Sicily to follow up Allied success in north Africa, and for a joint bomber offensive against Germany. Afterwards, Roosevelt stated the Allied demand for the Axis powers' unconditional surrender. ▷ 6.09

Castro, Fidel
(1927–) Cuban revolutionary who overthrew Fulgencio Batista in 1959 and repelled the counter-revolutionary Bay of Pigs invasion (1961) He became prime minister of Cuba in 1959 and president in 1976. His social reform program depended on Soviet aid, which was withdrawn in 1989. His Caribbean Marxist state has labored under American trade sanctions. ▷ 6.13, 6.14

Ceauçescu, Nicolae
(1918–89) Romanian communist leader from 1967. He pursued a policy of independence from the Soviet Union, criticizing the invasion of Czechoslovakia in 1968, but kept Romania within the Warsaw Pact. His Stalinist agricultural policies and regime based on nepotism and brutality brought him hatred, and he was executed with his wife, Elena, on 25 December 1989, following a popular revolution. ▷ 6.10

Central Intelligence Agency (CIA)
Agency established in 1947 to prepare intelligence reports for the president of the USA. Under Allen Dulles (director 1953–61), the CIA became involved in covert operations against opponents of the USA. Despite the Bay of Pigs fiasco, the CIA continued to be active throughout the world during and after the Cold War. ▷ 6.21

Central Pacific Forces
Forces assembled by Admiral C. W. Nimitz (1885–1966) at Pearl Harbor to drive the Japanese from the central Pacific and liberate the Philippines. Nimitz's command bypassed unimportant islands, using "atoll-hopping" to clear specific islands in the Marshalls and Marianas. Naval victories (Philippine Sea and Leyte) cleared the way for the liberation of the Philippines and the attack on Iwo Jima and Okinawa. ▷ 6.19

Central powers
Originally, the partners in the 1882 Triple Alliance (Germany, Austria-Hungary and Italy). The term now applies to the countries opposing the Allied powers in World War I: Germany and Austria-Hungary, joined by Turkey (29 October 1914) and Bulgaria (14 October 1915). ▷ 6.06

Chaco War
(1932–35) War between Paraguayan and Bolivian forces in the Gran Chaco region of northern Paraguay. Despite the leadership and training provided by the German general von Kundt, the Bolivians were forced to

accept a truce in 1935. Paraguay retained most of the Chaco by the Treaty of Buenos Aires (21 July 1938). ▷ 6.12

Chamberlain, Neville
(1869–1940) British statesman. Conservative member of Parliament from 1918, chancellor of the exchequer (1931–37), and prime minister from 1937 to 1940, he was the main architect of appeasement. Heavily criticized after the Munich agreement, he resigned on 10 May 1940, after the German occupation of Denmark and Norway, in favor of Winston Churchill. ▷ 6.07

Changsa, battles of
Battles fought by Jiang Jieshi's Nationalists to preserve this important railroad center in Hunan province and stem the Japanese advance along the Yangtze River inland. One consequence was the Japanese attack on French Indo-China in 1940 to cut another supply route to Chongqing, Jiang Jieshi's new capital. Changsa was ultimately lost to the Japanese. ▷ 6.19

Chechnya
Caucasian region populated by a Muslim hill people noted for their ferocity. Brought under Russian control in 1859 after a long struggle, risings continued after Chechnya became part of the Soviet Union. In 1944, Joseph Stalin deported the entire population to Central Asia; half died before Nikita Khruschev allowed them to return home in 1957. Chechnya declared independence from the Soviet Union and Russia on 1 November 1991. Civil war followed before Russian troops invaded on 11 November 1994. After a bloody, inconclusive conflict, a peace treaty was signed (29 August 1996) giving Chechnya autonomy but putting off the question of sovereignty until 2001. ▷ 6.11

Cheka
Secret police set up by Vladimir Ilyich Lenin in December 1917 under Felix Dzerzhinski. Responsible for the "Red Terror" that followed the assassination attempt on Lenin in August 1917, in 1922 it became the OGPU (later the NKVD, then the KGB). ▷ 6.15

Chemin des Dames, Battle of
(16 April–9 May 1917) World War I battle, also known as the "Nivelle Offensive" after the French commander in chief, in which attempts to use a creeping artillery barrage to shield advancing troops failed. Mutinies spread in response to the massive losses suffered, finishing the French army as an attacking force. Philippe Pétain replaced Nivelle on 25 April. ▷ 6.06

Chernobyl accident
Explosion at a nuclear power plant near Kiev, Ukraine, on 26 April 1986. Meltdown of the core was narrowly avoided and a concrete cap used to seal the damaged reactor, but

serious contamination of the surrounding area occurred and radioactive fallout was spread across Europe. ▷ 6.16

Chetniks
Serbian partisans, originally fighting for independence from the Ottoman empire. In World War II in Yugoslavia, Mihailovic's Chetniks fought the ruling Croatian Ustaše, the Germans and Tito's communist partisans. Allied-supported until late 1943, they were put down by Tito and the Red Army after July 1944. ▷ 6.09

Chiang Kai-shek
See Jiang Jieshi

China, People's Republic of
Republic proclaimed by Mao Zedong on 1 October 1949 after the People's Liberation Army had established control over mainland China. It suffered economic catastrophe after the Great Leap Forward (1958–60) and the Cultural Revolution (1966). In the 1960s China quarrelled with its ally the Soviet Union over ideological issues (the Sino-Soviet split) and became a nuclear power. The People's Republic was admitted to the United Nations in 1971. It was internationally reviled for the massacre of pro-democracy demonstrators in Tiananmen Square in 1989. Britain returned Hong Kong to Chinese control in 1997 on the expiry of its lease. The People's Republic still seeks control over Taiwan. Since Mao's death, socialist policies have largely been abandoned in favor of a mixed economy. Foreign investment is encouraged in special economic zones. ▷ 6.17, 6.20

China, Republic of (Nationalist)
Republic proclaimed on 1 January 1912 by Sun Yixiang. It survived Japanese invasions and the rise of the communists until 1945, when the ruling Nationalist Party (the Guomindang) went onto the defensive. Defeated by the People's Liberation Army in 1949, the republic was re-established in Taiwan, where the Nationalist government was recognized as the legitimate represen-tative of China by the United Nations until 1971. ▷ 6.17, 6.18, 6.19, 6.20

Christian Democracy
Moderate political movements such as the German Center Party (founded 1870) and the Italian Center Party (founded 1919) were formed to offer the new mass electorate an alternative to socialism. Conrad Adenauer's Christian Democratic Party, now led by Helmut Kohl, is one of many similar contemporary centrist parties. ▷ 6.10

Churchill, Winston
(1874–1965) British statesman. He was both a Conservative (1900–04 and 1925–64) and a Liberal (1906–22) member of Parliament. In an initially turbulent career, Churchill used

troops against striking miners while home secretary (1910–11), and he resigned as first lord of the admiralty after the failed GALLIPOLI landings. As chancellor of the exchequer (1924–29) he returned Britain to the gold standard. Becoming a staunch opponent of APPEASEMENT in the 1930s, Churchill entered the war cabinet in September 1939 and became prime minister in May 1940. He was an energetic, inspiring and imaginative leader and his oratory and cultivation of Anglo-American relations were vital to the war effort. Defeated in the general election of 1945 Churchill became prime minister again from 1951 to 1955, when he retired because of ill-health. He was knighted in 1953. ▷ 6.03, 6.06, 6.07, 6.08, 6.09

CIA
See CENTRAL INTELLIGENCE AGENCY

CIS
See COMMONWEALTH OF INDEPENDENT STATES

CISKEI
Former BANTUSTAN in South Africa adjacent to East London. Its independent status never received international recognition. It was reabsorbed into South Africa in 1991 and is part of eastern Cape Province. ▷ 6.28

CIVIL DISOBEDIENCE
The breaking of a law, considered unjust, by groups who reject the use of violence. The term was first used by the American poet and essayist Henry Thoreau in 1849. It became the policy of MOHANDAS GANDHI and the CIVIL RIGHTS MOVEMENT and some anti-nuclear protesters. ▷ 6.13, 6.18, 6.22

CIVIL RIGHTS MOVEMENT
Movement to end segregation and racial discrimination, particularly in the southern USA. It expanded under the leadership of MARTIN LUTHER KING (1929–68) to end racism in the entire USA. Its success was marked by civil rights legislation (1964–68). ▷ 6.13

CLEMENCEAU, GEORGES
(1841–1929) French statesman. A Radical deputy and senator, his first period as prime minister was devoted to tackling the waves of strikes afflicting France. From 1917 to 1920 he presided over French victory in World War I, but was criticized for being too lenient at the Paris Peace Conference and resigned in January 1920. ▷ 6.06, 6.07

CLINTON, BILL
(1946–) The 42nd president of the USA. He was DEMOCRATIC governor of Arkansas before winning the 1992 and 1996 presidential elections. Improving the economy and cutting the budget deficit at home, he has been active in foreign policy, helping to negotiate the DAYTON AGREEMENT and OSLO ACCORDS, but his presidency has been dogged by sexual and financial scandals. ▷ 6.11, 6.12, 6.21

COFFEE ACCORDS
Also known as the Washington Agreements, they were signed in 1940 with all the Central American producers. They guaranteed US purchases of coffee quotas at a time when European outlets were closed because of World War II. In return the USA acquired military bases. ▷ 6.12

COLD WAR
State of tension between the American-led west and the communist SOVIET UNION and its satellites from the late 1940s to the late 1980s. A breakdown of cooperation after World War II led to rival power blocs (the NORTH ATLANTIC TREATY ORGANIZATION and the WARSAW PACT), international crises (notably the BERLIN BLOCKADE and the CUBAN MISSILE CRISIS) and wars by proxy (notably the KOREAN WAR and the VIETNAM WAR). A period of DÉTENTE in the 1970s ended with a Soviet invasion of AFGANISTAN. In the 1980s, tensions were eased by MIKHAIL GORBACHEV's policies, which finally ended with dissolution of the Soviet Union. ▷ 6.03, 6.04, 6.05, 6.10, 6.13

COLLECTIVIZATION
The forcible reorganization of SOVIET agriculture on communist principles (1929–34). Undertaken to provide food for industrialization and to end the potential for peasant opposition, JOSEPH STALIN's brutal policy of grain requisition and mass deportations caused widespread death and famine.

COLONIALISM
The acquisition of foreign territory for settlement and exploitation. Following Spanish and Portuguese conquests in South America in the 15th and 16th centuries, most major European powers subsequently claimed extra-European territory, culminating in the "scramble for Africa" in the late 19th century. The BRITISH EMPIRE was the largest in the world before DECOLONIZATION began after World War II.

COMMONWEALTH OF INDEPENDENT STATES (CIS)
Association of ex-SOVIET states founded 1991 to replace the SOVIET UNION, comprising ARMENIA, Azerbaijan, BELARUS, KAZAKHSTAN, KYRGYSTAN, MOLDOVA, Russia, Tadjikistan, TURKMENISTAN, the UKRAINE and UZBEKISTAN. It was chaired by the Russian president, BORIS YELTSIN. ▷ 6.16

COMMONWEALTH OF NATIONS
Association of states formerly members of the BRITISH EMPIRE. The "British Empire and Commonwealth" ("Commonwealth" having being added after World War I to refer to the self-governing dominions of Canada, AUSTRALIA, New Zealand and South Africa) became the "British Commonwealth" after the DECOLONIZATION of INDIA and PAKISTAN in 1947 and the "Commonwealth of Nations" in 1949, reflecting its members' new status. ▷ 6.03, 6.04

COMMUNISM
Political theory promoting common ownership of the means of production, distribution and exchange. Articulated by Karl Marx and Friedrich Engels in the 19th century and developed in the 20th by VLADIMIR ILYICH LENIN and MAO ZEDONG. Communist regimes in eastern Europe and the SOVIET UNION collapsed between 1989 and 1991, but communism remains the official ideology in China, NORTH KOREA and CUBA. ▷ 6.15, 6.16, 6.17, 6.20, 6.21

CONCENTRATION CAMPS
Camps first used to detain prisoners of war by Spain in its war with CUBA (1895–98), and first used for enemy civilian population by Britain during the Second Anglo-Boer War (1899–1902). Developed as instruments of state control by the BOLSHEVIKS (GULAGS) and the NAZIS, who imprisoned their opponents and used them as forced labor. Some Nazi camps became DEATH CAMPS. ▷ 6.08, 6.09

CONGO, REPUBLIC OF
Formerly the Belgian Congo (the Congo Free State), the newly independent state in 1960 took the name of Republic of Congo. In 1971 the name was changed to ZAIRE. In 1992–95, conflict between President SESE SEKO MOBUTU and political opponents led to his overthrow (1997) and the name changed to Republic of Congo. ▷ 6.27

CONGRESS PARTY
Indian political party founded in 1885. Headed by MOHANDAS GANDHI and later by JAWAHARLAL NEHRU, the Indian National Congress voiced Indian demands for independence from Britain and remains the dominant force in Indian politics. ▷ 6.22

CONTRAS
Members of the Nicaraguan Democratic Front, who opposed the SANDINISTA Marxist-Leninist government (1979–90). Funded by the USA, most Contra units were based in Honduras, from where they launched their raids into NICARAGUA. They were disbanded after the National Opposition Union (UNO) won the 1990 elections. ▷ 6.14

COOLIDGE, CALVIN
(1872–1933) The 30th president of the USA. REPUBLICAN senator for Massachusetts and Warren Harding's vice-president, he became president in August 1923 on Harding's death and was elected in 1924. His presidency was characterized by an isolationist foreign policy and laissez-faire economics at home. ▷ 6.12

CORAL SEA, BATTLE OF THE
Battle fought off northeast Australia (6–8 May 1942) between Japanese and American carrier aircraft during a Japanese attempt to invade Port Moresby. Each side lost a carrier (the *Lexington* and the *Shobo*) and the Japanese were forced to abandon the invasion. ▷ 6.19

CORREGIDOR, BATTLE OF
Japanese siege, beginning in January 1942, of an island, transformed by the Americans into a fortress, off the Bataan peninsula in the Philippines. It surrendered in May and approximately 140,000 American and Filipino prisoners of war took part in the infamous Death March that followed. ▷ 6.19

CROATIA
European state. An Austro-Hungarian territory, after World War I it was part of YUGOSLAVIA. Croatian extremists actively opposed merging their Catholic nation with its Orthodox and Muslim neighbors, and during World War II Croatian fascists (Ustaše) formed a brutal NAZI puppet state, committing atrocities against Serbs, Bosnians, Jews and others. Under President Franjo Tudjman, Croatia declared independence from Yugoslavia on 7 October 1991 and fought with Serb nationalists and the federal Yugoslav government over disputed territory. ▷ 6.08, 6.08, 6.09, 6.11

CUBA
Island republic in the Caribbean. A Spanish colony, Cuba became an American protector-ate in 1902 after the Spanish-American war and won full independence in 1934. It declared war on the AXIS POWERS (December 1941). FULGENCIO BATISTA became dictator in 1952 and was overthrown by FIDEL CASTRO in 1959, after which Cuba became a member of the communist bloc and the scene of the BAY OF PIGS fiasco and the CUBAN MISSILE CRISIS. Communist rule has not brought prosperity, and almost 1 million Cubans have left since 1959. ▷ 6.12, 6.13, 6.14

CUBAN MISSILE CRISIS
Crisis arising on 22 October 1962 when President JOHN F. KENNEDY announced that American reconnaissance flights had revealed nuclear missiles in Cuba, sent from the SOVIET UNION. Kennedy ordered a "quarantine" of all offensive military equipment under shipment to Cuba. He stated that a missile attack from Cuba would bring "a full retaliatory response" on the Soviet Union. NIKITA KHRUSHCHEV agreed to remove the missiles and bombers from Cuba on 2 November, ending the most dangerous postwar crisis. ▷ 6.12, 6.13, 6.14

CULTURAL REVOLUTION
(1966–67) State-sponsored upheaval in China. Fearing the growth of elitism within the Communist Party, MAO ZEDONG announced "a new Maoism" to the youth of China in 1966. He gave them the right to rebel against those in authority or who exhibited bourgeois thoughts. Spearheaded by Madam Mao's RED GUARDS, they brought chaos to China and became themselves a law and order problem. The revolution culminated in a clash between the PEOPLE'S LIBERATION ARMY and Red Guards in Wuhan in 1967. Education, the countryside and city life all suffered from 1966 until Mao's death in 1976. ▷ 6.20

CURZON LINE
Demarcation line dividing ethnic Poles from Russians, Lithuanians and Ukrainians. It was proposed by British foreign secretary Lord Curzon after World War I, to run from Grodno through Brest-Litovsk to the Carpathians. The Poles secured large gains east of this line in the RUSSO-POLISH WAR, but it became the basis for the Polish-Soviet Union border at the World War II YALTA CONFERENCE. ▷ 6.07, 6.10

CZECH REPUBLIC
European state comprising Bohemia and Moravia, created when CZECHOSLOVAKIA divided in 1993. Prime Minister Václav Klaus's radical economic reforms produced growth, and the republic is in the first wave of eastern European states preparing to join the NORTH ATLANTIC TREATY ORGANIZATION and the EUROPEAN UNION. ▷ 6.11

CZECHOSLOVAKIA
State created from parts of Austria-Hungary (Bohemia, Moravia and SLOVAKIA) after World War I. Partitioned by the MUNICH AGREEMENT of 1938 and occupied by Germany in March 1939, it was liberated by the SOVIET UNION in 1944. A communist coup in February 1948 brought it firmly under Soviet control. In 1968 the Soviet Union crushed Alexander Dubček's attempt to liberalize the country (the PRAGUE SPRING), but in December 1989 the VELVET REVOLUTION overthrew communism and former dissident writer Václav Havel became president. The CZECH REPUBLIC and SLOVAKIA separated to form new states on 1 January 1993. ▷ 6.07, 6.08. 6.09, 6.10, 6.11

D-DAY
(6 June 1944) The day of the NORMANDY LANDINGS of World War II. ▷ 6.09

DALAI LAMA
Traditionally, the religious and temporal ruler of Tibet. The present Dalai Lama, Tenzin Gyatso, was born in 1935 and fled from Tibet after the 1950 Chinese invasion. He returned but fled a second time in 1959, taking refuge in India, when the Chinese suppressed a Tibetan rising. In 1989 he was awarded the Nobel Peace Prize and remains in exile. ▷ 6.22

DANZIG
See GDANSK

DARDANELLES
Narrow straits leading from the Aegean to the Black Sea, through which the ALLIES attempted to send a naval force to attack the Turkish capital, Constantinople (Instanbul), during World War I. The attack, (19 February-18 March 1915), failed and alerted the Turks, who were well-prepared for the subsequent GALLIPOLI CAMPAIGN. ▷ 6.06

DAWES PLAN
Proposals drafted in response to German hyper-inflation by American financier Charles

G. Dawes to reduce for a five year period the REPARATIONS imposed on Germany after World War I. Adopted in 1924–29, the scheme was followed by the similar Young Plan. ▷ 6.07

DAYTON AGREEMENT
Peace agreement ending the BOSNIAN CIVIL WAR, brokered by president of the USA, BILL CLINTON in Dayton, Ohio. Technically, Bosnia remained a unified state, but effectively the self-declared Serb Republic was given autonomy. ▷ 6.11

DE GAULLE, CHARLES
(1890–1970) French soldier-statesman. He led the Free French (those opposed to the VICHY regime's collaboration with Germany) during World War II. Elected president in 1945, he resigned in 1946 when his proposals to give the Fourth Republic a strong presidency were rejected. Forming the Rassemblement du Peuple Français in 1947, he became president again during the ALGERIAN CIVIL WAR in 1958, securing the executive power he demanded and founding the Fifth Republic. Committed to the idea of French leadership of Europe, he opposed British entry to the EUROPEAN ECONOMIC COMMUNITY because of Britain's American links, and withdrew France from the NORTH ATLANTIC TREATY ORGANIZATION (1966). He resigned in 1969. ▷ 6.09, 6.10

DE KLERK, F. W.
(1936–) President of South Africa (1989–91). He began dismantling APARTHEID, ordered the release of NELSON MANDELA (11 February 1990) and ensured there was no white backlash when Mandela became president in his place. ▷ 6.28

DEATH CAMPS
Nazi CONCENTRATION CAMPS dedicated to killing Jews, Gypsies and other "inferior races". Guards at AUSCHWITZ, Chelmno, Majdanek, Belzec and Treblinka and other camps shot, starved or gassed the inmates to death during the FINAL SOLUTION. ▷ 6.08, 6.09

DECOLONIZATION
The process of colonized extra-European territories becoming independent states, particularly the liquidation of European overseas empires after World War II. ▷ 6.01, 6.02, 6.03, 6.04, 6.05, 6.14, 6.18, 6.20, 6.21, 6.22, 6.23, 6.24, 6.27, 6.28

DEMOCRATIC PARTY
With the REPUBLICAN PARTY, one of the two major American political parties. Founded in 1828 and traditionally strong in the southern states, in the 20th century it propounded liberal policies such as the NEW DEAL and JOHN F. KENNEDY's and LYNDON BAINES JOHNSON's civil rights legislation. In foreign policy, the internationalism of WOODROW WILSON and his successors contrasted with Republican isolationism. Democratic presidents have included FRANKLIN DELANO

ROOSEVELT, HARRY S. TRUMAN, JIMMY CARTER, BILL CLINTON). ▷ 6.12, 6.13

DENG XIAOPING
(1902–97) Chinese political leader who became secretary-general of the Communist Party in 1954 but opposed MAO ZEDONG's excesses in the GREAT LEAP FORWARD. He was disgraced during the CULTURAL REVOLUTION but served under premier Zhou Enlai. He fell into disfavor again in 1976 but became deputy chairman of the party in 1977. As the most powerful man in China he led the country through a program of rapid modernization and encouraged economic links with the west. ▷ 6.23

DÉTENTE
Relaxation in COLD WAR tension during the 1970s. Pioneered by American diplomat HENRY KISSINGER and Presidents RICHARD NIXON and JIMMY CARTER, the period was characterized by US-Soviet and US-Chinese summits, the STRATEGIC ARMS LIMITATION talks and the HELSINKI AGREEMENTS. It ended with the Soviet invasion of AFGHANISTAN in 1979. ▷ 6.04, 6.10, 6.20

DIEM, NGO DINH
(1901–63) Vietnamese politician who became the first prime minister of South VIETNAM in June 1954. Bigoted and unpopular, he was opposed by the VIET CONG and requested aid from the USA. 16,000 American advisers arrived in 1956 but his subsequent lack of success led to his assassination. ▷ 6.21

DIEN BIEN PHU, BATTLE OF
Village and airstrip 354 kilometers (220 miles) west of Hanoi, fortified by the French. General VO NGUYEN GIAP's VIETMINH army surrounded the fortress in March 1954, closed the airstrip and frustrated the French air drops. The French surrendered on 7 May. The subsequent Geneva Accords led to a truce and French evacuation of INDO-CHINA. ▷ 6.20

DOLLFUSS, ENGELBERT
(1892–1934) AUSTRIAN chancellor (1932–34). He introduced an authoritarian constitution in March 1934 in response to political unrest in the GREAT DEPRESSION. Opposed to the ANSCHLUSS with Germany, he was killed by Austrian NAZIS attempting a coup. ▷ 6.06

DOMINO EFFECT
Phrase used by DWIGHT D. EISENHOWER in 1954 to express the fear that, if one country succumbed to COMMUNISM, adjacent states would also fall. It was envisaged that South VIETNAM's collapse could lead to the collapse of LAOS, Cambodia, THAILAND, BURMA and INDIA, and that Central American states were vulnerable in the same way. ▷ 6.21

DRESDEN BOMBING
(13–14 February 1945) Destruction of the German city of Dresden by ALLIED bombers during a controversial raid in World War II. Firestorms engulfed the city, killing between 50,000 and 100,000 people, many of them refugees from the SOVIET advance through eastern Germany. ▷ 6.09

DULLES, JOHN FOSTER
(1888–1959) American REPUBLICAN statesman. As secretary of state (1953–59) he developed "brinkmanship" (going to the brink of war to influence negotiations) and the threat of massive retaliation (full-scale nuclear attack) as a deterrent to any challenge to American interests. He was the architect of the SOUTH EAST ASIA TREATY ORGANIZATION. ▷ 6.21

DUST BOWL
The mid-western states of the USA during the GREAT DEPRESSION of the 1930s, when they were seriously affected by drought. ▷ 6.12

EAST ADEN
British protectorate in southern Arabia 1888–1967, comprising the ancient Arab state of Hadramaut. On independence it was united with WEST ADEN and since 1990 has formed part of YEMEN.

EAST GERMANY
See GERMAN DEMOCRATIC REPUBLIC

EAST PAKISTAN
See BANGLADESH

EAST TIMOR
Formerly Portuguese Timor, annexed by INDONESIA after Fretelin (Revolutionary Front of Independent East Timor) freedom fighters declared it independent (3 November 1975). A war of resistance against Indonesia has cost 200,000 civilian deaths. ▷ 6.23

EASTER RISING
(24–29 April 1916) Sinn Féin and IRA-led rebellion in Dublin to demand the immediate independence of IRELAND from Britain. It was put down by British troops. ▷ 6.06

EASTERN FRONT (WORLD WAR I)
Theater of war extending from the Baltic to the Ukraine, in which conflict between Germany and Austria-Hungary (the CENTRAL POWERS) and Russia remained an open war of movement, contrasting with the trench warfare on the WESTERN FRONT. Casualties were no less severe, however. Stopping the initial Russian advance at the BATTLE OF TANNENBERG (1914), the Central powers were victorious at Gorlice-Tarnow and the Masurian Lakes (1915) and halted the Brusilov and KERENSKY offensives (1916 and 1917). The BOLSHEVIKS ended hostilities after taking power in the OCTOBER REVOLUTION, the Central powers gaining large areas of Russia under the TREATY OF BREST-LITOVSK. ▷ 6.06

EC
See EUROPEAN COMMUNITY

ECSC
See EUROPEAN COAL AND STEEL COMMUNITY

EDEN, ANTHONY
(1897–1977) British statesman who became prime minister on WINSTON CHURCHILL's retirement in April 1955. After distinguished service in World War I, Eden became a Conservative member of Parliament (1923–57). He was foreign secretary from 1935 to 1938 (when he resigned in protest at APPEASEMENT), and again during World War II (1940–45). His health and reputation were broken by the SUEZ CRISIS, and he resigned as prime minister in January 1957. ▷ 6.07, 6.24, 6.25

EEC
See EUROPEAN ECONOMIC COMMUNITY

EIRE
See IRELAND

EFTA
See EUROPEAN FREE TRADE ASSOCIATION

EISENHOWER, DWIGHT DAVID
(1890–1969) The 34th president of the USA (1953–65). Commander of the ALLIED NORMANDY landings in World War II and first supreme Allied commander of the NORTH ATLANTIC TREATY ORGANIZATION (1951). The REPUBLICAN candidate, he was elected president in 1952 and re-elected in 1956, overseeing the ending of the KOREAN WAR, the MATSU AND QUEMOY crises and increased American prosperity. ▷ 6.09, 6.26

EL ALAMEIN, BATTLES OF
Two World War II battles at El Alamein, 96 kilometers (60 miles) west of Alexandria, Egypt. The first (30 June–25 July 1942) saw British and COMMONWEALTH troops under General Auchinleck halt ERWIN ROMMEL's advance on Cairo. The second (23 October–4 November 1942) began British General Montgomery's counteroffensive, which would drive Axis forces out of north Africa by May 1943. ▷ 6.08, 6.09

ERHARD, LUDWIG
(1897–1977) West German statesman. CONRAD ADENAUER's economics minister (1949–63), he oversaw the FEDERAL REPUBLIC OF GERMANY's "economic miracle", transformation from postwar ruin to Europe's leading economy. Taking over on Adenauer's retirement in October 1963, Erhard was less successful as chancellor and resigned in November 1966. ▷ 6.07

ESTONIA
Baltic state colonized by the Teutonic Knights in the 14th century, occupied by Sweden in the 16th century and annexed by Russia in the 18th. Independence, declared in 1918, was secured in war with Russia (1918–20). In 1934 President Päts established a dictatorship after unrest caused by the GREAT DEPRESSION. Invaded and annexed by the SOVIET UNION in

1940 under the NAZI-SOVIET PACT. It was occupied by Germany from 1941 to 1944. It won independence from the Soviet Union on 20 August 1991. ▷ 6.10, 6.11, 6.15, 6.16

EU
See EUROPEAN UNION

EUROPEAN COAL AND STEEL COMMUNITY (ECSC)
Organization established in 1952 incorporating the iron, coal and steel industries of France, West Germany, Italy and the BENELUX countries. The first of the European communities, it was integrated with the EUROPEAN ECONOMIC COMMUNITY and EURATOM (the European atomic energy agency) in 1967 to form the EUROPEAN COMMUNITY. ▷ 6.10

EUROPEAN COMMUNITY (EC)
European institution, set up in 1967, incorporating EURATOM, the EUROPEAN ECONOMIC COMMUNITY (EEC) and EUROPEAN COAL AND STEEL COMMUNITY. The original EEC members were joined by Britain, Denmark and IRELAND (1973), Greece (1981), Portugal and Spain (1985). The vehicle for movement to greater European unity, it created the MAASTRICHT TREATY setting up the EUROPEAN UNION (1991). ▷ 6.10, 6.11

EUROPEAN ECONOMIC COMMUNITY (EEC)
European free trade area created by the TREATY OF ROME (1958), with a European Parliament, a European Commission drafting and overseeing the implementation of legislation, and a European Court. Its members were the FEDERAL REPUBLIC OF GERMANY, France, Italy and the BENELUX countries. It was incorporated into the EUROPEAN COMMUNITY in 1967. ▷ 6.10

EUROPEAN FREE TRADE ASSOCIATION (EFTA)
Free trade area created in May 1960 by countries opposed to the eventual political union envisaged by the EUROPEAN ECONOMIC COMMUNITY (EEC). The founder members (AUSTRIA, Britain, Denmark, Norway, Portugal, Sweden and Switzerland) were later joined by Liechtenstein, FINLAND and Iceland. Britain left to join the EEC in 1973, as did Portugal in 1986, and Austria, Finland and Sweden in 1995. EFTA was formally dissolved on 1 January 1995. ▷ 6.10, 6.11

EUROPEAN UNION (EU)
Political association of the member states of the EUROPEAN COMMUNITY (EC), agreed under the MAASTRICHT TREATY (1992), incorporating the EC and working towards creation of common foreign, social policies etc. ▷ 6.10, 6.11

FALKLANDS WAR
Brief Anglo-Argentine war, the result of a long-standing dispute over sovereignty of the Falkland islands (Islas Malvinas), occupied by Britain since 1833. War broke out following the Argentinian invasion and occupation of the islands on 2 April 1982. A British task force was sent to recapture the islands and the Argentinian garrison surrendered on 24 June. The causes of the war remain unresolved. ▷ 6.05, 6.13

FAR EASTERN REPUBLIC
Ostensibly independent state in existence from 1920 to 1922 under Russian BOLSHEVIK control. After the defeat of ALEXANDER KOLCHAK's White forces in Siberia in 1919, Russia avoided a direct clash with occupying Japanese troops by establishing this puppet state. After the defeat of Japanese and other White forces in the RUSSIAN CIVIL WAR, it was incorporated into the SOVIET UNION in 1922.

FASCISM
Right-wing political ideology based on the idea of national rebirth and the cult of the leader, in which the fascist party gains TOTALITARIAN power. The Italian fascists under BENITO MUSSOLINI were the first to come to power, and were subsequently imitated by other violent mass movements across Europe, including ADOLF HITLER's Nazi Party. ▷ 6.02, 6.07, 6.08, 6.09

FEBRUARY REVOLUTION
The overthrow of NICHOLAS II of Russia in February 1917 after heavy defeats in World War I and social and economic problems. The Provisional government that took power was itself overthrown by the BOLSHEVIKS in the OCTOBER REVOLUTION. ▷ 6.15

FEDERAL REPUBLIC OF GERMANY
Republic created on 23 September 1949 from western-occupied Germany, when it had become clear that COLD WAR rivalry would not permit reunification of Germany. Under CONRAD ADENAUER and LUDWIG ERHARD it became the economic bulwark of western Europe. It was finally reunified with the GERMAN DEMOCRATIC REPUBLIC on 3 October 1990. ▷ 6.10

FINAL SOLUTION
Nazi term for the attempt to exterminate the Jews of Europe. ADOLF HITLER believed that Germans and other northern Europeans ("Aryans") were historically engaged in racial war with other "inferior races", and had long called for Jews to be "exterminated" and Slavs, Gypsies and others subjugated, deported or killed to create "living space" (*Lebensraum*) for Germans in eastern Europe. After the invasion of POLAND a brutal occupation regime shot Jews or confined them to ill-provisioned ghettoes; many Poles, and later Russians and other nationalities, were killed or deported. During the invasion of the SOVIET UNION in 1941 special killing squads (*Einsatzgruppen*) organized mass executions of Jews, and in 1942 DEATH CAMPS

were constructed, using poison gas for the same purpose. Around 6 million Jews are estimated to have been killed. ▷ 6.08, 6.09

FINLAND
Baltic state. Part of Sweden in the Middle Ages, then a Russian grand duchy from 1809, Finland seceded from Russia on 6 December 1917, establishing its independence in war with the BOLSHEVIKS (1918–20). The WINTER WAR of 1939–40 prevented a SOVIET takeover, but about 10 percent of territory was lost to the Soviet Union. Finland subsequently joined the German attack on the Soviet Union in 1941 before making peace in 1944, and driving the Germans out of northern Finland by April 1945. A member of the EUROPEAN FREE TRADE ASSOCIATION, it also enjoyed good postwar relations with the Soviet Union. It joined the EUROPEAN UNION in 1995. ▷ 6.07, 6.08, 6.09, 6.15, 6.16

FIVE YEAR PLANS
Radical attempts to modernize the Soviet economy. The First Five Year Plan was introduced by JOSEPH STALIN in 1928: COLLECTIVIZATION was to produce sufficient grain to feed an enlarged urban workforce, while state planners would concentrate on increasing heavy industrial production. Early five year plans were relatively successful, but later five year plans were less effective, the last being the Twelfth (1986–90). ▷ 6.15, 6.16

FOOTBALL WAR
(24–28 June 1969) A war between Honduras and El Salvador sparked by soccer fans fighting each other during the 1969 World Cup elimination matches. It followed two years of frontier disputes. After several air battles and an El Salvadoran invasion of Honduras, the Organization of American States arranged a truce. ▷ 6.14

FORD, GERALD
(1913–) The 38th president of the USA. A long-serving REPUBLICAN congressman, he became RICHARD NIXON's vice-president after Spiro Agnew's resignation in 1973, and president when Nixon resigned over the WATERGATE SCANDAL in 1974. He was defeated by JIMMY CARTER in the 1976 presidential election. ▷ 6.13

FRANCO, FRANCISCO
(1892–1975) Spanish general and dictator. Leader of the Right in the SPANISH CIVIL WAR, becoming head of state 1939. He strengthened the traditional elements in Spanish society, creating an authoritarian regime, through which he ruled until his death. ▷ 6.07, 6.10

FRANZ FERDINAND, ARCHDUKE
(1863–1914) Heir apparent to the Austro-Hungarian throne whose assassination in Sarajevo on 28 June 1914 by Serbian terrorists precipitated World War I. Austria-Hungary,

allied with Germany, took action against Russian-supported Serbia and a general war ensued. ▷ 6.06

FUAD I
(1868 –1936) King of Egypt (1917–36). He won effective independence for Egypt in 1922 when Britain promised not to intervene in Egyptian affairs unless they clashed with British interests. He survived to sign the 1936 Anglo-Egyptian Treaty that technically ended the British occupation of Egypt. ▷ 6.24

GAGARIN, YURI
(1934–68) Soviet cosmonaut. On 12 April 1961 he became the first man in space, orbiting Earth in the satellite Vostok I. ▷ 6.16

GALLIPOLI CAMPAIGN
Disastrous ALLIED attempt in World War I to attack TURKEY through the DARDANELLES. The Turks anticipated the landings (25 April and 6 August 1915), and Allied troops, largely Australians and New Zealanders, were prevented from advancing beyond their beachheads. They suffered heavy losses and had to be evacuated by 9 January 1916. WINSTON CHURCHILL, architect of the plan, resigned as first lord of the admiralty in the aftermath. ▷ 6.06

GANDHI, INDIRA
(1917–84) Indian politician. The daughter of JAWAHARLAL NEHRU, She was president of the Indian CONGRESS PARTY (1959–60) and prime minister (1966–77, 1980–84). She had enormous appeal for the people with her promise to reduce poverty, but her state of emergency in response to India's law and order problems lost her the 1977 election. She was assassinated in 1984. ▷ 6.05, 6.22

GANDHI, MOHANDAS ("MAHATMA")
(1869–1948) Indian nationalist leader who led the Indian National Congress in its quest for home rule. He adopted CIVIL DISOBEDIENCE as his political weapon in two campaigns: 1919–22 and the 1930 salt march to Dandi. He was jailed on both occasions but was released to attend discussions on the Indian constitution in 1931. He tried to end the Muslim-Hindu violence after independence (1947) but was assassinated in 1948. ▷ 6.18, 6.22

GANDHI, RAJIV
(1944–91) Indian politician and the eldest son of INDIRA GANDHI. He was a pilot in the Indian air force when his brother, Sanjay (1946–80), was killed. Rajiv took over his brother's parliamentary seat and became prime minister (1984–89) after his mother's death. He was assassinated by Tamil terrorists in 1991. ▷ 6.22

GDANSK
Formerly Danzig, a Prussian port on the Baltic, made a free city after World War I to give newly constituted POLAND access to the sea. Difficult relations with the city's largely German population led POLAND to establish the new port of Gdynia in 1924 in the POLISH CORRIDOR. A prominent target for German revisionists of the TREATY OF VERSAILLES, it was occupied by NAZI forces at the beginning of the invasion of POLAND in 1939. Incorporated into POLAND after World War II and renamed Gdansk, its shipyards provided the basis of support for the anti-government trade union SOLIDARITY. ▷ 6.10

GENERAL STRIKE (1926)
(4–12 May 1926) National strike held in Britain in support of miners' pay and conditions demands. Troops and volunteers carried on vital services, leading the Trades Union Congress to call off the strike. This provoked the anger of the miners, who did not return to work until August. ▷ 6.07

GENEVA CONFERENCE
International conference attended by Britain, France, the USA, SOVIET UNION and communist China, which closed 20 July 1954 with the signing of the Geneva Agreements ending French rule in INDO-CHINA. LAOS, Cambodia and VIETNAM became independent. Vietnam was divided along the 17th N parallel into a communist-controlled north and a western-aligned south. ▷ 6.04, 6.26

GERMAN DEMOCRATIC REPUBLIC
Republic constituted from Soviet-occupied eastern Germany on 7 October 1949 following the breakdown of cooperation between the wartime ALLIED POWERS at the beginning of the COLD WAR. Led by hard-liner Walter Ulbricht until 1971, it was a key member of the WARSAW PACT. However, in 1953 Soviet troops had to quash serious demonstrations against communist rule and in 1961 the BERLIN WALL was erected to stop emigration to the FEDERAL REPUBLIC OF GERMANY. Under Ulbricht's successor, Erich Honecker, relations with the west improved in response to West Germany's OSTPOLITIK. Following an anti-communist revolution and the fall of the IRON CURTAIN in 1989 the GDR became part of a reunified Germany (3 October 1990). ▷ 6.10

GERMAN EAST AFRICA
One of four African territories acquired by Bismarck at the 1884–85 Berlin Conference. During World War I General Paul von Lettow-Vorbeck, with 7,000 native troops, fought a brilliant guerrilla campaign against ALLIED invasions. After World War I the territory was mandated to Britain by the LEAGUE OF NATIONS, becoming the colony of Tanganyika (now TANZANIA). ▷ 6.24

GERMAN-POLISH NON-AGGRESSION PACT
Defensive pact signed on 26 January 1934. ADOLF HITLER sought to weaken the French system of alliances in eastern Europe which attempted to garrison Germany's eastern border with hostile states. ▷ 6.07

GIAP, VO NGUYEN
(1912–) Vietnamese soldier and statesman. Made defense minister by HO CHI MINH in 1946, he won the Battle of Langson 1950, repelled the French at Hoa Binh (1951–52) and then forced their surrender at DIEN BIEN PHU. He backed the VIET CONG, directed the TET OFFENSIVE and planned the 1975 armored advance on SAIGON. He is regarded as one of the most competent military commanders to emerge since 1945. ▷ 6.20

GOERING, HERMANN
(1893–1946) NAZI leader. A World War I fighter pilot, in 1933 he became minister president of Prussia in ADOLF HITLER'S first cabinet and subsequently head of the Luftwaffe. Initially he was very powerful, but his influence waned. He committed suicide after being sentenced to death at the NUREMBERG TRIALS. ▷ 6.07, 6.08, 6.09

GOLAN HEIGHTS
High ground in southwest SYRIA under ISRAELI military administration since 1967. It was the scene of a massive Syrian tank attack on Israel in 1973. ▷ 6.25, 6.26

GORBACHEV, MIKHAIL
(1931–) SOVIET leader. A communist bureaucrat in his native northern Caucasus, he entered the Politburo in 1979, becoming general secretary of the Communist Party and Soviet leader on 11 March 1985. He met American president RONALD REAGAN in summits at Geneva, Reykjavik and, in December 1987, Washington, where an agreement for the elimination of medium and short-range nuclear weapons was signed. His radical policies for the Soviet Union, *perestroika* ("restructuring") and *glasnost* ("openness"), led to demands for greater freedom, and in 1989–90 the eastern European countries overthrew their communist governments. Increasingly unpopular because of price rises and food shortages during liberalization of the economy, he saw his position fatally undermined by a coup by hard-line communists in August 1991 and by the prominent role played by Russian president BORIS YELTSIN in suppressing it. The republics of the Soviet Union seceded to form the COMMONWEALTH OF INDEPENDENT STATES. With Gorbachev's resignation on 25 December 1991, the Soviet Union dissolved. ▷ 6.10, 6.16

GREAT DEPRESSION
(1929–34) World economic slump precipitated by the collapse of the American stock market (the WALL STREET CRASH). Inflation and mass unemployment resulted from the breakdown of international trade, leading in continental Europe and Latin America to a flourishing of right-wing regimes. Britain and France attempted to reassert financial orthodoxy, while in the USA the NEW DEAL of FRANKLIN DELANO ROOSEVELT involved an increase in state intervention. ▷ 6.03, 6.07, 6.12

GREAT LEAP FORWARD
(1958–60) MAO ZEDONG's attempt to transform China's economy by creating large communes combining agricultural and industrial production, merging the existing cooperatives with private plots and industrializing the peasantry. Bad weather wrecked harvests and in 1961 the Communist Party formally abandoned the experiment, in which 20 million died from famine. ▷ 6.20

GREATER EAST ASIAN CO-PROSPERITY SPHERE
Japan's empire in the Far East (1942–45), symbolizing "Asia for the Asians". The term "Co-Prosperity" was meaningless as the empire was exploited to fuel the Japanese war economy. A Greater East Asia Conference was held in TOKYO in 1943. ▷ 6.18, 6.19

GREEK CIVIL WAR
(1946–49) Armed conflict between Greek communists and monarchists. Initially supported then abandoned by TITO, the communists were defeated by opponents benefiting from American aid supplied under the TRUMAN DOCTRINE. ▷ 6.10

GUADALCANAL, BATTLE OF
(1942-43) A lengthy campaign initiated to prevent Japanese air superiority in the Solomon Islands of the south Pacific. Marines landed on Guadalcanal and Tulagi Islands in August 1942 to face a tenacious enemy. Sea and air battles raged from October 1942 to February 1943. The Japanese eventually evacuated 18,000 troops after their first major defeat in the Pacific. ▷ 6.19

GUANTANAMO BAY
American naval base in eastern CUBA. US forces landed there in the Spanish-American War in 1898. After the 1901 Platt Amendment limited the powers of the Cuban government, the USA required Cuba to provide a naval base and coaling station there. ▷ 6.12

GUERNICA
Historic capital of the BASQUES, the first city to be destroyed from the air. German aircraft of the Condor Legion aiding FRANCISCO FRANCO's forces in the SPANISH CIVIL WAR bombed the city on 27 April 1937. ▷ 6.07

GUEVARA, CHE
(1928–67) Guerrilla and political leader who aided FIDEL CASTRO in the Cuban Revolution. He served in Castro's government until 1965, when he left to lead guerrilla groups in South America. Bolivian troops captured and shot him on 9 October 1967. ▷ 6.13, 6.14

GULAGS
Penal system for political prisoners made up of CONCENTRATION CAMPS in remote parts of the SOVIET UNION, in which 20 million inmates are estimated to have died. They were commonly the destination for victims of JOSEPH STALIN's PURGES and for those deported for alleged collaboration with the NAZIS, or for resisting COLLECTIVIZATION. ▷ 6.15, 6.16

GULF WARS
Two wars in the Persian Gulf region. The first (1980–88) began with an IRAQI invasion of IRAN to settle a frontier dispute. Heavy fighting on land, numerous air battles and the bombardment of Iran by Iraqi Scud missiles were followed by a peace in 1988 in which Iraq recognized existing borders. The second war (1990–91) began with an Iraqi invasion of KUWAIT and provoked intervention by an American-led UNITED NATIONS coalition force (23–28 February 1991), which expelled Iraq from Kuwait. Both wars caused immense damage to oil installations. ▷ 6.26

GUOMINDANG (KUOMINTANG, KMT)
The Chinese Nationalist Party (1919), which evolved under the leadership of SUN YIXIAN from the Chinese Revolutionary Party. It was remodeled in 1923–24 along Soviet lines in order to win support from the SOVIET UNION. It was led by JIANG JIESHI after 1925 and split from the communists in 1927. ▷ 6.17

HADRAMAUT
See EAST ADEN

HAIFENG
Together with Lufeng, a Chinese communist base in eastern Guangdong (1922–28). It was primarily a training school for peasant activists. The notion of a peasant uprising, as opposed to a city-based revolution, was pioneered at Haifeng by Peng Pia. His ideas influenced MAO ZEDONG, especially after the failure of the 1927 rebellions in Guangzhou and Nanchang. ▷ 6.17

HAILE SELASSIE (RAS TAFARI)
(1892–1975) Prince (Ras Tafari) and emperor of Ethiopia (1930–74). He fled to Djibouti and then to Britain after the Italian invasion on 3 October 1935. He went to Geneva to warn the LEAGUE OF NATIONS of the fascist peril in Africa. Restored by the British in 1941, he was deposed in 1974 and is worshipped by Rastafarians as Jah, the Messiah. ▷ 6.24, 6.27

HARDING, WARREN
(1865–1923) The 29th president of the USA, a REPUBLICAN senator elected president in 1920, but dying before completing his term. An isolationist, he opposed his predecessor WOODROW WILSON's internationalism and under him the USA did not join the LEAGUE OF NATIONS, although it did host the conference leading to signing of the WASHINGTON NAVAL AGREEMENTS. His administration was rocked by corruption scandals. ▷ 6.03, 6.12

HELSINKI AGREEMENTS
Agreements signed following a 35-nation conference held from 30 July to 1 August 1975. The west received acknowledgments from the eastern bloc of the importance of human rights in return for agreeing to exchange technical information. An agreement to reduce the risk of accidental war was also signed.

HERTZOG, JAMES
(1866–1942) Afrikaner general and commando leader in the Boer War. Founder of the National Party in 1912, he served as prime minister (1924–39) and disenfranchised African voters in 1936. He was unwilling to declare war on Germany in 1939 and was replaced by JAN SMUTS. ▷ 6.28

HINDENBURG, PAUL VON
(1847–1934) German soldier-statesman. He commanded German forces on the EASTERN FRONT in World War I with great success. Promoted to field marshal in November 1914, he became German army chief of staff in August 1916 and, effectively, military dictator, with control over all aspects of the war effort. Retiring in 1919, he was a successful right-wing candidate in the presidential elections of 1924 and 1931. In this office, he appointed ADOLF HITLER chancellor in 1933. ▷ 6.06, 6.07

HINDENBURG LINE
Series of defensive fortifications built behind German lines on the WESTERN FRONT in World War I, constructed from September 1916 onwards. German troops retreated behind it during February and March 1917. It was breached by Allied troops in late September 1918. ▷ 6.06

HIROHITO
(1901–89) Emperor of Japan (r.1926–89) who reluctantly approved the militarization of the country and its aggressive foreign policy but supported leaders advocating unconditional surrender in 1945. After the war he renounced his mythical imperial divinity and began a constitutional monarchy. ▷ 6.19, 6.20

HIROSHIMA
City on Honshu Island, Japan, the first to be destroyed by an atomic bomb (6 August 1945). The device, employing uranium 235, was carried in the American B-29 bomber *Enola Gay* and caused 78,150 instant deaths. ▷ 6.13, 6.19

HITLER, ADOLF
(1889–1945) Dictator of Germany and leader of the NAZI PARTY. He served as a soldier in World War I and after Germany's defeat joined the German Workers' Party and renamed it the National Socialist Workers' Party (NAZI PARTY). Jailed after a failed coup in Munich in 1923, he dictated his political testament *Mein Kampf* (My Struggle) to Rudolf Hess in 1924. Hitler became chancellor in 1933 and *Führer* (leader) in 1934. He immediately adopted anti-Semitic and anti-communist policies and an aggressive foreign

policy (appeased by European leaders). His invasion of POLAND (1 September 1939) finally provoked Britain and France to declare war, beginning World War II. Hitler's war leadership was erratic and played a significant role in Germany's eventual defeat. He eventually committed suicide in Berlin, probably on 30 April 1945. ▷ 6.07, 6.08, 6.09, 6.15

HIZBOLLAH

IRANIAN-inspired Shiite Muslim fundamentalist terrorist organization, based in south Beruit, LEBANON. The name means "Party of God". It was responsible for the hijacking of a TWA airliner at Cairo in 1985 and many subsequent acts of terrorism. ▷ 6.26

HO CHI MINH

North Vietnamese nationalist leader (1890–1969) who headed the VIETMINH struggle against the French (1946–54). He was president of North Vietnam (1954–65). He supported revolutionary movements in LAOS, Cambodia and South Vietnam and his determination to unite the two VIETNAMS inspired his people to endure years of American bombing of the North. ▷ 6.20, 6.21

HO CHI MINH TRAIL

A series of trails linking Hanoi with the VIET CONG in South VIETNAM, passing through eastern LAOS and Cambodia. It provided regular supplies to VIET CONG groups. Supply vehicles operated mainly at night to avoid American bombing. ▷ 6.21

HOLOCAUST

Jewish name for the NAZI attempt during World War II to exterminate the Jews of Europe (the FINAL SOLUTION). ▷ 6.08, 6.09

HOUPHOUET-BOIGNY, FÉLIX

(1905–93) West African statesman who ruled the republic of the Ivory Coast (Côte d'Ivoire) from independence in 1960 to his death in 1993. He retained close links with France and modeled his country's government on the constitution of the French Fifth Republic. ▷ 6.27

IBN SAUD, ABDUL AZIZ

(1880–1953) King of SAUDI ARABIA (r.1932–53). Because of Saudi oil reserves, he received aid from Roosevelt in World War II and supported the ALLIES in 1945. Hostile to Zionist ambitions and with no interest in democratic reform, he ruled SAUDI ARABIA as a conservative autocrat and strongly upheld the teachings of Wahabbi Islam. ▷ 6.24

IMF

See INTERNATIONAL MONETARY FUND

INCHON

Port on the west coast of Korea. It was the scene of the landings (15 September 1950) that transformed imminent defeat at Pusan into temporary victory for the United Nations

Command during the KOREAN WAR. It enabled the UNITED NATIONS forces to break out of Pusan and recapture Seoul. ▷ 6.20

INDIA, PARTITION OF

(15 August 1947) The division of British India into two independent republics, primarily Hindu India and Muslim PAKISTAN. The partition stemmed from the fears of Muslims – the majority in the northwest and northeast – that they would become a disadvantaged minority in a Hindu-dominated Indian state. The immediate consequences of partition were chaotic. Millions migrated to their new republics and an estimated half million were killed in communal violence. ▷ 6.22

INDO-CHINA

A term embracing the former French colonies of LAOS, Cambodia and Vietnam. The GENEVA CONFERENCE ruled that these should be independent in 1954 though the formal unification of North and South VIETNAM into an independent republic occurred only on July 1 1976. ▷ 6.20, 6.21

INDO-PAKISTAN WARS

Three wars between INDIA and PAKISTAN over the sovereignty of Kashmir (1947–49, 1965 and 1971). On the British withdrawal from India in 1947 the Hindu maharajah of Kashmir opted to join India, without consulting his mainly Muslim subjects, who rebelled. Pakistani forces occupied the western third of Kashmir, India the remainder. The United Nations-brokered 1949 cease-fire provided for a plebiscite on the future of Kashmir but this has never been held. The 1965 war saw fighting in the Punjab and Kashmir. Russian mediation at Tashkent persuaded the rival armies to withdraw. The 1971 war involved clashes in East and West Pakistan and the transformation of East Pakistan into independent BANGLADESH. Tension on the India–Pakistan border remains high as India accuses Pakistan of supplying and training separatist forces. ▷ 6.22

INDONESIA

Extensive archipelago in southeast Asia, formerly the Dutch East Indies and now an independent republic. Nationalists led by AHMED SUKARNO declared independence in 1945, which was finally recognized in 1949. AHMED SUKARNO ruled as president until 1967, but after the military suppressed a communist rising in 1965 real power rested with General Suharto (president 1968–98). Indonesia annexed West Irian (western New Guinea, now Irian Jaya) in 1963 and former Portuguese EAST TIMOR in 1975. Until the financial crisis of 1997–98 Indonesia was a leading TIGER ECONOMY. The crisis led to the resignation of Suharto in 1998. ▷ 6.23

INTERNATIONAL MONETARY FUND

United Nations agency established on 27 December 1946, its creation having been

agreed at the BRETTON WOODS CONFERENCE. It holds currency reserves used to assist countries with large balance of payments deficits. ▷ 6.04

INTIFADA

(The "shaking" or "throwing off" in Arabic) The name given to the PALESTINIAN uprising against the ISRAELIS in the WEST BANK and Gaza Strip in December 1987. By 1995 over 1,600 Jews and PALESTINIANS had died. ▷ 6.26

IRAN

The land known as Persia until 1935. The oil-rich country was ruled by the autocratic westernizing PAHLAVI DYNASTY (1925–79), but occupied by the ALLIES during World War II. The return of the exiled religious leader AYATOLLAH KHOMENEI in 1979 led to the overthrow of the monarchy and the establishment of a fundamentalist Shiite Islamic government. It fought IRAQ (1980–88) but remained neutral in the Second GULF WAR (1990–91). Hashemi Rafsanjani became president in 1989 and was re-elected in 1995. ▷ 6.25, 6.26

IRAQ

Oil-rich Middle Eastern republic. Formerly part of the Ottoman empire, it was mandated to Britain by the LEAGUE OF NATIONS in 1920. It became independent under a monarchy in 1932 but was reoccupied by the British in World War II after Axis sympathizers took over the government. The monarchy was overthrown in 1958 and since 1979 President SADDAM HUSSEIN has governed through his nine-man Revolutionary Command Council. Blamed by the United Nations Security Council for the first GULF WAR, Iraq was invaded by a UNITED NATIONS coalition in 1991 in response to its invasion of KUWAIT. Saddam's resistance to visits by UN weapons inspectors to "presidential sites" caused another international crisis in 1997–98. ▷ 6.24, 6.25, 6.26

IRELAND

Western European state. Under more or less effective English rule from the Middle Ages, it became part of the United Kingdom under the Act of Union (1801). Demand for self-government grew during the 19th century and a Home Rule Act was passed in 1914, only to be suspended because of the outbreak of World War I. This led to the EASTER RISING. War with Britain (1920–21) led to the Anglo-Irish Treaty of 6 December 1921, which gave southern Ireland independence (as the IRISH FREE STATE) but without control of foreign policy, and left the six (mainly Protestant) Ulster counties within the UK as NORTHERN IRELAND. Civil war ensued (1922–23), in which moderates accepting the treaty defeated its opponents led by Eamonn De Valera. However, De Valera became president in 1932, and was behind the establishment of southern Ireland as the independent state of Éire (the republic of Ireland) in 1937. Neutral during

World War II, Ireland joined the EUROPEAN COMMUNITY in 1973. ▷ 6.07, 6.10

IRISH FREE STATE
Autonomous state created in southern IRELAND in 1922. Britain retained sovereignty and control of foreign policy until full Irish independence in 1949. ▷ 6.07

IRON CURTAIN
An imaginary line dividing communist eastern Europe from western Europe. The term was popularized after its use by WINSTON CHURCHILL in a speech at Fulton, Missouri, on 5 March 1946. ▷ 6.07

ISRAEL
Jewish state established in Palestine in 1948. The establishment of a Jewish homeland was the chief objective of the ZIONIST MOVEMENT. Following World War I Palestine was mandated to Britain by the LEAGUE OF NATIONS and opened to Jewish immigration. Irreconcilable conflicts between Jewish settlers and native PALESTINIANS forced the UNITED NATIONS to agree the partition of Palestine into Jewish and Arab states in 1948, and the British withdrew on 13 May. Israel declared independence on 14 May and successfully defeated the attacks of its Arab neighbors, who refused to recognize it. ARAB-ISRAELI wars have also been fought in 1956, 1967 and 1973. The CAMP DAVID AGREEMENTS with Egypt in 1979 raised hopes of a lasting peace between Israel and its Arab neighbors but Israel's failure to implement in full its promises of self-rule for the PALESTINIANS have led to the INTIFADA and continuing tensions despite the creation of the Palestine National Authority in 1996. ▷ 6.25, 6.26

IWO JIMA, BATTLE OF
(19 February–24 March 1945) Battle on the center island of the Volcanos group in the north Pacific, 1221 kilometers (759 miles) from TOKYO. It was the fiercest US marine assault of World War II. 22,000 Japanese troops, entrenched in elaborate defenses, died almost to the man. Mount Suribachi was captured on 23 February after 6,891 US marines died. The island was subsequently used to launch bombing raids on Japan. ▷ 6.19

JAMMU AND KASHMIR
Northern Indian state currently divided between INDIA and PAKISTAN and scene of the INDO-PAKISTANI WARS and the Sino-Indian conflict of 1962. Indian and Pakistani foreign policy remains centered on the issue of this area's sovereignty. ▷ 6.22

JIANG JIESHI (CHIANG KAI-SHEK)
(1887–1975) Chinese revolutionary leader. He joined the government of SUN YIXIAN in 1918 as a military commander. He later headed the GUOMINDANG government (1928–49) and fought on the side of the ALLIES in World War

II. Defeated by the communists under MAO ZEDONG, he moved his capital to Chengdu and then evacuated his army to TAIWAN. He was president of Taiwan from 1949 to 1975. ▷ 6.17

JIANG ZEMIN
(1926–) Chinese politician, member of the Chinese Communist Party Polititburo in 1987. He was promoted Communist Party leader after the Tiananmen Square massacre and was sympathetic to economic reform and trade with the west. ▷ 6.23

JINNAH, MOHAMMED ALI
(1876–1948) Indian politician and founder of PAKISTAN. He was its first governor-general (1947–48). The charismatic leader of the MUSLIM LEAGUE, he supported Britain during World War II but demanded the creation of a separate Muslim state. Faced with the problems caused by partition – JAMMU AND KASHMIR and mass migration – and in poor health, he died in office. ▷ 6.22

JOHN PAUL II
(1920–) Pope, born Karol Wojtyla in POLAND, becoming archbishop of Cracow in 1964, cardinal in 1967, and pope on 22 October 1978. The first non-Italian pontiff since 1523, he provided inspiration for an anti-communist movement in POLAND and has visited many countries. During his pontificate, church teachings have remained conservative. ▷ 6.10

JOHNSON, LYNDON BAINES
(1908–73) The 36th president of the USA. DEMOCRATIC congressman and senator for Texas, he was elected JOHN F. KENNEDY's vice-president in 1960. He became president after Kennedy's assassination (1963), and was elected to a full term in 1964. Johnson's "Great Society" legislation included civil rights laws, the 1965 Education Act, and provision of medical care for the elderly ("Medicare"). Unpopular because of increasing American involvement in the VIETNAM WAR, he did not stand for re-election in 1968. ▷ 6.13, 6.26

JORDAN
Middle eastern kingdom, formerly part of the Ottoman empire. Renamed TRANSJORDAN in 1921, it was under British protection from 1923 to 1946. It became an independent kingdom in 1946 and was renamed Jordan in 1949. It occupied the WEST BANK from 1950 until this was occupied by ISRAEL in 1967. ▷ 6.24, 6.25, 6.26

JUTLAND, BATTLE OF
(31 May–1 June 1916) The only major naval battle of World War I, fought in the North Sea. The British Grand Fleet under Admiral Sir John Jellicoe failed to exploit numerical superiority over the German High Seas Fleet commanded by Admiral Reinhard Scheer, and sustained heavier losses. Despite this, British naval mastery was confirmed and the German

fleet did not leave port for the rest of World War I. ▷ 6.06

KAIFENG, BATTLE OF
(19 June 1948) Major battle of the Chinese Revolution, fought in Henan province after the communist general Chen Yi (1901–72) cut the railroad north of Kaifeng. This isolated the GUOMINDANG armies from north China. After initial successes, many Guomindang troops deserted and the rest surrendered. ▷ 6.17

KAISER WILHELMSLAND
German colony in northeast New Guinea (1884–1914). Occupied by AUSTRALIA (1914–21), it was mandated to Australia by the LEAGUE OF NATIONS and then united with Papua in 1945. ▷ 6.01

KAREN
A 3-million strong rebel minority in BURMA (Myanmar), one of several ethnic groups who were disappointed at failing to win their own independence in 1948. The Karen have consistently fought against the government, but since 1988 most of their bases in the southeast have been destroyed. ▷ 6.22

KATANGA
The name that Shaba province took when it seceded from the REPUBLIC OF CONGO in 1960. Governor Moise Tshombe's mercenary soldiers resisted central government attacks and the UNITED NATIONS intervened in 1961. Attempting to arrange a cease-fire, UN secretary-general Dag Hammarskjöld died when his aircraft crashed at Ndola. The secession ended in 1963. ▷ 6.27

KAUNDA, KENNETH
(1924–) Zambian politician, prime minister of Northern Rhodesia from January 1964 and president of independent ZAMBIA in October. His dictatorial rule led to widespread protest in 1990, and he was defeated in 1991 when he permitted democratic elections. ▷ 6.27

KAZAKHSTAN
Central Asian state. Part of the Russian empire from 1731, it became part of the SOVIET UNION in 1924. Under JOSEPH STALIN, its vast size and remoteness led to it being used as a destination for deported nationalities. It became independent on 16 December 1991. ▷ 6.05, 6.15, 6.16

KELLOGG–BRIAND PACT
Pact renouncing war, drafted by American secretary of state Frank Kellogg and French foreign minister Aristide Briand. Signed in Paris by nine countries on 27 August 1928, and subsequently by a further 56, the pact contained no provision for disciplining aggressors and was soon defunct. ▷ 6.07

KENNEDY, JOHN F.
(1917–63) The 35th president of the USA. DEMOCRATIC congressman and senator for

Massachusetts, in 1960 Kennedy was elected the youngest-ever and first Roman Catholic president of the USA. He introduced civil rights and social reform legislation at home. In foreign affairs, he forced Soviet leader NIKITA KHRUSCHEV to back down in the CUBAN MISSILE CRISIS. He helped to bring about the limited nuclear test ban treaty (August 1963) and increased American support for South Vietnam. He also created the "Alliance for Progress" for aid to Latin America and initiated the Apollo moon program (both in 1961). He was assassinated on 22 November 1963 in Dallas, Texas. ▷ 6.13, 6.26

KENYA

Former British East African colony. It was the scene of the MAU-MAU rebellion and a state of emergency (1952–60) involving the British armed forces. An estimated 13,000 people died in the violence. Kenya became independent on 12 December 1960, with JOMO KENYATTA as its first president. ▷ 6.27

KENYATTA, JOMO

(1890–1978) Kenyan politician who became the leader of the Kikuyu in 1946. Wrongly accused of planning MAU-MAU operations, he was jailed (1953–61) and emerged to lead the Kenyan African National Union. He visited London to discuss Kenya's future and became Kenyan prime minister in 1963 and president (1964–78). ▷ 6.27

KERENSKY OFFENSIVE

Last Russian offensive of World War I, named after Alexander Kerensky, minister of war in the Provisional government, which took power after the FEBRUARY REVOLUTION. An attack against Austro-Hungarian and German forces in Galicia was initially successful, but was halted by supply problems and German reinforcements. The Russian army fell apart under a counteroffensive, fatally weakening the Provisional government, which fell in the OCTOBER REVOLUTION). ▷ 6.06

KEYNES, JOHN MAYNARD

(1883–1946) British economist. A critic of the World War I peace settlement, which he attended as Britain's treasury representative. During the interwar period Keynes recommended reflating the economy with massive public spending, in contrast to orthodox government policy. He was a powerful advocate of a world bank. After World War II his ideas strongly influenced government policy until the election of MARGARET THATCHER. ▷ 6.07, 6.10

KGB

(Komitet Gosudarstvennoy Bezopasnosty – Committee for State Security) The name of the Soviet political police from 1954. The KGB was responsible for the harsh internal security system of the SOVIET UNION and external espionage. Its involvement in the 1991 coup

attempt against Mikhail Gorbachev led to its dissolution. ▷ 6.16

KHALKIN GOL, BATTLE OF

(August 1939) Clash on the Mongolian frontier between Soviet troops and Japanese forces advancing from MANCHURIA. Soviet victory led to the Soviet-Japanese neutrality pact of 1941 and Japan to expand through southeast Asia instead. ▷ 6.18

KHMER ROUGE

Communist guerrillas in Cambodia who captured the capital, Phnom Penh, in 1975 and toppled the Cambodian government. Their leader, Pol Pot, formed the People's Revolutionary Council to govern "Democratic Kampuchea" (1975–79) and began a genocide against any Cambodians thought to be tainted by western influences. The regime was overthrown by Vietnamese forces in 1979. Khmer Rouge guerrillas remained active in 1997–98. ▷ 6.21

KHOMEINI, AYATOLLAH RUHOLLAH

(1900–89) Religious and political leader of IRAN. He returned from exile on 11 February 1979 to create an Islamic republic and form a Islamic fundamentalist "government of God". His followers overran the American embassy in Teheran and took diplomats and personnel hostage. President JIMMY CARTER imposed trade sanctions and attempted an abortive rescue mission in April 1980. In 1989 Khomeni issued a *fatwa* (religious death sentence) for blasphemy against the British Muslim author Salman Rushdie, which has kept him in hiding ever since. ▷ 6.26

KHRUSCHEV, NIKITA

(1894–1971) Soviet leader. Born in the UKRAINE, Khruschev fought for the BOLSHEVIKS in the RUSSIAN CIVIL WAR and became a party functionary. Made First Secretary after JOSEPH STALIN's death in 1953, he gradually established himself as supreme Soviet leader. His ambitious administrative reforms upset the bureaucracy, and failures in the VIRGIN LANDS CAMPAIGN and CUBAN MISSILE CRISIS led to his deposition on 15 October 1964. He was succeeded by LEONID BREZHNEV. ▷ 6.16

KIM IL SUNG

(1910–94) North Korean soldier and politician who fought against the Japanese in World War II and became president when NORTH KOREA was established as a communist state in 1948. In 1950 his troops crossed the 38th parallel to begin the KOREAN WAR and he became absolute ruler in 1958, retaining the loyalty of the armed forces to his death. ▷ 6.20, 6.23

KING, MARTIN LUTHER

(1929–68) A charismatic Baptist minister from Atlanta, Georgia, who headed the CIVIL RIGHTS MOVEMENT in the USA. He led the bus protest in Montgomery, Alabama (1955–56),

and important marches in Washington (28 August 1963) and Selma, Alabama, (1965). He founded the Southern Christian Leadership Conference and was awarded the Nobel Peace Prize (1964). He was assassinated on 4 April 1968 in Memphis, Tennessee. ▷ 6.13

KIROV, SERGEI

(1886–1934) Soviet official. An active BOLSHEVIK organizer in the 1905 and 1917 revolutions and the RUSSIAN CIVIL WAR. A close ally of JOSEPH STALIN, he was appointed Leningrad Communist Party chief in 1926. His assassination, possibly on Stalin's orders, triggered the PURGES. ▷ 6.15

KISSINGER, HENRY

(1923–) American politician and expert on international affairs, appointed presidential security adviser in 1969 and secretary of state (1973–77). His famous "shuttle diplomacy" improved American relations with China and the SOVIET UNION, aided the withdrawal of troops from the VIETNAM WAR and established a "peace process" between Egypt and ISRAEL. He was awarded a Nobel Peace Prize. ▷ 6.21

KMT

See GUOMINDANG

KOHL, HELMUT

(1930–) German politician. Leader of the CHRISTIAN DEMOCRATS from 1973, in 1982 he became chancellor of a coalition formed with the Liberals. Continuing the OSTPOLITIK of his predecessors, Kohl also improved West Germany's relationship with the USA and France, pressing ahead with plans for European integration. In 1990 he became chancellor of a united Germany, presiding over the difficult re-integration of the east. ▷ 6.10, 6.11

KOLCHAK, ALEXANDER

(1874–1920) Russian admiral and civil-war leader. Commander of the Russian Black Sea fleet during World War I, after the OCTOBER REVOLUTION Kolchak became leader of the anti-Bolshevik White forces in Siberia. Proclaiming himself "Supreme Ruler" of Russia in October 1918, he was captured and executed by the Bolsheviks. ▷ 6.15

KOREA, PEOPLE'S REPUBLIC OF

See NORTH KOREA

KOREA, REPUBLIC OF

See SOUTH KOREA

KOREAN WAR

(1950-53) War that began on 25 June 1950 when North Korean forces invaded SOUTH KOREA. The UNITED NATIONS Security Council resolved to ask member states to intervene. (The SOVIET UNION was at the time boycotting the Council meetings and so was not present to veto the resolution against its ally.) US forces held a perimeter around Pusan long enough for General DOUGLAS MACARTHUR to launch the INCHON landings. UN forces advanced across the 38th parallel but were driven back by Chinese troops. The war stabilized along an immobile front until peace talks at Panmunjom ended hostilities on 27 July 1953. ▷ 6.03, 6.10, 6.20

KOSYGIN, ALEXEI
(1904–80) Soviet politician. Deputy chairman of the Council of People's Commissars during World War II (1940–46), he organized the evacuation of industry east of the Urals to avoid the German advance. Under LEONID BREZHNEV, he argued unsuccessfully for economic liberalization. ▷ 6.15, 6.16

KU KLUX KLAN
Society founded in Pulaski, Tennessee, in 1866 for the purpose of intimidating black and white REPUBLICANS in the American south with its hooded costumes, flaming crosses and associated brutalities. Congress outlawed it through the 1871 Ku Klux Klan Act, but it revived in 1915 as a national organization. After 1945 it evolved into a paramilitary white supremacist group.

KUOMINTANG (KMT)
See GUOMINDANG

KURDISTAN
A mountainous region in southeast TURKEY and parts of IRAN, IRAQ and SYRIA, homeland of 10 million Kurds. Promises by France, Britain and Iraq to establish an independent Kurdistan after World War I were never honored. Kurds in TURKEY suffered serious discrimination; many in Iraq were uprooted or exterminated after the GULF WAR despite the creation of a safe zone for Kurdish refugees in 1991. ▷ 6.26

KURSK, BATTLE OF
(5–15 July 1943) The largest tank battle in history. German forces were decisively defeated by Red Army forces defending a salient around the town of Kursk. The battle was the last German attempt in World War II to gain the strategic initiative on the Eastern Front. It confirmed the advantage that had swung to the Soviets since German defeat at STALINGRAD. ▷ 6.09

KUT, SIEGE OF
Turkish victory during the British invasion of Mesopotamia during World War I. Advancing towards Baghdad in 1915, the British commander, general Townshend (1861–1924), captured Kut but was besieged by the Turks. British relief forces failed to reach Kut and he surrendered on 29 April 1916. General Maude (1864–1917) retook Kut (January-February 1917) and captured Baghdad. ▷ 6.06

KUWAIT
Arab state of the Perian Gulf, founded in 1756 and a British protectorate from 1899 until its

independence in 1961. The oil-rich state was invaded by IRAQ in 1990 and its oil installations seriously damaged by an Iraqi scorched earth policy during Operation Desert Storm, which led to its liberation in the GULF WAR. ▷ 6.26

KYRGYSTAN
Central Asian state. Incorporated into the Russian Empire in 1864, it became part of the Turkestan Soviet republic in 1918 and a full member of the SOVIET UNION in 1936. A poor, remote member of the Soviet Union, it declared independence on 15 December 1990 under its popular president, Askar Akayev. ▷ 6.05, 6.16

LABOUR PARTY
British political party formed in 1900 as the Labour Representation Committee, renamed the Labour Party in 1906. Despite adopting an explicitly socialist constitution in 1918, the Labour governments of 1924 and 1929–31 lacked a parliamentary majority and did not introduce radical responses to the GREAT DEPRESSION. However, Clement Attlee's government (1945–51) won a landslide victory, and went on to establish a welfare state in accordance with the BEVERIDGE REPORT and nationalized major industries. Subsequent Labour governments in the 1960s and 1970s under Harold Wilson and James Callaghan upheld these policies until comprehensive defeat by the Conservative party under MARGARET THATCHER at the general elections of 1979 and 1983 eventually forced the party to modernize its policies and constitution. Having officially abandoned socialism in 1995, it was returned to power by a landslide victory in 1997 under Tony Blair.

LAOS
Southeast Asian state originating in the 14th century. In the 19th century it avoided annexation by THAILAND by appealing for French protection. Incorporated into French INDO-CHINA in 1893, it became independent in 1953 as the Lao People's Democratic Republic. Used as "safe area" by the VIET CONG, Laos was heavily bombed by the USA during the VIETNAM WAR. The Lao Patriotic Front and its armed wing, the PATHET LAO, seized power in 1975. ▷ 6.20, 6.21, 6.23

LATERAN TREATIES
Agreements signed 11 February 1929 between BENITO MUSSOLINI's fascist government and Pope Pius XII, regularizing the position of the papacy and Roman Catholic church in Italy. This had been disputed since the seizure of papal territories during Italian unification in the 19th century. The Vatican was now made an independent state and the church given a limited role in national life. ▷ 6.07

LATVIA
Baltic state. Colonized by the Teutonic Knights in the 14th century, annexed by

POLAND in the 16th century and by Russia in the 18th, it became independent under a communist government in 1918. A rival right-wing government under Karl Ulmanis won control after war with the Russian-supported communists and occupying German forces (1918–20). In 1934, Ulmanis assumed dictatorial powers in response to unrest caused by the GREAT DEPRESSION. In 1940 the country was invaded and annexed by the SOVIET UNION under the terms of the NAZI-SOVIET PACT, before German occupation (1941–44). Latvia declared its independence from the Soviet Union on 5 May 1990. ▷ 6.05, 6.06, 6.07, 6.08, 6.10, 6.11

LE DUAN
(1908–81) Vietnamese politician who, under the alias Ba ("second son"), helped direct the VIET CONG insurgency. After the death of HO CHI MINH, he emerged as the most powerful figure in Viet Nam, though the presidency was held by Ton Duc Than from 23 September 1969. ▷ 6.21

LE DUC THO
(1911–90) Vietnamese politician who led the North Vietnamese delegation to the Paris Conference on INDO-CHINA (1968–73). He won the Nobel Peace Prize (with HENRY KISSINGER) but declined the award. ▷ 6.21

LEAGUE OF NATIONS
Precursor of the UNITED NATIONS, founded on 24 April 1919 at the Paris Peace Conference following World War I as a body for the peaceful resolution of international disputes. The brainchild of American president WOODROW WILSON, it was successful in administering Germany's ex-colonies as mandates and in dealing with refugee resettlement and minor crises during the 1920s, but the refusal of the USA (under President WARREN HARDING) to join meant it was powerless over large states. In the 1930s Japanese, German and Italian aggression went effectively unpunished. It was succeeded by the UNITED NATIONS in 1946. ▷ 6.01, 6.02, 6.07, 6.12, 6.15, 6.18, 6.24, 6.28

LEBANESE CIVIL WAR
(1975–89) A protracted conflict in LEBANON between Christian and Muslim militias, exacerbated by ISRAELI (1978, 1982) and SYRIAN (1976–81) incursions, by PALESTINE LIBERATION ORGANIZATION (PLO) guerrillas and by a multinational peacekeeping force (1982–84). An Israeli siege of Beirut (June–September 1982) forced the evacuation of the PLO and a Syrian withdrawal from LEBANON. Civil strife continued and the USA evacuated its Beirut embassy in 1989. A partial agreement for a cease-fire came at Taif, SAUDI ARABIA, in September 1989. ▷ 6.25, 6.26

LEBANON
Middle Eastern republic. Formerly part of the Ottoman empire, its modern boundaries were

created by the French in 1920, to whom the area was mandated after World War I. Lebanon became independent in 1943 but French troops remained there until 1946. Lebanon was progressively destabilized in the 1960s and 1970s by conflict between its Christian and Muslim population and by the ARAB-ISRAELI CONFLICT, leading to the outbreak of the LEBANESE CIVIL WAR. A measure of political stability has returned since the cease-fire. ▷ 6.24, 6.25, 6.26

LEE KUAN YEW
(1923–) Singapore politician. He was the founder of the People's Action Party in 1954 and became prime minister of the republic of Singapore in 1959. He removed Singapore from MALAYSIA in 1965. When he resigned in 1990, Singapore had become one of the most successful economies in east Asia. ▷ 6.23

LEND-LEASE SCHEME
Means adopted by the then still neutral USA for supplying countries at war with NAZI Germany and Japan during World War II. The Lend-Lease Act (11 March 1941) gave war material to Britain, the SOVIET UNION, China and over 35 other nations for the duration of the war, increasing American productive capacity and influence. ▷ 6.08, 6.12

LENIN, VLADIMIR ILYICH
(1870–1924) Russian revolutionary. Born the son of a nobleman in Simbirsk on the middle Volga and trained as a lawyer, he was exiled to Siberia (1897–1900) and subsequently left Russia. He became head of the BOLSHEVIK faction of the Russian Social Democrats in 1903. Arriving in Russia after the FEBRUARY REVOLUTION of 1917, he led the Bolsheviks to power in the OCTOBER REVOLUTION. Head of the new Soviet government, he was seriously wounded in an assassination attempt on 30 August 1918 but presided over the victory of the communists in the RUSSIAN CIVIL WAR and the introduction of NEW ECONOMIC POLICY. Suffering three strokes between May 1922 and March 1923, he died on 21 January 1924. His "testament", detailing the faults of potential successors including LEON TROTSKY and JOSEPH STALIN, was suppressed after his death. ▷ 6.15

LEYTE GULF, BATTLE OF
(23–26 October 1944) Japan's final effort to snatch victory in the central Pacific. Its plan to destroy all American amphibious forces was wrecked in four component battles (Sibuyan Sea, Surigao Strait, East Samar and Cape Engano). Almost all the 64 Japanese ships were sunk or damaged, most as a result of American air attacks. ▷ 6.19

LHASA REBELLION
(1958–59) Tibetan uprising. Khamba tribesmen had resisted the Chinese since the invasion of Tibet in 1950. Their resistance spread to the Tibetan capital, Lhasa, but

newly built military highways enabled the Chinese to rush 250,000 PEOPLE'S LIBERATION ARMY troops to Lhasa, forcing the DALAI LAMA to flee to Tezpur in India. ▷ 6.22

LIBYA
North African state. Part of the Ottoman empire from 1511 to 1911, when it was conquered by Italy, Libya was occupied by Britain during World War II and became independent in 1951 under King Idris I. The discovery of oil in 1959 led to rapid economic growth and social tensions. On 1 September 1969 MUAMMAR QADHAFI seized power, winning support for his Arab COMMUNISM which celebrated Libya's Islamic traditions and rejected western values. Qadhafi's support for terrorist organizations led to the American bombing of Tripoli in April 1986. ▷ 6.09, 6.24, 6.25, 6.27

LIN BIAO
(1907–71) Chinese communist soldier and politician. His troops assisted in the capture of Shenyang (1947), the siege of Beijing (1949) and the capture of Guangzhou (1949). He led the PEOPLE'S LIBERATION ARMY into Korea in (1950) and was promoted marshal (1955). He advised the VIET CONG and was regarded as the heir to MAO ZEDONG. Accused of conspiring against Mao, he tried to escape to Russia but died when his Trident jet crashed in Mongolia. ▷ 6.17

LINEBACKER II
(18–29 December 1972) Operational name for a maximum-effort American air strike during the VIETNAM WAR against the Hanoi and Haiphong areas. It was the final effort of the air war against North Vietnam in which half of Strategic Air Command's B-52s inflicted such heavy damage that LE DUC THO was forced to sign a peace agreement with HENRY KISSINGER. ▷ 6.21

LITHUANIA
Baltic state. Europe's last pagan kingdom, it adopted Christianity only in 1386. In dynastic union with POLAND (1368), it was absorbed by POLAND (1569) then annexed by Russia (1795), becoming independent in 1918. Vilnius, the capital, was seized by Polish forces in 1920 and Memel was awarded to Lithuania under the TREATY OF VERSAILLES, creating tensions during the interwar period. Antanas Smetona took power as dictator in 1926. It was invaded and annexed by the SOVIET UNION under the NAZI-SOVIET PACT (1940) before NAZI occupation (1941–44). It was the first Soviet state to become independent of the Soviet Union, (11 March 1990). ▷ 6.06, 6.08, 6.10, 6.11, 6.15, 6.16

LITTLE ENTENTE
Series of defensive treaties between Romania, CZECHOSLOVAKIA and YUGOSLAVIA concluded between 1920 and 1921, aimed at preventing AUSTRIA and Hungary regaining territory lost

after World War I. France made treaties with Czechoslovakia (1925) and YUGOSLAVIA (1927), and POLAND (1925), but attempts to use the entente to prevent German expansion in eastern Europe were undermined by Polish-Czechoslovak rivalry (over TESCHEN) and the GERMAN-POLISH NON-AGGRESSION TREATY (1934). ▷ 6.07

LITTLE ROCK
City in Arkansas, USA. After the United States Supreme Court ruled that segregation in schools was unconstitutional (1954), Governor Faubus stated that Arkansas was not ready for a "complete and sudden mixing of the races". President DWIGHT D. EISENHOWER was forced to send in federal troops to enable Afro-American children to enter Little Rock's Central High School (1957). ▷ 6.13

LOCARNO, TREATIES OF
A series of treaties signed 1 December 1925 aimed at preventing a violent alteration of the peace settlement agreed after World War I. Represented by GUSTAV STRESEMANN, Germany confirmed its borders with Belgium and France and the demilitarization of the RHINELAND in treaties guaranteed by Britain and Italy, and also signed arbitration agreements with France, Belgium, POLAND and CZECHOSLOVAKIA. However, Germany's eastern borders remained unconfirmed. ▷ 6.07

LONG MARCH
(1934–35) The breakout by the Chinese communists from their base in Jiangxi to the hills of Shaanxi and YAN'AN. The epic story of the march became a legend: it ensured the survival of the Chinese Communist Party and witnessed the rise of MAO ZEDONG, thereafter called Chairman Mao. ▷ 6.17

LOS ALAMOS
A new "laboratory town" in New Mexico, USA, north of Santa Fe. In 1942 it was selected as the center for the development of atomic weapons under the direction of Robert Oppenheimer. Its test site was at Alamogordo, where the first nuclear explosion occurred on 16 July 1945. ▷ 6.13

LUDENDORFF OFFENSIVES
Collective description for the last German offensives of World War I, named after General Erich Ludendorff. Three attacks in 1918, mounted successively near Arras (21 March–5 April), along the Lys in Flanders (9–29 April) and along the Aisne (27 May–6 June) made spectacular progress, but this proved impossible to sustain in the face of heavy casualties. ▷ 6.06

MAASTRICHT TREATY
Agreement signed 10 December 1991 by the EUROPEAN COMMUNITY countries establishing the EUROPEAN UNION and setting a timescale for further European integration. Introduction of a single European currency was planned,

with Britain and Denmark reserving the right to retain their present currencies instead. ▷ 6.07

MacArthur, Douglas
(1880–1964) American general. He was a divisional commander in World War I and a field marshal in the Philippine army (1936). He conducted the defense of the Philippines (1941–42). Supreme Allied commander in the southwest Pacific in World War II, he commanded the assaults on New Guinea and the Philippines. He received the Japanese surrender in Tokyo Bay (2 September 1945), became supreme Allied commander in Japan, directed the defense of the Pusan perimeter in the Korean War and, brilliantly, landed troops at Inchon. His advocacy of air attacks on China led to his dismissal by President Harry S. Truman (April 1951). ▷ 6.19, 6.20

Macedonia
Balkan region under Ottoman rule from 1317 to 1913. The Internal Macedonian Revolutionary Movement, founded in 1893, agitated for independence, but after the Balkan wars Macedonia was partitioned between Greece, Serbia (later Yugoslavia) and Bulgaria. Northern Macedonia was not independent until 1993, after the dissolution of Yugoslavia. Tension with Greece over territorial questions and its large Macedonian minority followed. ▷ 6.07, 6.10

Macmillan, Harold
(1894–1986) British statesman. Macmillan was elected a Conservative member of Parliament in 1924, becoming a progressive economic thinker and opponent of appeasement. The minister for housing in Winston Churchill's 1951 government, he was minister of defense (1954–55), foreign secretary (1955) and chancellor of the exchequer (1955–57) before succeeding Anthony Eden as prime minister in 1957. His attempts to get Britain into the European Economic Community and approval of African decolonization were forward-thinking. Economic prosperity helped him win the 1959 general election. In 1963 he resigned as prime minister, and was created earl of Stockton in 1984. ▷ 6.07, 6.10, 6.27

Maginot line
Defensive fortifications along France's borders with Germany and Luxembourg, named after minister of war André Maginot. Constructed in 1929–34 to defend against German invasion, they were ineffective in 1940. German troops bypassed them by advancing through the Ardennes (May–June). ▷ 6.07, 6.08

Malan, D. F.
(1874–1959) South African politician who helped steer the National Party towards a policy of separate development for the races. While prime minister (1948–54) he introduced the discriminatory legislation of apartheid, notably the 1950 Group Areas Act. ▷ 6.28

Malawi
East African republic located west and south of Lake Malawi. Formerly the British colony of Nyasaland, it achieved independence in 1964 and became a republic in 1966. Dr Hastings Banda became president in 1966 and life president in 1971. Multiparty opposition overthrew his authoritarian rule and Bakili Muluzi became president in 1994. ▷ 6.27, 6.28

Malaysia
Federation of the 11 states of the former protectorate of Malaya (which became independent in 1957); joined by Sabah, Sarawak and Singapore in 1963. Singapore withdrew in 1965. ▷ 6.20, 6.23

Manchuria
Industrial region in northeast China (the provinces of Jilin, Liaoning and Heilongjiang). It was occupied by Japan from 1931 to 1945, when it formed the "independent" state of Manzhougou, and by the Soviet Red Army in 1945. The Guomindang fought unsuccessfully to retain the region (1946–48). People's Liberation Army troops were based here in 1950 prior to their crossing of the Yalu River during the Korean War. ▷ 6.17, 6.18, 6.20

Mandela, Nelson
(1918–) South African politician. The son of a chief, he was married to Winnie Mandela from 1955 to 1992. He was prominent in the banned African National Congress, jailed for treason in 1964. Released in 1990, he negotiated with president F. W. de Klerk to secure the end of apartheid. He was elected president of South Africa on 9 May 1994. He preserved racial harmony and in 1995 his government passed the Promotion of National Unity and Conciliation Act. ▷ 6.28

Manzhougou
Puppet state. After the Japanese army overran Manchuria (1931–32) it established the republic of Manzhougou (Manchukuo) on 9 March 1932. The last Qing emperor, Pu Yi, was enthroned by the Japanese on 1 March 1934 to rule the empire of Manzhouguo. It collapsed in 1945. ▷ 6.02, 6.18, 6.19

Mao Zedong
(1893–1976) Chinese political leader and Marxist philosopher. One of the founders of the Chinese Communist Party in 1921, he emerged as leader during the Long March. He led resistance to the Japanese and the Guomindang (1937–45) and led the Chinese revolution that created the People's Republic in 1949. He instituted the Great Leap Forward and the Cultural Revolution. His ideas were reinterpreted by Deng Xiaoping but he remains a revered figure in China. ▷ 6.17, 6.20, 6.23

Marco Polo Bridge incident
(7 July 1937) Incident deliberately manufactured by Japanese officers southwest of

Beijing. Skirmishes between Japanese and Chinese troops near the bridge led to a brief cease-fire and then to a full Japanese attack on Beijing 29 July 1937. The resulting Sino-Japanese war lasted until 1945. ▷ 6.18

Marcos, Ferdinand
(1917–89) Filipino politician and a resistance fighter during the Japanese occupation (1942–45). He was president from 1965 to 1986 but was exiled after a record of political executions and embezzlement. ▷ 6.23

Marne, Battle of the
(5–11 September 1914) World War I battle in which French forces halted the advance of the German army 25 kilometers (16 miles) from Paris, as it attacked following the Schlieffen Plan. Victory prevented France being knocked out of World War I with a lightning blow, and obliged Germany to fight on two fronts, against both France and Russia. A Second Battle of the Marne (15–20 July 1918) was a highly successful Allied counterattack following defeat of the German Ludendorff Offensive, and began the driving back of German forces which continued until the end of the war in November. ▷ 6.06

Marshall Aid
American aid program for European countries devastated by World War II, named after the US secretary of state George C. Marshall. Economic assistance was provided to prevent destabilized western European countries succumbing to communism. Eastern European countries were forced by the Soviet Union to decline offers of Marshall Aid. ▷ 6.10

Matsu and Quemoy
Heavily defended islands off southwest China, at present under Taiwanese control. Claimed by the People's Republic of China, they were shelled by the People's Liberation Army in the 1954–55 Formosan crisis. ▷ 6.20

Mau Mau
Secret society founded in 1948–49 among the Kikuyu, Meru and Embu of peoples of Kenya to expel the British colonial rulers. It involved ritual oath-taking and was organized as a mini-state, with a political and military hierarchy. It began a campaign of intimidation in 1952. A state of emergency (20 October 1952–12 January 1960), with land and air attacks, eliminated most groups by 1956. ▷ 6.27

McCarthy, Joseph
(1908–57) American politician. Senator for Wisconsin from 1946, he claimed in 1950, in the early days of the Cold War, that many government officials were communists or communist sympathizers. Paranoia following the fall of China to communism and the Soviet acquisition of nuclear arms enabled McCarthy to lead a witch-hunt within the American establishment until his power was curtailed in 1954. ▷ 6.13

McNamara, Robert

(1916–) American statesman. President of the Ford Motor Company before becoming John F. Kennedy's secretary of state in 1961, he was originally a proponent of American involvement in the Vietnam War, but he resigned in 1968 in protest at the war's conduct and became president of the World Bank (1968–81). ▷ 6.21

Megiddo, Battle of

(19–21 September 1918) World War I battle. British troops under General Allenby, assisted by the RAF and Arabs under T. E. Lawrence and Feisal (leader of the Arab Revolt), won a decisive victory in the Palestine campaign, defeating Turkish forces led by the German general Liman von Sanders and making possible the seizure of Damascus. ▷ 6.06

Menem, Carlos

(1935–) Argentine politician. He led the Perónist (Justicialist) party in 1963, became president of Argentina in 1989 and was re-elected 1995. He began a successful privatization program in 1991, reduced annual inflation to 5 percent, but still faced a major unemployment problem in 1995–96. ▷ 6.13

Mensheviks

Moderate faction of the Russian Social Democratic Party believing in a transition to workers' power after a period of democratic capitalist development, who split with the Bolsheviks in 1903. Politically active after the February Revolution of 1917, they were persecuted by the Bolsheviks following the October Revolution. ▷ 6.15

Midway, Battle of

(4–6 June 1942) One of the decisive battles of World War II, fought in the central Pacific between the Japanese and American carrier fleets. It blocked Japanese hopes of capturing Midway's airfields, while the loss of all four of their carriers and 275 airplanes robbed them of future initiatives. American success in this battle was aided by a knowledge of Japanese naval codes. ▷ 6.19

Mobutu, Sese Seko

(1930–) African soldier and politician. In 1965 he seized power in Congo (renamed Zaire in 1971) and was elected president in 1970. His was a one-party state despite his promise of multi-party democracy in 1990. Although his term of office expired in 1991, he remained in power until overthrown in 1997. ▷ 6.27

Moldova

Southeastern European state. Under Turkish control from the 16th to the 18th centuries, in the 19th century the region was partitioned between Russia and Romania. In 1918, Romania annexed Russian-ruled Moldova (Bessarabia), which Russia reclaimed in 1940 (Romania occupying it again from 1941 to 1944). The modern state of Moldova,

including territory east of its traditional border on the Dniester added during the Soviet era, became independent of the Soviet Union on 27 August 1991. The population is mainly ethnic Romanian, but with significant minority groups. The Gagauzy in the south were granted independence in 1994, but the self-declared Russian/Ukrainian republic of Dnestr remains unrecognized. ▷ 6.05, 6.11, 6.16

Moscow, Battle of

World War II battle in which German troops, advancing on Moscow from October 1941 after the successful Barbarossa campaign, were halted and pushed back by a combination of autumn rains, the onset of winter and Soviet counterattacks. The Germans advanced to within 20 kilometers (12 miles) west of the Soviet capital in late November, but by January the front lay 150 kilometers (95 miles) west of Moscow. ▷ 6.08

Mountbatten, Lord Louis

(1900–79) British statesman. One of Queen Victoria's grandsons, he served in the Royal Navy during World War I and World War II, becoming supreme allied commander in southeast Asia (1943–46). Viceroy of India during its transition to independence, he later became first sea lord (1955–59) and chief of defense staff (1959–65). He was killed by Irish nationalist extremists. ▷ 6.10, 6.19, 6.22

Moussadeq, Mohammed

(1880–1967) Iranian prime minister (1951–53). He nationalized the Anglo-Iranian Oil Company on 2 May 1951, and the Abadan refineries closed down. Britain unsuccessfully contested his actions in the International Court of Justice and the frustrated oil companies developed reserves in Kuwait. Iran's economy collapsed, Moussadeq was deposed and an international consortium (principally British Petroleum) took over the company's affairs. ▷ 6.25

Mozambique

Republic on the southeast African coast, formerly a Portuguese colony established in the 17th century. Nationalist resistance (1964–75) led to independence in June 1975 and a Marxist People's Republic was established. Rhodesia and South Africa encouraged armed opposition and a new multiparty republic was created in 1990. ▷ 6.27, 6.28

Mubarek, Hosni

(1928–) Egyptian politician who succeeded Anwar al-Sadat as president in 1981. He maintained Egypt's commitment to the Middle East peace process, opposed Iraq's invasion of Kuwait in 1990 and has attempted to contain Muslim fundamentalist attacks on tourists and government officials. ▷ 6.26

Mugabe, Robert

(1925–) African politician jailed for his opposition to the Smith regime in Rhodesia

(1964–75), he was leader of the Zimbabwe African National Union and became prime minister of independent Zimbabwe in 1980. Elected president in 1987, he has progressively redistributed white-owned farmland to government supporters. ▷ 6.28

Mujahideen

("Holy warriors") Afghan Muslim guerrillas who engaged in civil war against prime minister Hafizullah Amin's communist government in 1979. Soviet intervention (24 December 1979) led to war between the Soviet Union and the American- and Pakistani-backed Mujahideen, who occupied the mountainous areas and retained partial control of Kandahar. The Soviets withdrew in 1989 though the civil war continued. ▷ 6.22

Mujibur Rahman, Sheikh

(1920–75) Bangladeshi politician who helped found the Awami League in 1949 to win independence for East Pakistan. He won the 1970 general election and after the 1972 Indo-Pakistan War became the first prime minister of independent Bangladesh. He was assassinated in 1975. ▷ 6.22

Mukden

Modern Shenjang, the scene of the "1931 incident" when the Japanese contrived a bomb explosion on the nearby South Manchurian Railroad on 18 September 1931. Claiming it was the work of Chinese saboteurs attacking Japanese commerce, the Japanese army occupied the city and began its conquest of Manchuria. ▷ 6.02

Munich agreement

Agreement between Britain, Germany, France and Italy made on 29 September 1938 for a peaceful German annexation of the Sudetenland which, with its large German population, Adolf Hitler was threatening to seize militarily. British prime minister Neville Chamberlain believed the agreement, part of the policy of appeasement, would satisfy Hitler, but in March 1939 Germany occupied the rest of Czechoslovakia. ▷ 6.07

Muslim Brotherhood

A fundamentalist Muslim association founded in Egypt in 1928 by Hassan al-Banna. It carried out several political assassinations. With popular support, it persuaded King Farouk to join in the First Arab-Israeli War. Its members tried to assassinate Gamal Abdel Nasser in 1954 and six were executed. ▷ 6.24

Muslim League

Association founded in 1906 in India by Muslims anxious to have their national identity recognized and respected. Some sought their own nation state (the term "Pakistan" was current by 1933) and this was ambition fostered by Mohammed Ali Jinnah, who became Pakistan's first governor-general. ▷ 6.22

MUSSOLINI, BENITO
(1883–1945) Italian fascist dictator. Combining socialism with nationalism, he founded the fascist movement in 1919. Taking power following the "March on Rome" in 1922, he created a one-party state and embarked on an expansionist foreign policy, pacifying LIBYA (1923–31), invading Abyssinia (1935–36) and annexing Albania (1939). Allied with ADOLF HITLER from 1936, Italy joined World War II in June 1940 but was unsuccessful in its Balkan and North African campaigns. Deposed in July 1943, before Italy signed an armistice with the Allies, Mussolini was made head of the puppet republic of Salo by the Germans, who took control of northern Italy in September 1943. He was killed by partisans at the end of World War II. ▷ 6.07, 6.08, 6.09

MY LAI MASSACRE
Massacre of unarmed South Vietnamese by American soldiers at this hamlet on 16 March 1968. The hamlet was wrongly identified as My Khe, reputedly the headquarters of the 48th battalion of the VIET CONG and part of the large village of Son My, shaded as "Pinkville" on American maps. ▷ 6.21

MYANMAR
See BURMA

NAFTA
See NORTH AMERICAN FREE TRADE AGREEMENT

NAGASAKI
Japanese city on Kyushu coast, target of the second American atomic attack, (9 August 1945). Some 36,000 people died instantly. The plutonium weapon ("Fat Man") dropped from a B-29 bomber had the same destructive power as the HIROSHIMA bomb. Nagasaki has since been rebuilt. ▷ 6.19

NANSEN, FRITJOF
(1861–1930) Pioneering Norwegian polar explorer, academic and statesman. Between 1921 and 1930 he worked as a LEAGUE OF NATIONS commissioner resettling refugees. He was awarded the Nobel Peace Prize in 1922.

NASSER, GAMAL ABDEL
(1918–70) Egyptian soldier and politician who helped to overthrow King Farouk in 1952. He was prime minister (1954–56) and toppled General Neguib to become president of Egypt (1956–70). His nationalization of the Suez Canal provoked the 1956 SUEZ CRISIS. His determination to eliminate ISRAEL led to the 1967 SIX DAY WAR. He began the War of Attrition against Israel on 8 March 1969 but failed to destroy the BAR LEV LINE. He died in office. ▷ 6.25

NATIONAL SOCIALISM
ADOLF HITLER's variant of FASCISM, based on an alleged historical conflict between the races. Hitler called for a totalitarian regime in Germany followed by extermination of the Jews and the subjugation of other "inferior races" in eastern Europe. ▷ 6.07, 6.08, 6.09

NATO
see NORTH ATLANTIC TREATY ORGANIZATION

NAZI PARTY
(Nationalsozialistische Deutsche Arbeiterpartei – German National Socialist Workers' Party) Political party founded in 1919 as the German Workers' Party. Its name was changed in 1920, ADOLF HITLER becoming leader in 1921. It was banned after Hitler's abortive putsch of 1923, but refounded in 1925. Hitler developed an ideology of NATIONAL SOCIALISM. The Nazi Party was the only legal party in Germany after 5 July 1933. ▷ 6.07, 6.08, 6.09

NAZI-SOVIET PACT
Agreement made on 23 August 1939 between Germany and the SOVIET UNION. Ostensibly a non-aggression treaty, it had secret clauses for partitioning POLAND and bringing the Baltic states under Soviet control. These were implemented in September 1939. The treaty was negated by the German invasion of the Soviet Union in June 1941. ▷ 6.07

NE WIN
(1911–) Burmese general who formed an emergency government (1958–60) and then transformed BURMA (Myanmar) into a one-party military state. In 1981 he relinquished office in favor of a civilian, U San Yu, but continued to dominate the government, even after martial law ended in 1992. ▷ 6.20

NEHRU, JAWAHARLAL
(1889–1964) Indian politician who became president of the Indian National Congress in 1929. The first prime minister of India (1947–64), he adopted a strong moral attitude towards international affairs and, though he was neutral throughout the COLD WAR, he dispatched Indian army medical corps units to the KOREAN WAR. He was anxious to modernize India, to introduce industrialization and to reduce Hindu prejudice towards change. He was criticized for his caution in dealing with JAMMU AND KASHMIR and China's invasion of Tibet. His daughter was INDIRA GANDHI. ▷ 6.18, 6.22

NEP
See NEW ECONOMIC POLICY

NEW DEAL
Name given to American president FRANKLIN DELANO ROOSEVELT's program of economic and social reforms (1933–39) to combat the effects of the GREAT DEPRESSION. It introduced public works schemes and government bodies to regulate the economy. ▷ 6.12

NEW ECONOMIC POLICY (NEP)
Leninist measure re-introducing limited free enterprise to Soviet Russia (1921–28). Peasants were allowed to sell a proportion of their grain to encourage production. It succeeded War Communism, the forcible requisition of grain by the BOLSHEVIKS in the RUSSIAN CIVIL WAR, which had led to famine. It ended with the introduction of COLLECTIVIZATION. ▷ 6.15

NICARAGUA
Central American republic. Independent in 1838, it was occupied by American troops (1912–25, 1926–33), initially at the request of the government. It was ruled (from 1936 to 1979) by the Somoza family. Anastasio Somoza, dictator from 1967 to 1979, lost American aid and the Marxist SANDINISTA party came to power. America's response was to back the CONTRAS, resulting in further civil war. The SANDINISTAS were defeated in elections in 1990, and Violeta Chamorro became president. ▷ 6.12, 6.13, 6.14

NICHOLAS II
(1868–1918) Russian czar (r.1895–1917). He was a committed autocrat whose prestige suffered during the RUSSO-JAPANESE WAR, and he was forced to grant limited parliamentary concessions after the revolution of 1905. Increasingly unpopular during World War I (having unwisely taken personal control of the Russian army in 1915) he abdicated in March 1917 after the FEBRUARY REVOLUTION and was subsequently murdered by the BOLSHEVIKS. ▷ 6.15

NIXON, RICHARD
(1913–94) the 37th president of the USA. A REPUBLICAN congressman and senator, he was DWIGHT D. EISENHOWER's vice-president (1953–61), losing the 1960 presidential election to JOHN F. KENNEDY. Elected president in 1968, he stepped up American involvement in the VIETNAM WAR but was forced to withdraw American forces in 1973. He devalued the dollar and withdrew from the BRETTON WOODS system in 1968. Pursuing DÉTENTE, he recognized the PEOPLE'S REPUBLIC OF CHINA (1971) and began the STRATEGIC ARMS LIMITATION talks. He won the 1972 election before resigning over the WATERGATE SCANDAL in 1974. ▷ 6.04, 6.13, 6.16, 6.21

NKRUMAH, KWAME
(1909–72) Ghanaian politician. He organized a nationalist party in 1947 and became prime minister of the Gold Coast in 1952. He continued as prime minister after the Gold Coast became independent from Britain as Ghana in 1957 and was president from 1960 to 1966. He created a one-party state, was a committed Pan-Africanist and espoused Marxist principles. He was deposed by a military coup while visiting Beijing and became co-head of state in Guinea. ▷ 6.27

NONALIGNED MOVEMENT
Term used to describe nations prepared to mediate in disputes between the American and Soviet superpowers. At BANDUNG in 1955, it was thought that nonaligned nations might

develop a third force in world politics. The first nonaligned conference was held in Belgrade in September 1961, chaired by JAWAHARLAL NEHRU and KWAME NKRUMAH. In 1992, 108 nations attended the Jakarta conference but by then the emergence of the oil-rich nations and their relationships with the great powers had rendered the movement largely ineffective. ▷ 6.04

NORIEGA, MANUEL
(1939–) Panamanian soldier and politician, and a powerful influence on Panama's governments from 1983 to 1989. He worked for the American CENTRAL INTELLIGENCE AGENCY but in 1987 was accused of drug-trafficking. American troops invaded Panama on 20 December 1989 to arrest him and he surrendered in 1990. He was convicted of racketeering in Miami on 9 April 1992. ▷ 6.14

NORMANDY LANDINGS
Amphibious and airborne landings of American, British and Canadian forces under DWIGHT D. EISENHOWER's command beginning the ALLIED liberation of NAZI-occupied Europe. They were launched on 6 June 1944 (D-DAY) and were the largest seaborne operation in history. ▷ 6.09

NORTH AMERICAN FREE TRADE AGREEMENT (NAFTA)
Agreement negotiated by President GEORGE BUSH with Canada and Mexico and supported by President BILL CLINTON. It created the largest free trade area in the world. It won Senate approval on 21 November 1993. ▷ 6.13

NORTH ATLANTIC TREATY ORGANIZATION (NATO)
Permanent supra-national military organization created after the outbreak of the KOREAN WAR in 1950 to supplement the North Atlantic Treaty, a defensive pact signed on 4 April 1949 in response to a perceived threat from the SOVIET UNION and its allies. It comprises Britain, Belgium, Canada, Denmark, France (which withdrew from the military command structure in 1966), Iceland, Italy, Luxembourg, the Netherlands, Norway, Portugal, the USA, Greece (joined 1952, left 1974, rejoined 1979), the FEDERAL REPUBLIC OF GERMANY (joined 1955) and Spain (joined 1982). After the COLD WAR, NATO redefined its role, setting up the Partnership for Peace, giving former WARSAW PACT countries associate status while considering their applications for full membership. ▷ 6.10, 6.11

NORTH KOREA
State formed in 1948 as the communist Democratic People's REPUBLIC OF KOREA after the division of Korea along the 38th parallel. Its invasion of SOUTH KOREA (24 June 1950) caused the KOREAN WAR. Aid from Russia and China ended in 1991 and 1993 respectively, damaging the economy and the people's quality of life. ▷ 6.20, 6.23

NORTH YEMEN
The Yemen Arab Republic, created in 1962. A civil war (1962–70) ended in a republican victory. Oil production began in 1987 and in 1989 moves began to unite with the People's Democratic REPUBLIC OF YEMEN in the south. Unification occurred on 22 May 1990 to form the REPUBLIC OF YEMEN. ▷ 6.24, 6.26

NORTHERN EXPEDITION
JIANG JIESHI's campaign against the communists to win control of northern and eastern China. Two armies left Guangzhou in July 1926 and advanced on Wuhan and CHANGSA. By March 1927 Jiang was in Shanghai. On 12 April his soldiers began exterminating communists (the White Terror), defeating their armies in battles along the Yangtze. On 4 June 1928 he was in Beijing. He now controlled several provinces, forcing the communists to flee to Jiangxi. ▷ 6.17

NORTHERN IRELAND
The six counties of Ulster, which remained part of the United Kingdom when IRELAND (which continued to claim Northern Ireland) gained independence in 1921. Civil disorder and violence between Catholic republican terrorists and Protestant loyalists from the late 1960s to the 1990s left over 3,000 dead and necessitated a strong British military presence. An attempt to end the conflict by giving Ireland a say in the government of Northern Ireland under the Sunningdale Agreement (1973) failed. An IRA cease-fire in 1994 led to talks at which proposals for the creation of cross-border institutions in return for the south dropping its claim to the north were agreed by most parties (1998). ▷ 6.10

NUREMBERG TRIALS
Trials of nearly 200 leading NAZIS by the ALLIES after World War II, taking place in Nuremberg (1945–46). Most defendants were given prison sentences, though a few were sentenced to death for crimes against humanity. Many lesser-ranking figures escaped prosecution, provoking criticism from later generations. ▷ 6.10

NYERERE, JULIUS
(1922–) Tanzanian politician who became leader of the Tanganyika African Association, transforming it into the Tanganyika African National Union in 1954. He was prime minister of independent Tanganyika in 1961 and president in 1962. When Zanzibar united with Tanganyika in 1964, forming TANZANIA, he continued as president (1964–85) and was head of the ORGANIZATION OF AFRICAN UNITY. His troops invaded UGANDA and toppled IDI AMIN in 1979. ▷ 6.27

OAS
See ORGANIZATION OF AMERICAN STATES

OAU
See ORGANIZATION OF AFRICAN UNITY

OCTOBER REVOLUTION
Second Russian revolution of 1917, in which the BOLSHEVIKS overthrew the Provisional government which had taken power after the FEBRUARY REVOLUTION but become unpopular because of Russia's continued involvement in World War I. Bolshevik control was secured in the RUSSIAN CIVIL WAR. ▷ 6.15

OGADEN
Arid region of eastern Ethiopia. It was annexed by Italy in 1935 and liberated by British forces in 1941. Somalia invaded the Ogaden in 1977 and encountered Soviet-equipped Ethiopians backed by Cuban volunteers and Soviet advisers. In 1978 Ethiopia regained the region. Sporadic guerrilla warfare continued. ▷ 6.27

OKINAWA
Japanese island group in the Ryukyu Islands and scene of the greatest land battle in the PACIFIC WAR. American forces commanded by General Buckner (killed in the battle) landed on 1 April 1945 to begin a campaign lasting until 2 July. 7,613 US marines and soldiers died; about 100,000 Japanese soldiers and civilians were killed. Simultaneously, fierce naval and air battles were in progress. Japan lost the huge *Yamato* battleship. Kamikazes sank 36 American ships, and 4903 American sailors died. The heavy casualties helped persuade the USA to use atomic weapons against Japan. America restored Okinawa to Japan in 1972. ▷ 6.19

OPEC
See ORGANIZATION OF PETROLEUM EXPORTING COUNTRIES

ORGANIZATION OF AFRICAN UNITY (OAU)
Organization established in 1963, now with 52 member African nations committed to unity, cooperation and security. Founded in Addis Ababa, its present headquarters, it was united against South African APARTHEID but has rarely been able to settle conflicts. ▷ 6.27

ORGANIZATION OF AMERICAN STATES (OAS)
Regional organization established in 1948 to promote peace and economic cooperation in the Americas. The headquarters of the OAS is at Washington DC. One representative from each of the 33 member states sits on its ruling General Assembly.

ORGANIZATION OF PETROLEUM EXPORTING COUNTRIES (OPEC)
Cartel founded in 1960 to standardize oil prices among its members: Algeria, Gabon, INDONESIA, IRAN, IRAQ, KUWAIT, LIBYA, Nigeria, Qatar, SAUDI ARABIA, Venzuela and the UNITED ARAB EMIRATES. Membership has since changed, partly because of the formation in 1968 of the Organization of Arab Petroleum Exporting Countries. ▷ 6.04, 6.13, 6.25

ORTEGA, DANIEL
(1945–) Nicaraguan soldier who led the Sandinista National Liberation Front in 1966 and helped overthrow Anastasio Somoza in 1979. President of NICARAGUA in 1985, he handed over power to Violeta Chamorro in 1990. ▷ 6.14

OSLO ACCORDS
(1993) Interim settlement of the ARAB-ISRAEL CONFLICT. The peace process between ISRAEL and the PALESTINE LIBERATION ORGANIZATION (PLO), begun in Madrid in 1990, achieved nothing. Secret talks began in Oslo in 1993, leading to the Declaration of Principles on Interim Self-Government (13 September 1993). The PLO renounced terrorism. Israel recognized the PLO and promised to vacate the Gaza Strip and Jericho. A permanent settlement was projected for 1999. ▷ 6.26

OSTLAND
Name given to LATVIA, LITHUANIA, ESTONIA and western BELARUS (1941) as part of Greater Germany. The NAZI aim was to colonize and exploit economically these territories for the benefit of Germany. They became slave states in which almost all Jews and gypsies were murdered. Ostland was reconquered by the Red Army in 1944–45. ▷ 6.08, 6.09

OSTPOLITIK
West German chancellor WILLY BRANDT'S foreign policy of establishing closer ties with eastern Europe, especially with the GERMAN DEMOCRATIC REPUBLIC, during the COLD WAR. The FEDERAL REPUBLIC OF GERMANY recognized the German Democratic Republic's borders in 1970, and in 1972 the two Germanies formally recognized each other's existence. ▷ 6.10

PACIFIC RIM
The nations of east and southeast Asia (China, Japan, TAIWAN, SOUTH KOREA, MALAYSIA, Singapore, THAILAND, INDONESIA and the Philippines) whose economies accelerated after 1975, producing consumer goods for the world at large. Prosperous Hong Kong was restored to China, itself a newly industrializing economy, in 1997. ▷ 6.05, 6.23

PACIFIC WAR (WORLD WAR II)
When the Japanese attacked PEARL HARBOR (7 December 1941) their plan was to conquer southeast Asia and the Pacific Ocean as far as Midway and then, by defending its perimeter, force the USA to submit. After initial successes Japan experienced a slow but general defeat in the face of ALLIED (mainly American) material superiority. They lost control of the sea at MIDWAY. Their eastern perimeter was smashed by American forces at TARAWA, Kwajalein and in the Solomons. Their western perimeter was undermined by COMMON-WEALTH victories at Imphal and Kohima. As the Americans drew closer (1944–45), air attacks saturated Japan with bombs. Soviet

forces overran Japanese-occupied MANCHURIA in August 1945. President HARRY S. TRUMAN planned to invade Japan in 1945–46 but the nuclear strikes on HIROSHIMA and NAGASAKI brought Japanese surrender before this. ▷ 6.19

PAHLAVI DYNASTY
Iranian ruling family. Reza Khan, prime minister of IRAN, was elected Reza Shah Pahlavi in 1925. In 1941 he abdicated in favor of Mohammed Reza Shah Pahlavi (1919–80). His westernizing policies brought protests and Shah Pahlavi fled Iran in 1979 to be succeeded by AYATOLLAH RUHOLLAH KHOMEINI. The former shah died in Egypt. ▷ 6.24, 6.25

PAKISTAN
Muslim state formed in 1947 from territories east and west of India, known as East and WEST PAKISTAN. West Pakistan was much the larger territory and a secessionist movement developed in the east. Pakistan became a republic within the COMMONWEALTH in 1956 and an Islamic republic in 1965. In 1972 President ZULFIKAR ALI BHUTTO withdrew the country from the Commonwealth. He was replaced by General ZIA UL-HAQ in 1978 and executed. Pakistan has since found political stability hard to achieve. Territorial disputes with India over JAMMU AND KASHMIR have led to the three INDO-PAKISTAN WARS (1947–49, 1965, 1971). Defeated by Indo-Bangladeshi forces in 1971, it recognized the independence of East Pakistan as BANGLADESH. Pakistan's nuclear program caused the USA to terminate aid in 1998. ▷ 6.22

PALESTINE LIBERATION ORGANIZATION
Organization founded in 1964 and joined in 1967–68 by AL FATAH and other terrorist groups. By 1989 it was widely recognized as representing a Palestine state. Terrorist attacks on ISRAEL from Lebanese bases led to two Israeli invasions (1978 and 1982). It withdrew from west Beirut in 1982. YASSIR ARAFAT became PLO president in 1989 and in 1996 he became leader of the Palestine National Authority. ▷ 6.25

PALESTINE NATIONAL AUTHORITY
The executive power of the PALESTINIAN state as defined by the OSLO DECLARATION. It is headed by YASSIR ARAFAT. Legislative power is held by the Palestinian Council. It has jurisdiction over the Gaza Strip and Jericho. ▷ 6.26

PALESTINIANS
The Arab inhabitants of the former British mandate of Palestine, mainly Muslim but including many Christians. The ARAB-ISRAELI CONFLICT has scattered 5 million Palestinian refugees around the world. About 700,000 are Israeli citizens. About 660,000 live in Jericho and the Gaza Strip. ▷ 6.24, 6.25, 6.26

PAN-AMERICAN CONGRESS
Congress created as a reaction to the American-dominated Pan-American Union

(1890). Congresses were held in different Latin American venues to debate commercial, financial, economic and security issues. The congress held in Lima on 26 December 1938 issued the Declaration of Peru, opposing all foreign intervention. ▷ 6.12

PAPUA NEW GUINEA
State comprising eastern New Guinea. The south (Papua) was occupied by Britain in 1884 and subsequently passed under AUSTRALIAN administration. The north became a German colony (German New Guinea) in 1884. German New Guinea was occupied by Australia in 1914, and after World War I it was mandated to Australia by the LEAGUE OF NATIONS. It was the scene of fierce battles between Australian and Japanese forces in 1942–45. The two territories, united and renamed Papua New Guinea in 1971, achieved independence in 1975. Rich in economic resources, the country has faced sabotage from a secessionist group, the Bougainville Revolutionary Army. ▷ 6.03, 6.04, 6.05, 6.18, 6.19, 6.20, 6.23

PARIS AGREEMENT (1973)
Agreement reached in talks between HENRY KISSINGER and LE DUC THO in Paris, which led to the end of American involvement in the VIETNAM WAR. An initial agreement on a cease-fire in Vietnam was reached on 23 January 1973. The cease-fire agreement was signed in Paris on 27 January. ▷ 6.21

PASSCHENDAELE (THIRD BATTLE OF YPRES)
Notorious World War I battle, fought on the WESTERN FRONT from 31 July to 6 November 1917. ALLIED troops attempting to break German lines in Belgium made only minor advances, suffering over 300,000 casualties in reaching the village after which the battle is named. Continuous bombardment had turned the low-lying battlefield into a quagmire, making progress almost impossible. ▷ 6.06

PATHET LAO
Laotian communist guerrilla movement in conflict with government forces (1954–75). Backed by North VIETNAM, it won control of LAOS and abolished the monarchy. Its political wing, the Lao People's Revolutionary Party, created the one-party Lao People's Democratic Republic in 1975. ▷ 6.21

PEARL HARBOR
American naval and air base on the island of Oahu, Hawaii, attacked on 7 December 1941 by Japanese carrier airplanes. They sank or damaged 18 American warships and more than 2,400 Americans died. This "day of infamy" brought the United States into World War II. ▷ 6.02, 6.12, 6.18, 6.19

PEOPLE'S LIBERATION ARMY (PLA)
Created in YAN'AN from the nucleus of the 8th communist Chinese Route Army, which made

no distinction between the ordinary people and the soldiers: "the people are the water, the soldiers of the 8th Route Army are the fish; the fish cannot live without water," said MAO ZEDONG. Victorious in the Chinese Revolution, the PLA has campaigned in Tibet, KOREA, Aksai Chin, Thag La and VIETNAM and suppressed the pro-democracy protests in China itself in 1989. ▷ 6.17, 6.18, 6.20, 6.22

PERÓN, EVA

(1919–52) Argentine radio and cinema star. She married JUAN PERÓN in 1945 and became a popular political figure, devoted to helping the poor. She won women the right to vote and ran for vice-president in 1951. ▷ 6.13

PERÓN, JUAN

(1895–1974) Argentine soldier and politician who, with other officers, rebelled against President Castillo in 1943. He was elected president in 1946 and maintained support for his dictatorial rule by favoring industrial workers against other classes. Because of inflation and church hostility he was overthrown in 1955. He returned as president in 1973 and died in office. ▷ 6.13

PÉTAIN, PHILIPPE

(1856–1951) French soldier and statesman. Commander of French forces in World War I after the ruinous CHEMIN DES DAMES offensive, he won respect by using his men sparingly. He became prime minister on 17 June 1940, making peace with the invading Germans and ruling collaborationist VICHY FRANCE. A death sentence passed on him after the ALLIED victory in 1945 was later commuted to life imprisonment. ▷ 6.06, 6.08, 6.09

PHALANGISTS

Political party founded in LEBANON by Pierre Gemayel, a Maronite Christian, in 1936 to counterbalance Muslim demands for union with SYRIA. Hostile to the disruptive presence of the PALESTINE LIBERATION ORGANIZATION, it became a military force in 1975 and supported ISRAELI invasions in 1978 and 1982. ▷ 6.26

PILSUDSKI, JOSEF

(1867–1935) Polish dictator. Leader of a Polish volunteer army during World War I, he became head of state and army chief of staff on independence. Victorious in the RUSSO-POLISH WAR, he retired from politics in 1922 before becoming dictator of an authoritarian regime (1926–35). ▷ 6.07

PLA

See PEOPLE'S LIBERATION ARMY

PLO

See PALESTINE LIBERATION ORGANIZATION

POLAND

Eastern European state founded in the 10th century, partitioned at the end of the 18th century between Prussia, Russia and Austria. Reconstituted after World War I, its eastern frontier was defined by the CURZON LINE. Poland won extra territory during the RUSSO-POLISH WAR (1920–21) The foreign policy of General JOSEF PILSUDSKI's authoritarian regime (1926–35) left POLAND isolated, and, despite belated British and French support, it was partitioned again between Germany and the SOVIET UNION under the NAZI-SOVIET PACT in September 1939. It came under overall German control (1941–44) before incorporation into the Soviet bloc after World War II. Both occupation regimes deported or killed large numbers. POLAND's modern frontiers were defined by the ALLIES at the YALTA and POTSDAM CONFERENCES. After World War II, opposition to communist rule resulted in serious demonstrations in 1956, and grew in the late 1970s and 1980s with the accession of Polish Pope JOHN PAUL II and the emergence of the independent trade union SOLIDARITY. The communist regime fell in 1989 and Solidarity leader Lech Walesa was elected president in 1990, but the former communists remain powerful. ▷ 6.07, 6.08, 6.09, 6.10, 6.11

POLAND, GENERAL GOVERNMENT OF

Area of POLAND, including Warsaw, Cracow and Lublin, not annexed by Germany after its invasion of 1939, and placed instead under the rule of German NAZI, Hans Frank.

POLISARIO

(Popular Front for the Liberation of Saguia el Hamra and Rio de Oro) Guerrilla organization demanding independence for the WESTERN SAHARA. Originally formed to fight Spanish rule, after the Spanish withdrawal in 1973 it opposed the Moroccan and Mauritanian forces that occupied the country. ▷ 6.27

POLISH CORRIDOR

Strip of territory assigned to POLAND after World War I, dividing East Prussia from the rest of Germany. Envisioned as a means of keeping Germany weak, it flouted the principle of national SELF-DETERMINATION on which the post-World War I settlement was based, fueling German resentment. ▷ 6.07

POTSDAM CONFERENCE

(17 July–2 August 1945) Conference of the "Big Three" ALLIED POWERS held after the end of World War II. Attended by JOSEPH STALIN, HARRY S. TRUMAN and WINSTON CHURCHILL

THE POPES FROM 1914	
Benedict XV	1914–22
Pius XI	1922–39
Pius XII	1939–58
John XXIII	1958–63
Paul VI	1963–78
John Paul I	1978
John Paul II	1978–

(who was replaced on 28 July by Clement Attlee following the LABOUR PARTY's victory in a British general election). It was agreed that Germany was to be preserved as a unified state (although subsequent COLD WAR rivalry prevented this), and that territory in eastern Germany would be transferred to POLAND as compensation for realigning the Polish-Soviet border along the CURZON LINE. ▷ 6.10

PRAGUE SPRING

Czechoslovak leader ALEXANDER DUBCEK's attempt to create "socialism with a human face" in the spring of 1968, reforming the Communist Party and its hidebound administrative institutions. The initiative was ended and Dubcek dismissed after WARSAW PACT troops invaded on 20 August. ▷ 6.10

PREMADASA, RANASINGHE

(1924–93) SRI LANKAN politician. As prime minister from 1978 to 1988 he introduced ambitious social policies. He became president in 1988 and faced hostility from the militant TAMIL TIGERS. His use of the army to attack rebel strongholds led to his assassination in 1993. ▷ 6.22

PROHIBITION

A ban on the manufacture, transportation and sale of alcoholic drinks in the USA under the 18th Amendment to the constitution. It led to bootlegging and organized crime. Enforcement required the strengthening of the Federal Bureau of Investigation. In 1933 the 21st Amendment repealed Prohibition. ▷ 6.12

PU YI

(1906–67) The last of the Qing dynasty to rule China (1908–12 and, briefly, during 1917). After his deposition he chose to be called Henry. When the Japanese created MANZHUGOU, he became its chief executive. The Japanese then enthroned him as its emperor on 1 March 1933. Tried and pardoned for war crimes after World War II, he became a private Chinese citizen. ▷ 6.18

PURGES, STALIN'S

The execution or deportation of millions of Soviet citizens for trumped-up crimes against the state during JOSEPH STALIN's brutal consolidation of his authority over the SOVIET UNION in the 1930s. The murder of SERGEI KIROV in 1934 was a pretext for show trials of leading communists, which began in 1936, and purges of the armed forces in 1938. Between 3 and 8 million people are estimated to have died. ▷ 6.15, 6.16

QADHAFI, MUAMMAR

(1942–) LIBYAN leader who overthrew King Idris (1969) and declared a republic. He retains the rank of colonel and his title is "leader of the revolution and supreme commander of the armed forces". He has intervened in the affairs of North African states, clashed with the USA and suffers

UNITED NATIONS sanctions, partly because of his refusal to hand over suspected international terrorists for trial. ▷ 6.25

QUEMOY
See MATSU AND QUEMOY

RABIN, YITZHAK
(1922–95) ISRAELI general and statesman and the first Israeli-born prime minister (1974–76) when he succeeded Golda Meir. An outstanding military planner, he was chief of staff in the SIX DAY WAR and defense minister from 1984. He favored PALESTINIAN self-government and was assassinated on 4 November 1995. ▷ 6.26

RACE TO THE SEA
Series of battles during World War I. Following the halt of the German advance through France in 1914 at the BATTLE OF THE MARNE, both sides attempted to turn the other's northern flank. When the English Channel prevented further northward movement, they dug trenches and the stalemate that characterized the WESTERN FRONT ensued. ▷ 6.06

RAPALLO, TREATY OF
Treaty in which Germany and Russia recognized each other diplomatically and agreed to cooperate economically. Secret clauses provided for German military exercises banned under the TREATY OF VERSAILLES to take place in Russia. ▷ 6.07

RAS TAFARI
See HAILE SELASSIE

REAGAN, RONALD
(1911–) The 40th president of the USA. A former actor, Reagan unsuccessfully contested the REPUBLICAN presidential nomination in 1968 and 1976, before being elected president in 1980 and re-elected in 1984. He introduced stringent economic policies at home, and his foreign policy included bombing LIBYA (1986) and supporting right-wing guerrilla organizations in South America. Initially highly critical of the SOVIET UNION, after 1986 he developed a productive relationship with MIKHAIL GORBACHEV. ▷ 6.05

RED GUARDS
Originally a group of students who paraded before MAO ZEDONG at a Qinghua University rally in Beijing in 1966. He called on them to be the advance guard of the CULTURAL REVOLUTION. Thousands more joined, creating havoc across China. One group fought a battle with the PEOPLE'S LIBERATION ARMY in Wuhan in 1967. ▷ 6.20

REPARATIONS
Payments demanded by the ALLIES from the defeated CENTRAL POWERS after World War I as compensation for damage caused by the war. The sums demanded of Germany led to a non-fulfilment campaign, to hyper-inflation

and to French occupation of the RUHR (1923). Revised downwards by the DAWES PLAN of 1924, the sum was again reduced by the Young Plan of 1929, before demands for reparations were suspended in response to the GREAT DEPRESSION (1931). After World War II, the western Allies claimed small amounts in reparations, in comparison to the SOVIET UNION's extensive demands. ▷ 6.07

REPUBLICAN PARTY
With the DEMOCRATS one of the two main American political parties, founded in 1854. Despite being the party of Abraham Lincoln, in the 20th century it generally adopted a conservative approach to social and economic questions. It is traditionally isolationist in foreign policy, but DWIGHT D. EISENHOWER, RICHARD NIXON and RONALD REAGAN projected American power around the globe during the COLD WAR. ▷ 6.12, 6.13

REZA PAHLAVI, MOHAMMED
See PAHLAVI DYNASTY

RHEE, SYNGMAN
(1875–1965) Korean politician, the first elected president of SOUTH KOREA (1948) and its leader throughout the KOREAN WAR. Only a month after winning his fourth presidential election (1960) he was forced to resign and died in exile. ▷ 6.20

RHINELAND, GERMAN REOCCUPATION OF
(7 March 1936) Reoccupation by German troops of this industrial region bordering France, which had been made a demilitarized area under the TREATY OF VERSAILLES. With international attention focused on BENITO MUSSOLINI's invasion of Abyssinia, the action went unchallenged, and it encouraged ADOLF HITLER to further make assaults on the post-World War I order. ▷ 6.07

RHODESIA
Former British African colony, embracing Northern Rhodesia (a protectorate in 1924 and part of the Central African Federation from 1953 to 1963) and the colony of Southern Rhodesia (self-governing from 1923 and also a member of the federation). It was named after the British imperialist Cecil Rhodes. Northern Rhodesia became independent as ZAMBIA in 1964. Ian Smith, prime minister of Southern Rhodesia, made a unilateral declaration of independence in 1965 in an attempt to preserve white minority rule, provoking Britain to impose economic sanctions. After a period of intensifying civil war, British control was briefly restored in 1979. White rule ended and Rhodesia became officially independent in 1980 as ZIMBABWE. ▷ 6.04, 6.27, 6.28

ROME, TREATY OF
Treaty creating the EUROPEAN ECONOMIC COMMUNITY signed on 25 March 1957 by France, the FEDERAL REPUBLIC OF GERMANY, Italy and the BENELUX countries. ▷ 6.10

ROMMEL, ERWIN
(1891–1944) German field marshal. He commanded a tank division during the invasion of France in 1940 and with distinction led German forces in north Africa (1941–43). Charged with defending northern France against Allied invasion, he was wounded during the NORMANDY landings. Discovered to be part of a plot to assassinate ADOLF HITLER, he committed suicide. ▷ 6.08, 6.09

ROOSEVELT, FRANKLIN DELANO
(1882–1945) The 32nd president of the USA. A DEMOCRAT, he was assistant secretary to the navy (1913–20) and governor of New York from 1929, before being elected president in 1932. His NEW DEAL legislation for combating the GREAT DEPRESSION earned him re-election in 1936. After winning the 1940 election, he offered help under the LEND-LEASE SCHEME to countries fighting Nazi Germany, and after PEARL HARBOR took the USA into the war. The only president to serve third and fourth terms in office (he was re-elected in 1944), he died in office, having been crippled with polio since 1921. ▷ 6.03, 6.08, 6.09, 6.12

RUHR
Industrial area of Germany occupied by France in 1923 for non-payment of German REPARATIONS. After World War II it was administered by an international committee (1949–53) before being incorporated into the FEDERAL REPUBLIC OF GERMANY. ▷ 6.07, 6.10

RUSSIAN CIVIL WAR
Conflict between the BOLSHEVIKS, who seized power in the OCTOBER REVOLUTION of 1917, and assorted anti-communists, the Whites. Beginning in August 1918, the Whites, led by ALEXANDER KOLCHAK in Siberia and Anton Denikin in southern Russia, and assisted by detachments from foreign powers, revolutionary minorities and others, were initially successful. The BOLSHEVIKS' control of central Russia proved crucial against their disunited Russian opponents, and they established themselves as rulers of the country, although at the same time they lost territory in the RUSSO-POLISH WAR. War Communism, their policy of forcible grain requisition, caused widespread famine and was replaced by the NEW ECONOMIC POLICY in 1921. ▷ 6.15

RUSSO-POLISH WAR
War between POLAND and BOLSHEVIK Russia. After World War I, newly-constituted Poland refused to accept the Russo-Polish frontier delineated by the CURZON LINE. Taking advantage of the RUSSIAN CIVIL WAR, Poland occupied Russian territory in 1919 and invaded the UKRAINE in April 1920. The Bolshevik response drove the Poles back to Warsaw by August 1920, but the Poles counterattacked and at the Peace of Riga (18 March 1921) they gained a new border 200 kilometers (125 miles) east of the Curzon line. ▷ 6.15

RWANDA-URUNDI
Central African territory mandated to Belgium after World War I, a UNITED NATIONS trust territory after 1945. Rwanda became independent in 1962 but ethnic conflict between Hutus and Tutsis led to civil war and, in 1990–94, to genocide and the flight of 2 million refugees. Urundi became independent Burundi in 1962 and experienced similar ethnic conflict. ▷ 6.01, 6.02, 6.03, 6.24

SAAR
German coal-producing region under LEAGUE OF NATIONS' trusteeship for 15 years after World War I, as part of the attempt to limit German power. At a plebiscite in 1935, 90 percent of its population voted for re-incorporation into Germany. After World War II it was again internationally administered, before coming back under German control in 1957. ▷ 6.07, 6.10

SADAT, ANWAR AL-
(1918–81) President of Egypt (1970–81). He planned with SYRIA to attack ISRAEL in the YOM KIPPUR WAR, but visited Jerusalem in 1977 to met MENACHEM BEGIN at CAMP DAVID and signed a peace treaty that recognized the sovereignty of Israel. He was assassinated in 1981. ▷ 6.05, 6.25, 6.26

SADDAM HUSSEIN
(1937–) IRAQI dictator, president and chairman of the Revolutionary Command Council since 16 July 1979. He has ruthlessly suppressed internal opposition by Kurdish separatists, Shiite Muslims and political dissidents. He attacked IRAN in the first GULF WAR (1980–88) and provoked a second by annexing KUWAIT (1990). An international coalition army forced his withdrawal and his agreement to permit a UNITED NATIONS special commission of weapons experts to destroy his stockpile of nuclear, chemical and biological weapons and missiles in 1991. His failure to cooperate in this led to an international crisis in 1997–98. ▷ 6.25, 6.26

SADCC
See SOUTHERN AFRICAN DEVELOPMENT COORDINATION CONFERENCE

SAIGON
Capital city of South Vietnam from 1954 and headquarters of South Vietnamese and American military forces during the VIETNAM WAR. Attacked during the TET OFFENSIVE, it was evacuated by American forces in 1973. It was occupied by North Vietnam in 1975 and renamed Ho Chi Minh City. ▷ 6.21

SAKARYA RIVER, BATTLE OF THE
(24 August–16 September 1921) Decisive battle in TURKEY during the 1920–22 Greek-Turkish War. Turkish troops, commanded by KEMAL ATATÜRK, blocked the Greek advance on Ankara and went on to capture the Greek strongholds of Afyon and Smyrna. ▷ 6.07

SAKHALIN
Island in the Sea of Okhotsk. Russia annexed northern Sakhalin in 1853 and took southern Sakhalin in 1900, before losing it again in the Russo-Japanese War (1905). All of Sakhalin was occupied by White forces (1918–20) during the RUSSIAN CIVIL WAR, then by Japan until 1925, when northern Sakhalin was incorporated into Soviet Russia. In 1945 the SOVIET UNION took advantage of World War II to annex southern Sakhalin, possession of which remains a source of tension between Russia and Japan. ▷ 6.19, 6.20

SALT
See STRATEGIC ARMS LIMITATION TREATIES

SANDINISTAS
Nicaraguan Marxist guerrillas, who took over NICARAGUA (1979–90) under DANIEL ORTEGA after the overthrow of the Somoza clan. They were named after their revolutionary hero, Auguste Sandino (1895–1934), murdered on the orders of Anastasio Somoza, a National Guard commander. The Sandinista government was defeated in 1990 elections. ▷ 6.14

SAUDI ARABIA
Oil-rich kingdom in the Arabian peninsula, comprising Nejd and Hejaz, united by ABDUL AZIZ IBN SAUD in 1927 and named Saudi Arabia in 1932. A founder member of the ARAB LEAGUE, it was pro-Arab in the ARAB-ISRAELI CONFLICT. A founder member of the ORGANIZATION OF PETROLEUM EXPORTING COUNTRIES, it joined the 1973 oil boycott that raised world prices. It was active in the 1991 GULF WAR against SADDAM HUSSEIN. ▷ 6.24, 6.25, 6.26

SCHENGEN AGREEMENT
Agreement between France, West Germany and the BENELUX countries (14 June 1985), providing for free movement of people, goods and services across their borders. Signed by Italy in 1990, Spain and Portugal in 1991 and Greece in 1992. ▷ 6.10, 6.11

SCHLIEFFEN PLAN
General Alfred von Schlieffen's 1905 plan for a German invasion of France. To avoid fighting France and its ally Russia simultaneously, in the event of war Germany was to defeat France quickly, advancing through Belgium before swinging round to capture Paris. Troops could then be rushed to the Russian front. However, in 1914 the advance was halted at the BATTLE OF THE MARNE, and its failure obliged Germany to fight a long war for which it was unprepared. ▷ 6.06

SEATO
See SOUTH EAST ASIA TREATY ORGANIZATION

SELF-DETERMINATION
The idea that national groups should be allowed to rule themselves. It was championed by American president WOODROW

WILSON after World War I, who believed it would end the dynastic rivalries and squabbling over territory which had led to World War I. In practice, the great ethnic complexity of central and eastern Europe made it impossible to satisfy rival groups' demands. The creation of multi-ethnic states (YUGOSLAVIA, CZECHOSLOVAKIA), the exclusion of many Germans from Germany and the ban on ANSCHLUSS between Germany and AUSTRIA all undermined the principle. ▷ 6.07

SERBS, CROATS AND SLOVENES, KINGDOM OF THE
See YUGOSLAVIA

SÈVRES, TREATY OF
Peace treaty between the ALLIES and the Ottoman empire after World War I. TURKEY lost Adrianople (Edirne), Eastern Thrace and Smyrna (Izmir) to Greece, and Rhodes and the Dodecanese to Italy. SYRIA was made a French LEAGUE OF NATIONS mandate, and IRAQ, Palestine and TRANSJORDAN were mandated by Britain. The treaty was never ratified. The Turkish leader KEMAL ATATÜRK won Smyrna and Adrianople back from Greece militarily, and negotiated the more lenient Treaty of Lausanne (1923). ▷ 6.07

SHAMIR, YITZHAK
(1915–) ISRAELI right-wing politician who had led the Stern Gang of Jewish terrorists (1940–48) during the British mandate in Palestine. As prime minister (1983–84, 1986–92), he opposed any dialogue with the PALESTINE LIBERATION ORGANIZATION. He was succeeded by YITZHAK RABIN. ▷ 6.26

SHARPEVILLE MASSACRE
(March 21 1960) Massacre in an African township 65 kilometers (40 miles) south of Johannesburg, where 69 people were killed during an anti-APARTHEID protest. Demonstrators against the pass-laws threw away their identification cards, marched on the police station and demanded to be arrested. The government mounted a full scale military operation, involving jet airplanes and armored cars, and opened fire during a scuffle. ▷ 6.28

SHATT AL-ARAB
The confluence of the Rivers Tigris and Euphrates, about 193 kilometers (120 miles) in extent and forming part of the boundary between IRAN and IRAQ, a constant source of frontier dispute. Iraq seized control of it in 1980, instigating the first GULF WAR (1980–88). Much of the conflict revolved around Khorramshar and Abadan, stubbornly defended by Iran. ▷ 6.26

SIHANOUK, PRINCE
(1922–) King of Cambodia (r.1941–55) and prime minister (1955–70). Overthrown by American-backed Lon Nol, he took refuge in Beijing and formed an alliance with Pol Pot. He returned to become head of state but was

removed by the KHMER ROUGE in 1976. Elections under United Nations control created a democratic government and he was elected king on 23 September 1993. ▷ 6.21

SIHANOUK TRAIL
Supply route across Cambodia (Kampuchea) linking VIET CONG positions with Kompong Som (Sihanoukville), Cambodia's principal port. The main supply destinations were Fish Hook and Parrot's Beak (both in Cambodia) and the Bulge. Its existence was not admitted until April 1966. It was closed in March 1970. ▷ 6.21

SINO-JAPANESE WAR
War between China and Japan that began on 7 July 1937 as a result of the MARCO POLO BRIDGE INCIDENT. It continued until 1945, though from 1941 is usually considered as part of World War II. Japanese attacks included systematic bombing raids from bases in Kyushu, TAIWAN and Korea and the use of specially designed assault landing ships. The GUOMINDANG survived largely through aid from the SOVIET UNION following the 1937 Sino-Soviet Treaty. Japanese forces occupied much of China until 1945. ▷ 6.02, 6.18

SINO-SOVIET TREATY (1950)
Treaty of friendship and alliance between the PEOPLE'S REPUBLIC OF CHINA and the SOVIET UNION. MAO ZEDONG visited Moscow in December 1949 and in this February 1950 agreement JOSEF STALIN promised China advantageous trade arrangements and military protection against a resurgent Japan. ▷ 6.20

SIX DAY WAR
(5–10 June 1967) War between ISRAEL and the Arab states of Egypt, SYRIA, JORDAN and IRAQ. Arab mobilization (400,000 troops, 2,430 tanks and 650 combat aircraft) provoked pre-emptive Israeli air strikes that destroyed the Arab air forces. Israeli forces then occupied the WEST BANK, Jerusalem, Gaza, the Sinai peninsula and the GOLAN HEIGHTS. ▷ 6.25

SLOVAKIA
Central European republic, a NAZI puppet state during World War II. The more rural part of postwar COMMUNIST CZECHOSLOVAKIA, Slovaks considered themselves oppressed by Czech domination. After the collapse of communism, Slovakia separated from the CZECH REPUBLIC, becoming independent on 1 January 1993. ▷ 6.07, 6.08, 6.09, 6.11

SLOVENIA
Adriatic state incorporated into YUGOSLAVIA after World War I. It had close links with AUSTRIA, having been part of Austria-Hungary since the 13th century. Partitioned between Austria and Italy in World War II, it was the first Yugoslav republic to seek statehood after the end of the COLD WAR and is the most prosperous of the former Yugoslav republics. Independence, declared on 21 June 1991, was recognized by the Serb-dominated federal government after brief hostilities. ▷ 6.07, 6.11

SMUTS, JAN
(1870–1950) Prime minister of South Africa (1919–24, 1939–45). An Afrikaner general in the Second Anglo-Boer War, he invaded Cape Colony and in 1902 signed the Treaty of Vereeniging. In World War I he commanded forces that overran GERMAN EAST AFRICA and SOUTH-WEST AFRICA, and he was a signatory to the TREATY OF VERSAILLES. He was made a British field marshal in 1941. ▷ 6.28

SOLIDARITY
POLISH trade union, founded on 1 August 1980 in GDANSK and led by Lech Walesa, that opposed COMMUNISM in POLAND in the 1980s. About 80 percent of Polish workers joined before it was banned in December 1981. Legalized in 1988, it fielded candidates in the country's first postwar democratic elections in 1989 and won. After it became involved in government its popularity waned dramatically. ▷ 6.10, 6.16

SOMME, BATTLE OF THE
World War I battle, a concerted British attempt to break through German lines along the River Somme on the WESTERN FRONT. It resulted in massive losses for minor gains. It was launched on 1 July 1917 with a huge but ineffective artillery barrage followed by frontal assaults on heavily defended positions. ALLIED losses were 61,000 killed and injured on the first day and 615,000 by the end of the offensive in November. The German army lost 650,000 men and was forced to retreat to the HINDENBURG line in February 1917. ▷ 6.06

SOUTHERN AFRICAN DEVELOPMENT COORDINATION CONFERENCE (SADCC)
Ten African states (Angola, BOTSWANA, Lesotho, MALAWI, MOZAMBIQUE, Namibia, Swaziland, TANZANIA, ZAMBIA, ZIMBABWE) in association from 1980 to improve their economies and limit South Africa's influence. SAADCC was redefined in 1992 as the Southern African Development Community, primarily to promote economic integration in imitation of the 1975 Economic Community of West African States. ▷ 6.28

SOUTH EAST ASIA TREATY ORGANIZATION (SEATO)
Pact established in 1954 after the KOREAN WAR to resist communist aggression. Its signatories were the United Kingdom, the USA, AUSTRALIA, France, New Zealand, PAKISTAN, the Philippines and THAILAND. Pakistan withdrew in 1972. It was decided to dissolve the organization in 1975. ▷ 6.21

SOUTH KOREA
The REPUBLIC OF KOREA, established in 1948. Its invasion by NORTH KOREA in 1950 precipitated the KOREAN WAR. An economic and educational transformation (1963–80), concentrating on consumer industries and export markets, made it one of the most prosperous of the TIGER ECONOMIES prior to 1998. ▷ 6.20, 6.23

SOUTH-WEST AFRICA
A German colony captured by South African troops in 1914. Mandated by the LEAGUE OF NATIONS to South Africa, it was illegally retained by South Africa after 1945. The UNITED NATIONS recognized it as Namibia in 1968. It achieved independence as Namibia in 1990. ▷ 6.01, 6.02, 6.05, 6.27, 6.28

SOVIET UNION (UNION OF SOVIET SOCIALIST REPUBLICS, USSR)
Created on 30 December 1922, following the BOLSHEVIK victory in the RUSSIAN CIVIL WAR. Nominally a federation of Russia, UKRAINE, BELARUS and Transcaucasia, its power was centralized in Moscow. As more republics were created, other administrative entities were established for smaller ethnic minorities. It was attacked by Germany in 1941, and the war at first went badly, but after STALINGRAD the Germans were steadily rolled back, with the Soviet Red Army in Berlin by April 1945. Soviet casualties are estimated at 20 million, and the Soviet Union's contribution was a major factor in the defeat of NAZI Germany. At the peak of its power and influence in the immediate postwar period, when it dominated eastern Europe through the WARSAW PACT, in the 1980s the Soviet Union faced increasingly serious economic problems. Formally dissolved on 30 December 1991 after revolts by the nationalities, its successor was the non-communist, loosely-affiliated COMMONWEALTH OF INDEPENDENT STATES. ▷ 6.15, 6.16

SOWETO
Acronym for South West Township, home of the labor force for Johannesburg, South Africa, and scene of violence after students protested against the teaching of Afrikaans in African townships. Between 16 and 25 June 1976, 76 students died. ▷ 6.28

SPUTNIK I
The first artificial satellite in space, launched by the SOVIET UNION on 4 October 1958, giving NIKITA KRUSCHEV a propaganda coup and shocking the west. ▷ 6.04, 6.16

SRI LANKA
The former British colony of Ceylon, which achieved independence in 1948 as a dominion within the COMMONWEALTH. It became a republic in 1972, adopting its present name meaning "resplendent island". Tamil separatist riots and the assassination of Prime Minister Bandaranaike in 1959 led to a prolonged guerrilla war by the TAMIL TIGERS in the north of the island. ▷ 6.04, 6.05, 6.22

ST-GERMAIN, TREATY OF
Peace treaty concluding hostilities between the ALLIES and AUSTRIA in World War I, signed

on 10 September 1919. Austria-Hungary was dismembered and CZECHOSLOVAKIA, the KINGDOM OF THE SERBS, CROATS AND SLOVENES (later YUGOSLAVIA), AUSTRIA and Hungary became separate states. Galicia was lost to POLAND, the Bukovina to Romania and South Tyrol to Italy. Austrian ANSCHLUSS with Germany was forbidden. Austria's army was limited to 30,000 men and the country was obliged to pay reparations. ▷ 6.07

STALIN, JOSEPH

(1879–1953) SOVIET dictator. Born in Georgia, he joined the BOLSHEVIKS in 1903 and was active in the OCTOBER REVOLUTION and the RUSSIAN CIVIL WAR. Limited intellectually but an effective administrator, he was commissar for nationalities before becoming general secretary of the Communist Party of the Soviet Union (1922). By 1927 he had emerged as VLADIMIR ILYICH LENIN's successor, having played his opponents off against one another. In 1929 he began the COLLECTIVIZATION of agriculture, to complement the industrialization of the Soviet Union through the First FIVE YEAR PLAN (launched 1928). Increasingly paranoid, in the 1930s he initiated a series of massive PURGES to cement his power. Having concluded the NAZI-SOVIET PACT in 1939, he was surprised by ADOLF HITLER's invasion of the Soviet Union in 1941, but eventually victorious and responsible for the Soviet Union's cooption of eastern Europe into an unofficial empire. He was posthumously denounced by NIKITA KHRUSCHEV in 1956. ▷ 6.02, 6.07, 6.08, 6.09, 6.15, 6.16, 6.19

STALINGRAD, BATTLE OF

World War II battle. After this Soviet city was captured by German forces in September 1942, ADOLF HITLER forbade his army to withdraw when Soviet troops counterattacked. After a bitter siege, 200,000 Germans surrendered (31 January–2 February 1943). The defeat was the turning point in World War II in Europe, marking the beginning of Soviet ascendancy on the eastern front. ▷ 6.08, 6.09

STRAIT OF HORMUZ

Strait separating the northern tip of Oman (Musandam peninsula) and IRAN. It provides access to the Persian Gulf and is technically policed by Oman. Of immense strategic importance in the Middle East, it was mined during the GULF WAR between Iran and IRAQ (1980–88). ▷ 6.26

STRATEGIC ARMS LIMITATION TREATIES (SALT)

Two US-Soviet treaties helping to formalize DÉTENTE. SALT I, signed 26 May 1972, regulated the deployment of anti-ballistic missiles and imposed a five-year moratorium on intercontinental ballistic missile construction. SALT II, signed June 1979, was not ratified by the USA because of the Soviet invasion of AFGHANISTAN. ▷ 6.04

STRESEMANN, GUSTAV

(1878–1929) German statesman. A National Liberal politician before World War I, he helped form the center-right German People's Party in 1918. As German chancellor (August-–November 1923) he defused the RUHR crisis, and as foreign secretary (1923–29) restored Germany's international reputation, getting reparations reduced under the DAWES PLAN (1924), signing the TREATY OF LOCARNO (1925) and joining the LEAGUE OF NATIONS (1926). His death was a blow to hopes of a peaceful revision of the VERSAILLES settlement. ▷ 6.07

STROESSNER, ALFREDO

(1912–) Paraguayan soldier and politician. President from 1954 to 1989, he was South America's longest surviving dictator. General Andrés Rodriguez overthrew him in a military coup. ▷ 6.13

SUDETENLAND

Ethnically German area of Moravia, part of Austria-Hungary until World War I, after which it was incorporated into CZECHOSLOVAKIA, then annexed by Germany under the MUNICH AGREEMENT of 1938. The German population was expelled after World War II. It is part of the present CZECH REPUBLIC. ▷ 6.07

SUEZ CRISIS

Crisis prompted by Egyptian leader GAMAL ABDEL NASSER's nationalization of the British-owned Suez Canal on 26 July 1956. Britain and France sponsored an ISRAELI invasion (29 October) before occupying the canal zone themselves on 5 November. Diplomatic pressure by the American government forced a humiliating withdrawal (6–7 November) and acceptance of nationalization, highlighting the decline of British power after World War II. ▷ 6.04, 6.24, 6.25

SUKARNO, AHMED

(1901–70) INDONESIAN nationalist who founded the Indonesian Nationalist Party (1927) and cooperated with the Japanese occupation forces in World War II. He was president of Indonesia (1949–67) and conducted a "confrontation" with MALAYSIA (1963–67) that flared into an undeclared war involving British troops. He withdrew Indonesia from the UNITED NATIONS in 1965 and retired in 1967. ▷ 6.18

SUN YIXIAN (SUN YAT-SEN)

(1866–1925) Chinese revolutionary, founder of the GUOMINDANG and briefly president of the Chinese Republic in 1912. He retired in favor of YUAN SHIKAI. His Three Principles of the People (freedom, democracy, "livelihood") revitalized the Guomindang in 1924. He was the first great Asian nationalist. ▷ 6.17

SYRIA

Eastern Mediterranean Arab republic. Formerly part of the Ottoman empire, it was mandated to France in 1920 and occupied

by the ALLIES from 1941 to 1946, though technically independent from 1944. It was briefly joined with Egypt as the UNITED ARAB REPUBLIC (1958–61). In the SIX DAY WAR in 1967, it lost the GOLAN HEIGHTS to ISRAEL. It intervened in the LEBANESE CIVIL WAR but this was countered by Israel in 1982. It joined the UNITED NATIONS coalition against IRAQ in 1991. ▷ 6.08, 6.09, 6.24, 6.25, 6.26

TAIWAN

Island state off southeast China. Japanese from 1895 to 1945, it was established by the refugee GUOMINDANG as NATIONALIST CHINA in 1949, occupying the Chinese seat in the UNITED NATIONS until 1971, when it was expelled in favor of the PEOPLE'S REPUBLIC OF CHINA. TAIWAN has a well-educated workforce, is a world leader in computer and television manufacture and is one of the most successful of the TIGER ECONOMIES. Beijing claims it as a Chinese province. ▷ 6.04, 6.05, 6.17, 6.18, 6.20, 6.23

TAJIKISTAN

Central Asian state. Coming under Russian rule in the 19th century, it was incorporated into the Soviet state after 1917 and made a full republic of the SOVIET UNION in 1929. A remote region, it remained undeveloped during the Soviet era. After independence (9 September 1991), ethnic rivalry led to civil war between former communists and Islamic fundamentalists, the communists regaining power in 1994. ▷ 6.05, 6.16, 6.22

TAMIL TIGERS

The military arm of the Tamil ethnic group (the Liberation Tigers of Tamil Elam), a minority in SRI LANKA. They have conducted a secessionist campaign in the north of the island. Government forces were gaining the upper hand in 1995–96. ▷ 6.22

TANNENBERG, BATTLE OF

(23–31 August 1914) World War I battle at which German forces under PAUL VON HINDENBURG and Erich Ludendorff halted the advance of Russian forces through East Prussia before driving them back at the battles of the Masurian Lakes and Gorlice-Tarnow. ▷ 6.06

TANZANIA

East African republic, formerly the British colonies of Tanganyika and Zanzibar. Tanganyika became independent 1961, Zanzibar in 1963. The two united on 26 April 1964 to form Tanzania though separatism is now an issue. Under JULIUS NYERERE it was a one-party state (1977–92). ▷ 6.27, 6.28

TARAWA, BATTLE OF

(20–24 November 1943) World War II battle for a Japanese-occupied atoll in the central Pacific. Attacked by the US 2nd Marine Division, 4,700 Japanese defenders put up a fierce resistance. Only 17 survived. Marine

BRITISH PRIME MINISTERS 1783–1916					
Herbert Henry Asquith	Liberal	1908–16	Winston Churchill	Conservative	1951–55
David Lloyd George	Coalition	1916–22	Anthony Eden	Conservative	1955–57
Andrew Bonar Law	Conservative	1922–23	Harold Macmillian	Conservative	1957–63
Stanley Baldwin	Conservative	1923–24	Alex Douglas–Home	Conservative	1963–64
Ramsay MacDonald	Labour	1924	Harold Wilson	Labour	1964–70
Stanley Baldwin	Conservative	1924–29	Edward Heath	Conservative	1970–74
Ramsay MacDonald	Labour/National	1929–35	Harold Wilson	Labour	1974–76
Stanley Baldwin	National	1935–37	James Callaghan	Labour	1976–79
Neville Chamberlain	National	1937–40	Margaret Thatcher	Conservative	1979–90
Winston Churchill	Coalition	1940–45	John Major	Conservative	1990–97
Clement Attlee	Labour	1945–51	Tony Blair	Labour	1997–

losses were heavy and the battle taught the USA hard lessons for the future conduct of the PACIFIC WAR. ▷ 6.19

TEHERAN CONFERENCE
(28 November–1 December 1943) ALLIED conference attended by WINSTON CHURCHILL, FRANKLIN DELANO ROOSEVELT and, for the first time, JOSEPH STALIN. A joint US-British invasion of France, long demanded by Stalin, was scheduled for 1944. The SOVIET UNION also agreed to join the war against Japan after Germany was defeated. ▷ 6.09

TESCHEN
Central European grand duchy, Habsburg-ruled from the 18th century. Possession was disputed by POLAND and CZECHOSLOVAKIA after World War I. Partitioned between them by the LEAGUE OF NATIONS in 1920, it was annexed by Poland in 1938 under a minor clause of the MUNICH AGREEMENT and partitioned again in 1945. ▷ 6.07

TET OFFENSIVE
(January–February 1968) VIETNAM WAR offensive launched by the North Vietnamese army and the VIET CONG during the Tet holiday truce period. Most towns and cities in South Vietnam were attacked and the campaign, which completely surprised the American and South Vietnamese forces, was a psychological victory for North Vietnam. ▷ 6.21

THAILAND
Kingdom in southeast Asia. Known as Siam before 1939, its origins go back to the 14th century. It was the only southeast Asian state not subjected to European colonial rule. Occupied by Japan in World War II, it provided the USA with bases during the VIETNAM WAR. Ill-planned tourist and manu-facturing developments have made its capital Bangkok one of the most crowded cities in Asia. ▷ 6.18, 6.19, 6.20, 6.21, 6.23, 6.25

THATCHER, MARGARET
(1925–) British prime minister. A research chemist and lawyer by training, she was elected as a Conservative to Parliament in 1959 and served as minister of education and science (1970–74). Elected party leader in 1975, she became prime minister in 1979. Her privatization of state-owned industries and her assault on the welfare state marked a turning point in postwar politics. Initial unpopularity was assuaged by British victory in the FALKLANDS WAR and, following re-election in 1983, she won the crucial battle in her war with the trade unions when she defeated the miners' strike of 1984–85. In foreign policy, her relations with MIKHAIL GORBACHEV and RONALD REAGAN were highly profitable. Elected again in 1989 after an economic boom, she resigned in 1990 amid controversy over her proposed poll tax when a cabinet revolt broke out in opposition to her anti-European views. ▷ 6.10

THIEU, NGUYEN VAN
(1923–) Vietnamese soldier and politician. Deputy prime minister of South Vietnam from 1964 to 1965, he became president in 1965 and head of state until the fall of SAIGON in 1975. He has since lived in exile. ▷ 6.21

THIRD WORLD
Term to describe developing countries outside the First World (the west) and the Second World (the former communist countries). Located mainly in Africa, Asia and Latin America, it is subdivided by the World Bank into low income, middle income and upper income countries (e.g. India, Nigeria and Brazil, respectively). Following the BANDUNG CONFERENCE during the COLD WAR, most Third World countries adopted an anti-colonial, anti-racist, non-aligned stance. The collapse of the SOVIET UNION, poverty in its former satellite states and the rise of prosper-ous PACIFIC RIM economies has made the term less meaningful. ▷ 6.13, 6.22, 6.23, 6.27

TIANANMEM SQUARE MASSACRE
(4 June 1989) Massacre of students at "The Gate of Heavenly Peace", the main square in Beijing. They assembled to celebrate the reforms of Hu Yaobang and deplore the restrictions imposed by DENG XIAOPING. Their demonstration coincided with MIKHAIL GORBACHEV's visit to the city and was tele-vized worldwide. Agitators also aroused workers in Beijing and in other Chinese cities. Fearing political chaos, the government ordered the army to suppress the demon-strators. Many hundreds were killed and thousands arrested. ▷ 6.23

TIGER (DRAGON) ECONOMIES
Rapidly growing southeast Asian economies during the 1970s and 1980s that were some-times built on insecure financial foundations. THAILAND, the Philippines, SOUTH KOREA and MALAYSIA concentrated 65 percent of their exports on specialist markets and depended heavily on loans. Slower growth in Japan, beginning in 1991–92, spread to TAIWAN and SINGAPORE, but the three still accounted for 17 percent of world export of goods from 1996 to 1997. In 1997–98 a financial crisis in southeast Asia resulted in currency devalu-ations and falling stock-market prices. ▷ 6.23

TITO (JOSIP BROZ)
(1892–1980) Yugoslavian leader. General secretary of the Communist Party from 1937, he led the country's communist partisans in World War II. Having defeated the rival CHETNIKS as well as the Germans, after World War II Tito refused to allow YUGOSLAVIA to become a Soviet satellite. He broke decisively with Moscow in 1948. His rule gave the country a unity it had previously lacked, and which did not last long after his death. ▷ 6.10

TOJO, HIDEKI
(1885–1948) Japanese soldier and politician. He was promoted general in 1941 and became prime minister. He was set on a conflict with the USA and, as wartime leader, simultaneously held the posts of foreign and home affairs, commerce, industry and education. He was dismissed in 1944 and executed as a war criminal in 1948. ▷ 6.19

TOKYO
Originally Edo, renamed Tokyo when it became the Japanese capital in 1868. It was destroyed by an earthquake in 1923, rebuilt and then largely destroyed by American bombing in 1944–45. A raid by 150 B-29 bombers on 10 March 1945 caused a firestorm in which 72,000 people died. Japan's surrender was signed on board the USS *Missouri* in Tokyo Bay on 2 September 1945. ▷ 6.18, 6.19

TONGKING CRISIS

Political crisis in the USA after 7 August 1964, when President LYNDON BAINES JOHNSON told the American people that North Vietnamese warships had attacked American destroyers in the Gulf of Tonking. (In fact, the destroyers were protecting South Vietnamese personnel attacking North Vietnam.) The US Senate Tonking Gulf Resolution authorized the president to take all necessary measures to deal with North Vietnamese aggression. ▷ 6.21

TOTALITARIANISM

State control of all aspects of national life. STALIN'S SOVIET UNION and NAZI Germany were such regimes. ▷ 6.07, 6.15, 6.16

TRANSJORDAN

See JORDAN

TRANSKEI

A territory in eastern Cape Province, South Africa, defined as a self-governing BANTUSTAN in 1976. It did not receive international recognition. ▷ 6.28

TRIANON, TREATY OF

Peace treaty made after World War I between the ALLIES and Hungary, signed on 4 June 1920. Hungary lost two-thirds of the territory it held in 1914 (when it was part of Austria-Hungary), including Ruthenia and SLOVAKIA (to CZECHOSLOVAKIA), CROATIA (to the KINGDOM OF THE SERBS, CROATS AND SLOVENES) and Transylvania (to Romania). ▷ 6.07

TROTSKY, LEON

(1879–1940) BOLSHEVIK revolutionary. Born in the UKRAINE of Jewish parents, he was originally a MENSHEVIK before joining VLADIMIR ILYICH LENIN's Bolsheviks in May 1917. Playing key roles in the OCTOBER REVOLUTION and RUSSIAN CIVIL WAR, he also negotiated the TREATY OF BREST-LITOVSK (1918). Outmaneuvered by JOSEPH STALIN in the power struggle following Lenin's death, he was dismissed as commissar for war (1925), exiled (1929) and finally murdered in his refuge in Mexico City on Stalin's orders. ▷ 6.15

TRUMAN, HARRY S.

(1884-1972) The 33rd president of the USA. DEMOCRATIC senator for Missouri from 1935, he became vice-president in 1944 and took over the presidency on FRANKLIN DELANO ROOSEVELT's death in April 1945. He authorized the dropping of atomic bombs on Japan. Forced to accept Soviet dominance in eastern Europe after World War II, he took the USA into the COLD WAR, announcing the TRUMAN DOCTRINE (1947), ordering MARSHALL AID (1947), joining the NORTH ATLANTIC TREATY ORGANIZATION and entering the KOREAN WAR (1950). His attempts to introduce liberal "Fair Deal" legislation at home were frustrated by Congress. Victorious at the 1948 election, he retired in 1953. ▷ 6.03, 6.17, 6.19

TRUMAN DOCTRINE

American foreign policy defined by President HARRY S. TRUMAN in a speech made 14 March 1947. He pledged to help "free peoples… resisting attempted subjugation by armed minorities or by outside pressures". A clear determination to oppose the spread of Soviet power, it was the precursor to MARSHALL AID and one of the first moves in America's COLD WAR with the USSR. ▷ 6.03, 6.10

TUPAMAROS GUERRILLAS

Uruguayan urban guerrilla force established in 1963 and named after Tupac Amaru, an 18th-century rebel hero. Government forces brought them under control in 1981. ▷ 6.13

TURKEY

Republic established in 1923 in southeast Europe and Anatolia, following the abolition of the Ottoman sultanate in 1922. It was given a secular constitution by its first president, KEMAL ATATÜRK. Neutral until 1945, it entered World War II on the side of the ALLIES. It joined the NORTH ATLANTIC TREATY ORGANIZATION in 1952 and sent troops under UNITED NATIONS command to the KOREAN WAR. It occupied northern Cyprus in 1974 and has taken repressive action against Kurdish nationalists within its borders. ▷ 6.07, 6.08, 6.09, 6.10, 6.11, 6.24, 6.25, 6.26

TURKMENISTAN

Central Asian state. It was conquered by Russia in the late 19th century, and a revolt in 1916 was followed by an unsuccessful struggle for independence during the RUSSIAN CIVIL WAR. Under Soviet control from 1920, it became a full Soviet republic in 1925. COLLECTIVIZATION settled its nomadic population, but the region remained poor. After independence (27 October 1991) close links were maintained with Russia and communists retained power. ▷ 6.05, 6.16, 6.22

U NU

(1907–95) Burmese nationalist who with AUNG SAN helped govern BURMA under Japanese supervision (1942–45). He became president after independence and introduced democratic procedures and socialist policies. Challenges came from KAREN and communist guerrillas. He won the 1960 elections but was overthrown by NE WIN. ▷ 6.20

U-2 INCIDENT

Diplomatic crisis following the shooting-down of an American U-2 reconnaissance aircraft over the SOVIET UNION on 1 May 1960, worsening already-tense COLD WAR relations and ending DWIGHT D. EISENHOWER's hopes of holding talks with NIKITA KHRUSCHEV. The plane's captured pilot, Gary Powers, was traded for a Soviet spy in 1962. ▷ 6.04

UGANDA

British East African protectorate (1894–1962) that became a republic in 1967. Milton Obote became president in 1966 and introduced socialist policies in 1970. He was overthrown by IDI AMIN in 1971. A Tanzanian invasion toppled Amin in 1979 and elections restored Obote (in office 1980–85). Under President Museveni political parties are banned until 2000. ▷ 6.01, 6.04, 6.05, 6.27

UKRAINE

Eastern European state. Falling under Russian control in the 17th and 18th centuries, it declared independence with German assistance in January 1918, before being conquered by the Poles during the RUSSO-POLISH WAR and coming under BOLSHEVIK control in June 1920. Its grain-producing lands being vital to the SOVIET UNION, it suffered heavily during COLLECTIVIZATION. In World War II it was occupied by German forces from 1941 to 1944. Traditionally strongly nationalistic, it declared independence on 24 August 1991 and rapidly liberalized its economy. ▷ 6.11, 6.15, 6.16

UNION OF SOVIET SOCIALIST REPUBLICS

See SOVIET UNION

UNITED ARAB EMIRATES

Formerly the Trucial States, the seven emirates of Abu Dhabi, Ajman, Dubai, Fujairah, Ras al-Khamai, Shahjah and Um al-Qaiwain in southeast Arabia. They united on 2 December 1971. Each emirate has a separate government but with representation in a Supreme Council. The president is elected. ▷ 6.04, 6.05, 6.26

UNITED ARAB REPUBLIC

The union of Egypt and SYRIA from February 1958 that ended in September 1961 when SYRIA broke away. Egypt retained the title until 1971. ▷ 6.25

PRESIDENTS OF THE UNITED STATES OF AMERICA FROM 1913

Woodrow Wilson	Democrat	1913–21	John F. Kennedy	Democrat	1961–63
Warren G. Harding	Republican	1921–23	Lyndon B. Johnson	Democrat	1963–69
Calvin Coolidge	Republican	1923–29	Richard M. Nixon	Republican	1969–74
Herbert Hoover	Republican	1929–33	Gerald Ford	Republican	1974–77
Franklin D. Roosevelt			Jimmy Carter	Democrat	1977–81
	Democrat	1933–45	Ronald Reagan	Republican	1981–89
Harry S. Truman	Democrat	1945–53	George Bush	Republican	1989–93
Dwight D. Eisenhower			Bill Clinton	Democrat	1993–2001
	Republican	1953–61	George W. Bush	Republican	2001–

UNITED NATIONS ORGANIZATION (UN)
International body working for world peace and social justice, a more powerful successor to the LEAGUE OF NATIONS. The UN has intervened with varying degrees of success in the KOREAN WAR, the Second GULF WAR and other conflicts, and runs specialized agencies, such as the INTERNATIONAL MONETARY FUND and World Health Organization. Established on 26 June 1945, it is presided over by a general secretary, but real power lies with the Security Council, composed of the USA, Russia, Britain, France, and the PEOPLE'S REPUBLIC OF CHINA (admitted in 1971, when the GUOMINDANG regime on TAIWAN ceased to be recognized as the official Chinese government). With the power to veto resolutions, Security Council members paralysed much UN decision-making during the COLD WAR. At the same time the number of nations in the General Assembly, each with equal voting rights, rose dramatically, giving a greater say to countries from the developing world. ▷ 6.03, 6.04, 6.05, 6.08, 6.11, 6.20, 6.22, 6.25, 6.26, 6.27

UNTOUCHABILITY ACT
(1955) Indian legislation forbidding high-caste Hindus to discriminate against harijans (untouchables), one of many attempts in India to change long-established customs through parliamentary action. The state guaranteed harijans employment through special job reservations. ▷ 6.22

USSR
See SOVIET UNION

UZBEKISTAN
Central Asian state. Annexed by Russia in the mid-19th century, Uzbekistan became a full Soviet republic in 1925. It was the main center for cotton production in the SOVIET UNION. Corruption was endemic and the region remained very poor. Ethnic tension between Uzbeks and Mekhetian Turks deported from Georgia by JOSEPH STALIN in 1944 resulted in massacres of Turks in 1989. After independence, (31 August 1991), former communist leader President Karimov continued to rule dictatorially. ▷ 6.15, 6.16

VARGAS, GETÚLIO
(1883–1954) Brazilian politician who ran for president in the 1930 Brazilian elections. Although defeated, he took over with support from the army and was dictator from 1930 to 1945. He regained the presidency by constitutional means in 1950, but widespread opposition caused him to commit suicide. ▷ 6.12

VELVET REVOLUTION
Name given to the peaceful transition from COMMUNISM to democracy in CZECHOSLOVAKIA. After a general strike (27–29 November 1989) the communist government agreed to give up its political monopoly. Dissident leader Václav

Havel became president on 29 December, and free elections were held in June 1990. ▷ 6.10

VERDUN, BATTLE OF
(21 February–16 December 1916) World War I battle. German commander-in-chief Erich von Falkenhayn hoped to draw French troops into a battle of attrition around the symbolically important fortified town of Verdun, and "bleed them white". The ALLIES lost 400,000 men, but German losses were also high (350,000) and Falkenhayn was replaced by HINDENBURG in August 1916. ▷ 6.06

VERSAILLES, TREATY OF
Peace treaty made between the ALLIES and Germany after World War I. Germany was forced to accept responsibility for starting the war and required to pay REPARATIONS. It lost 13 percent of its territory, much of it in industrial areas (including Alsace-Lorraine to France) and the POLISH CORRIDOR. Danzig (GDANSK) became a free city and the SAAR came under LEAGUE OF NATIONS trusteeship, as did Germany's colonies, as mandates. Germany's army was limited to 100,000 men and tank and air forces were prohibited. The treaty provoked massive resentment in Germany and led many, such as ADOLF HITLER, to seek a radical break with the post-World War I system. ▷ 6.07

VERWOERD, HENDRIK
(1901–66) Afrikaner politician and minister of native affairs (1950–58), the leading exponent of APARTHEID. He became prime minister of South Africa (1958–66) and was assassinated in office. ▷ 6.28

VICHY FRANCE
Collaborationist state set up in southern France on 10 June 1940 under PHILIPPE PÉTAIN. It co-operated with NAZI Germany until November 1942, when ALLIED landings in north Africa led to German occupation of Vichy territory. ▷ 6.08, 6.09

VICTORIA POINT
Located in southern Myanmar (BURMA), it is one of two bases loaned to China to provide access to the Indian Ocean. China supplies equipment to the Myanmar armed forces and is the major source of financial aid. Other Asian countries regard the presence of China in the Indian Ocean as a threat to stability. ▷ 6.22

VIET CONG
South Vietnamese communist forces in the VIETNAM WAR. ▷ 6.20, 6.21

VIETMINH
(Vietnam Doc Lap Minh – League for Vietnamese Independence) Party founded by HO CHI MINH in 1941. It formed the first postwar Vietnamese government. Its armed forces led by VO NGUYEN GIAP defeated the French at DIEN BIEN PHU. ▷ 6.18, 6.20, 6.21

VIETNAM
Southeast Asian state whose origins date to 939. Vietnam was part of French INDO-CHINA from 1884 until occupied by Japan (1940–45). French control was restored after World War II but VIETMINH resistance forced the French to withdraw in 1954 when Vietnam was partitioned along the 17th parallel with a communist government at Hanoi and a pro-western government in SAIGON. The south survived only with American support, including, from 1965 to 1973, intervention by American forces (the VIETNAM WAR). The south survived less than two years after American troops withdrew. In 1975 Vietnam was reunified as the Socialist Republic of Vietnam. ▷ 6.03, 6.05, 6.20, 6.21, 6.23

VIETNAM WAR
(1964–75) War between communist North Vietnam and South Vietnam and (1965–73) the USA. The USA had supported South Vietnam since the French withdrawal in 1954, but the TONGKING CRISIS led to the commitment of American combat troops, whose numbers exceeded 500,000 by 1968. The Americans believed they were winning the war by 1967, but the unexpected TET OFFENSIVE shook their confidence. By 1970 the war had spilled over into LAOS and Cambodia, both of which were destabilized by the interventions of communist and American forces. The war was unpopular in the USA. This sapped the morale of American troops, and peace negotiations began in 1968, culminating in an American withdrawal in 1973. Fighting continued in divided Vietnam and ended with the communist capture of SAIGON in 1975. American fatalities in the war were 58,000. The Vietnamese lost 2–3 million. ▷ 6.10, 6.20, 6.21

VIRGIN LANDS CAMPAIGN
Soviet leader NIKITA KHRUSCHEV's attempt from 1954 to boost the SOVIET UNION's agricultural production by cultivating the steppes of northern KAZAKHSTAN and western Siberia. In 1956 the "virgin lands" yielded half the total harvest for the Soviet Union, but soil erosion invalidated the initiative as a long-term solution. ▷ 6.16

VITTORIO VENETO, BATTLE OF
(24 October–3 November 1918) World War I battle on the Italian Front. Italian troops, aided by a British detachment, broke Austro-Hungarian lines and took 425,000 prisoners, forcing Austria-Hungary to sue for peace (3 November). ▷ 6.06

VOJVODINA
Austro-Hungarian territory incorporated into Serbia after World War I (a small part being awarded to Romania). It was occupied by Germany from 1941 to 1944. Multi-ethnic, with a small Serbian majority, it was granted autonomy in 1946 and, with Kosovo, granted representation in the federal government

under YUGOSLAVIA's 1974 constitution. Serbia's reassertion of control over Vojvodina and Kosovo in 1988–89 was one of the causes of Yugoslavia's break up. ▷ 6.11

WALL STREET CRASH
Name given to the American stock market crash of 24 October 1929, which precipitated the GREAT DEPRESSION. ▷ 6.02, 6.12

WALVIS BAY
Harbor and railroad terminus on the Namibian coast in southern Africa. A British colony from 1878, it later formed part of South Africa, which transferred it to Namibia in 1994. ▷ 6.28

WARSAW PACT
Military alliance made on 14 May 1955 between the SOVIET UNION and its satellites in eastern Europe: Albania (which suspended its membership in 1961 and left 1969), Bulgaria, CZECHOSLOVAKIA, the GERMAN DEMOCRATIC REPUBLIC, Hungary, POLAND and Romania. Integrating the communist countries into a counterpoint to the NORTH ATLANTIC TREATY ORGANIZATION, it was also a means of keeping them under Soviet control. Warsaw Pact troops crushed the uprisings in Hungary (1956) and Czechoslovakia (1968). The pact was dissolved on 1 April 1991. ▷ 6.10, 6.11

WASHINGTON NAVAL AGREEMENT
Agreement reached when President WARREN HARDING invited powers with interests in the Pacific to attend the 1921 Washington Naval Conference. It specified battleship and aircraft carrier tonnages in the ratio 5:5:3 for Britain, America and Japan. The USA reduced its naval threat to Japan by limiting fortifications in the Philippines, The "Open Door" principle of unimpeded commerce with China was reaffirmed. ▷ 6.02

WATERGATE SCANDAL
American political scandal. In 1972 reporters Carl Bernstein and Bob Woodward revealed that President RICHARD NIXON had authorized bugging of the opposition DEMOCRATIC PARTY candidate during that year's presidential elections. After a Supreme Court investigation confirmed his involvement Nixon resigned (9 August 1974), to be succeeded by Vice-President GERALD FORD. ▷ 6.04, 6.13

WEST ADEN
A Federation of south Arabian emirates under British protection from 1903. It was joined to the colony of ADEN in 1963. In 1967 Britain recognized the National Liberation Front, withdrew its troops and the Republic of the South Yemen, incorporating EAST ADEN, emerged. In 1990 it united with NORTH YEMEN to form the REPUBLIC OF YEMEN. ▷ 6.24

WEST BANK
The area west of the River Jordan incorporated into the kingdom of JORDAN in 1948. It

was occupied by the ISRAELIS in the 1967 SIX DAY WAR. The OSLO ACCORDS and the 1995 Taba Accord anticipated Israeli withdrawal during 1998 and its transfer to the Palestine National Authority. ▷ 6.24, 6.25, 6.26

WEST GERMANY
See FEDERAL REPUBLIC OF GERMANY

WEST INDIES, FEDERATION OF THE
Federation originally planned in 1947 and formed in 1958 from ten British Caribbean colonies, with its capital at Port of Spain, Trinidad. Jamaica was unwilling to subsidize the poorer islands and seceded in 1961. It was dissolved on May 31 1962. ▷ 6.14

WEST PAKISTAN
The western wing of PAKISTAN. The term has not been used since the independence of East Pakistan (as BANGLADESH) in 1971 made it obsolete. ▷ 6.22

WESTERN EUROPEAN UNION (WEU)
Military alliance, founded in 1954 to tie West Germany into an exclusively European organization, following the decision to rearm it and incorporate it into the NORTH ATLANTIC TREATY ORGANIZATION (NATO). The importance of the WEU was negated by American involvement in NATO. Its members are Belgium, France, Germany, Italy, Luxembourg, the Netherlands, Portugal (joined 1989) Spain (joined 1989) and Greece (joined 1994). ▷ 6.10, 6.11

WESTERN FRONT (WORLD WAR I)
After the initial German advance of 1914 was halted at the BATTLE OF THE MARNE (thwarting the SCHLIEFFEN PLAN), both sides tried unsuccessfully to outflank the other in the RACE TO THE SEA. Deadlock followed, with defensive trench systems running from Belgium to the Swiss border. Attempts to break through with massed infantry attacks (for example, the battles of Champagne and Artois in 1915, of the SOMME and VERDUN in 1916, and of PASSCHENDAELE and the CHEMIN DES DAMES in 1917) resulted in massive losses with little territorial gain. From 1917 the conflict gradually became one of movement once again as both sides learned to devolve command to smaller, more flexible troop units. In February and March 1917 the Germans retreated to the HINDENBURG line before specialized assault troops made large gains in the LUDENDORFF OFFENSIVES of 1918, but exhausted Germany's resources in the process. Allied counterattacks advanced to the German border by the end of the war in November 1918. ▷ 6.06

WESTERN SAHARA
Territory in northwest Africa, formerly the Spanish Sahara (1884–1976). After the end of Spanish rule, it was divided between Morocco and Mauritania (which surrendered its claim 1979). The continuing Moroccan occupation is

opposed by the Polisarios (Popular Front for the Liberation of Saguia el Hamra and Rio de Oro). ▷ 6.04, 6.05, 6.27

WILHELM II
(1859–1941) German kaiser. Temperamental and autocratic, he dismissed Otto von Bismarck as chancellor soon after his accession in 1888, surrounded himself with a military coterie and set Germany on an expansionist course that culminated in World War I. Deposed as kaiser on 10 November 1918, he fled to the Netherlands where he lived until his death. ▷ 6.06

WILSON, WOODROW
(1854–1924) The 28th president of the USA. A law professor who served briefly as a DEMOCRATIC senator (1911-13), he was elected president in 1912. He launched an anti-corruption, tax- and tariff-cutting, "New Freedom" program. Initially determined to keep the USA out of World War I, Wilson was able to shape the postwar settlement after America's entry in February 1917. However, he failed to secure Senate approval for American membership of the LEAGUE OF NATIONS. He suffered a debilitating stroke in September 1919. ▷ 6.01, 6.06, 6.07, 6.12

WINTER WAR
(30 November 1939–12 March 1940) Conflict between the SOVIET UNION and FINLAND. After establishing suzerainty over LATVIA, LITHUANIA and ESTONIA under the terms of the NAZI-SOVIET PACT, the Soviet Union responded to Finland's refusal to agree to the stationing of Soviet troops on its territory by invading. FINLAND surrendered after pinning down a huge Soviet army for more than a year and was forced to cede 10 percent of its territory. ▷ 6.08

XUZHOU, BATTLE OF
(1948–49) A major PEOPLE'S LIBERATION ARMY victory when the GUOMINDANG armies deserted the battlefield. The decisive battle of the Chinese Civil War, it opened the communist advance to the Yangtze and persuaded the Nationalists to surrender Beijing. ▷ 6.17

YAHYA KHAN
(1917–80) Pakistani soldier who served in the British army during World War II. He was president from 1969 and dispatched troops to crush the democratically elected Awami League in East Pakistan, causing a civil war and his resignation in 1971. ▷ 6.22

YALTA CONFERENCE
(4–11 February 1945) Meeting in the Crimea of the three principal ALLIED leaders of World War II, WINSTON CHURCHILL, FRANKLIN DELANO ROOSEVELT and JOSEPH STALIN. The division of Germany and AUSTRIA into four zones of occupation (France being accepted as the fourth partner in the alliance by JOSEPH

STALIN) was agreed, and the CURZON LINE agreed as the new border between POLAND and the SOVIET UNION. ▷ 6.09

YAMAMOTO, ISOROKO
(1888–1943) Japanese admiral and distinguished naval strategist who in 1935 was already advocating the use of aircraft carriers to win future wars. He planned the attack on PEARL HARBOR and the early Japanese successes in the Pacific. He mismanaged the MIDWAY operation and the Solomons campaign. He was killed when American fighters intercepted his aircraft on 18 April 1943. ▷ 6.19

YAN'AN
Town in Shaanxi province, China, and the destination of the LONG MARCH. It was the headquarters of the Chinese Communist Party (1937–49) though it was briefly captured by the GUOMINDANG armies after MAO ZEDONG had abandoned it as a base in 1947–48. ▷ 6.17, 6.20

YELTSIN, BORIS
(1931–) Russian leader. A communist apparatchik from Sverdlovsk, Boris Yeltsin was made first secretary of the Moscow Communist Party by MIKHAIL GORBACHEV in 1985, and appointed to the Politburo in 1986. Criticizing Gorbachev for the slow pace of *perestroika*, in 1990 he became chairman of the Russian Supreme Soviet. Elected as the first Russian president in June 1991, he cemented his power by foiling the conservative coup against Gorbachev of August 1991. Leading the breakaway COMMONWEALTH OF INDEPENDENT STATES, he secured full independence for Russia. However, his market reforms produced unrest, and parliamentary dissent resulted in a siege of the White House (Russian parliament building) in November 1993, after which he won greater presidential powers. Despite health problems, frequent changes of government personnel and the disastrous conflict in CHECHNYA he was re-elected in 1996. ▷ 6.11, 6.16

YEMEN, REPUBLIC OF
Formed on 22 May 1990 by the union of the Yemen Arab Republic and the People's Democratic Republic of Yemen. It incurred Arab wrath when it supported SADDAM HUSSEIN in 1991. Despite its oil exports, it is the poorest of all Arab states, with most Yemeni engaged in subsistence farming. ▷ 6.05, 6.24, 6.26

YOM KIPPUR WAR
The fourth war of the ARAB-ISRAELI CONFLICT. On 6 October 1973 Egyptian and Syrian troops launched Operation Badr on the unsuspecting Israelis celebrating Yom Kippur. Arab nations warned the USA that intervention could stop oil supplies. Nevertheless, the USA supplied Israel with tanks, airplanes and ammunition. The ORGANIZATION OF PETROLEUM EXPORTING COUNTRIES banned oil exports to the USA and quadrupled the price of oil. Meanwhile, Israeli counterattacks resulted in the defeat of SYRIA and an advance across the Suez Canal. The great powers and the UNITED NATIONS were anxious to end hostilities but a cease-fire was broken by the Israelis and, fearing Soviet intervention on the Arab side, the USA went on nuclear alert. The final cease-fire was on 24 October. The USA cancelled the nuclear alert on 31 October. ▷ 6.04, 6.25

YUAN SHIKAI
(1859–1916) Chinese soldier and politician charged with restoring order during the Chinese Revolution. He made a truce with the revolutionaries and became president of the new republic when the emperor abdicated on 13 February 1912. He was little more than an ambitious warlord who meekly accepted the Twenty-One Demands presented by Japan in 1915. His announcement that he proposed to be emperor caused a rebellion and he died of a heart attack in Beijing. ▷ 6.17

YUGOSLAVIA
Adriatic state created from former Austro-Hungarian territories after World War I. Originally known as the kingdom of the Serbs, Croats and Slovenes, its name was changed in 1929 to promote national unity. It was ruled by ALEXANDER I until his assassination in 1934. After invasion by Germany in 1941 a Croat Ustaše fascist state took power, killing many Serbs, Jews and others. Of the various partisan groups opposing the Germans and Ustaše, TITO's communists emerged the strongest after the war. Tito broke with the SOVIET UNION in 1948, and thereafter maintained Yugoslavia's independence. He suppressed ethnic rivalries, but after his death in 1980 Serbia, led by Slobodan Milošević sought to increase its power with the federation. In response SLOVENIA seceded in 1990 and a secessionist CROATIA fought the Serb-dominated federal government for disputed territory. The BOSNIAN CIVIL WAR (1992–95) continued the country's dismemberment. ▷ 6.07, 6.08, 6.09, 6.10, 6.11

ZAIRE
See CONGO, REPUBLIC OF

ZAMBIA
Republic in south-central Africa, formerly the British protectorate of Northern RHODESIA (1924–53). It joined the 1953 Central African Federation on the recommendation of governor Roy Welensky and when this dissolved in 1963 elections brought KENNETH KAUNDA's Independence Party to power. Zambia became independent in 1964. The Chinese-built TanZam railroad was built in 1975 to facilitate exports. Democratic parties, banned since the 1970s, were permitted to campaign in 1990. ▷ 6.27, 6.28

ZAPATISTAS
Peasant Indians who began an armed revolt in Chiapas, Mexico, in January 1994 to publicize corruption in local government. They formed the Zapatista National Liberation Army and rebelled again (December 1994–February 1995). The government began talks to define the rights of indigenous people. The organization takes its name from the Mexican peasant revolutionary Emiliano Zapata. ▷ 6.14

ZIA UL-HAQ
(1924–88) PAKISTANI general who served in World War II and in the INDO-PAKISTAN WARS (1965, 1971). He was president from 1978 to 1988 and banned democratic parties, introducing martial law. He endorsed the execution of ZULFIKAR ALI BHUTTO and died in an air crash. ▷ 6.22

ZIA UR-RAHMAN
(1935–81) BANGLADESHI soldier who helped to secure the independence of Bangladesh. He was president from 1977 to 1981, securing international aid and claiming that his introduction of martial law was a temporary arrangement. Disillusioned army officers assassinated him in Chittagong. ▷ 6.22

ZIMBABWE
The former British African colony of Southern Rhodesia. It takes its name from Great Zimbabwe, an ancient African city. Southern Rhodesia's prime minister Ian Smith made a unilateral declaration of independence in 1965, making the colony independent of Britain as RHODESIA, under a white minority government. Independence was not recognized by Britain, which imposed sanctions for 14 years. Meanwhile, African guerrilla forces, notably the Zimbabwe African National Liberation Army and the Zimbabwe People's Revolutionary Army, fought the white Rhodesians. Matters were resolved at the Lusaka and Lancaster House conferences in 1979 and ROBERT MUGABE's independent republic of Zimbabwe emerged on 18 April 1980. ▷ 6.05, 6.28

ZIONIST MOVEMENT
Movement formed to establish a Jewish state in Palestine (Eretz Israel). Theodor Herzl (1869–1904) is regarded as the father of Zionism (he published his *Der Judenstaat* in 1896). Tel Aviv was founded in 1909; the first kibbutz was built at Degania on the Jordan River in 1910. The British foreign secretary, Arthur Balfour, favored a Jewish homeland in Palestine (BALFOUR DECLARATION, 1917) but a British proposal for partition was rejected by the Arabs in 1936. The UNITED NATIONS partition plan of 1947 led to ARAB-ISRAELI CONFLICT and the British withdrew from Palestine. ISRAELI independence was proclaimed on 14 May 1948. ▷ 6.05, 6.24

Acknowledgments & Index

Text, timelines and maps
The authors and publishers readily acknowledge the work of a large number of scholars and published works, on which they have drawn in the preparation of this atlas. Many of these works remain in print, and can be used as reliable secondary reading on the many topics covered in this atlas. Among them are the following:

Adams, AE, Matley, IM, and McCagg, WO *An Atlas of Russian and East European History* (London 1967)
Ajayi, JFA and Crowder, Michael (eds) *Historical Atlas of Africa* (Cambridge and New York 1985)
al Faruqi, Ismail Ragi (ed) *Historical Atlas of the Religions of the World* (New York and London 1974)
Almond, M, Black, J, McKitterick, R, and Scarre, C *The Times Atlas of European History* (London and New York 1994)
Ardagh, John with Jones, Colin *Cultural Atlas of France* (London and New York, 1991)
Ashdown, P. *Caribbean History in Maps* (London and New York 1979)
Banks, A *A Military Atlas of World War I* (London 1989)
Barraclough, G (ed) *The Times Atlas of World History* (4th ed , London 1993 and New York 1994)
Bayley, Christopher (ed) *Atlas of the British Empire* (London and New York 1989)
Blunden, Caroline and Elvin, Mark *Cultural Atlas of China* (London and New York, 1986)
Bolton, Geoffrey (ed) *The Oxford History of Australia* (Oxford and Melbourne 1994)
Brown, Dee *The American West* (New York 1994)
Campbell, John (ed) *The Experience of World War II* (London and New York 1989)
Chadwick, Henry and Evans, Gillian R (eds) *Atlas of the Christian Church* (London and New York, 1987)
Cohn-Sherbok, D *Atlas of Jewish History* (London and New York 1994)
Coles, JM and Harding, AF *The Bronze Age in Europe* (London 1979)
Collcutt, Martin, Jansen, Marius and Kumakura, Isao *Cultural Atlas of Japan* (London and New York, 1988)
Cotterell, A *East Asia* (London 1993, New York 1995)
Darby, HC and Fullard, Harold *The New Cambridge Modern History Atlas* (Cambrdge 1970)
Davis, Norman *Europe: a History* (Oxford and New York 1996)
Dear, ICB and Foot, MRD (eds) *The Oxford Companion to the Second World War* (Oxford and New York 1995)
de Lange, Nicholas *Atlas of the Jewish World* (London and New York, 1984)
Elliott, JH (ed) *The Hispanic World* (London and New York 1991)

Fage, JD and Oliver, R (eds) *The Cambridge History of Africa* (Cambridge and New York 1975–)
Fage, J.D. *An Atlas of African History* (London 1978)
Falkus, M and Gillingham J *Historical Atlas of Britain* (London and New York revised ed 1987)
Fernández-Armesto, Felipe (ed) *The Times Atlas of World Exploration* (London and New York, 1991)
Freedman, Lawrence *Atlas of Global Strategy* (London and New York, 1985)
Gilbert, Martin *The Atlas of Jewish History* (London and New York 5th ed 1996)
Gilbert, Martin *Atlas of The Holocaust* (London 1982, New York 1993)
Griffiths, Ieuan I *The Atlas of African Affairs* (London 1984)
Grosser Historischer Weltatlas (3 volumes (Munich 1981)
Hall, DGE *A History of South-east Asia* (4th ed 1981)
Handlin, O. *The History of the United States* (New York 1967)
Hartman, Tom *A World Atlas of Military History 1945–1984* (New York 1985)
Hermann, A *Historical and Commercial Atlas of China* (Cambridge Mass., 1935)
Holt, PM, Lambeth, AKS and Lewis, B (eds) *The Cambridge History of Islam* (Cambridge 1970–)
Homberger, E. *Historical Atlas of North America* (London and New York 1995)
Hosking, G *A History of the Soviet Union* (London 1985)
Johnson, Gordon, Bayly, C and Richards JF *The New Cambridge History of India* (Cambridge 1987–)
Johnson, Gordon *Cultural Atlas of India* (London 1995, New York, 1996)
Kinder, H and Hilgemann, W *Atlas of World History* (2 vols, Munich, London and New York 1974)
Kulke, H and Rothermund, D *A History of India* (London 1990)
Langer, William L *An Encyclopedia of World History* (5th ed, London and New York 1973)
Lee, K *A New History of Korea* (Cambridge, Mass 1988)
McEvedy, Colin and Jones, Richard *Atlas of World Population History* (London 1978)
Milner, CA., O'Connor, C.A. and Sandweiss, M *The Oxford History of the American West* (Oxford and New York 1994)
Milner-Gulland, Robin with Dejevsky, Nikolai *Cultural Atlas of Russia and the Soviet Union* (London and New York, 1989)
Moore, RI (ed) *The Hamlyn Historical Atlas* (London 1981)
Murray, Jocelyn *Cultural Atlas of Africa* (London and New York, 1981)
Nile, Richard and Clerk, Christian *Cultural Atlas of Australia, New Zealand and the South Pacific* (London and New York, 1995)
Nock, O.S. *World Atlas of Railways* (London 1978)
Parker, W.H. *An Historical Geography of Russia* (London 1968)

Paxton, John *The Statesman's Yearbook Historical Companion* (London 1988)
Porter, A.N. (ed) *Atlas of British Overseas Expansion* (London 1991)
Pounds, Norman JG *An Historical Geography of Europe* (Cambridge 1990)
Riasanovsky, NV *A History of Russia* (Oxford and New York 5th ed 1993)
Roberts, JM *The Hutchinson History of the World* (London 1976)
Robinson, Francis *Atlas of the Islamic World since 1500* (London and New York, 1982)
Roolvink, R *Historical Atlas of the Muslim People* (Amsterdam 1974)
Schmidt, KJ *An Atlas and Survey of South Asian History* (New York and London 1995)
Schwartzberg, Joseph E (ed) *A Historical Atlas of South Asia* (Chicago and London, 2nd ed 1992)
Segal, Aaron *An Atlas of International Migration* (London and New Jersey 1993)
Shepherd, William R *Shepherd's Historical Atlas* (New York and London, 9th ed 1974)
Sinclair, Keith (ed) *The Oxford Illustrated History of New Zealand* (Oxford and Auckland 1990)
Sinor, D (ed) *The Cambridge History of Early Inner Asia* (Cambridge 1990)
Spence, J *God's Chinese Son* (London and New York 1996)
Spence, J *The Search for Modern China* (London and New York 1990)
Spence JE (ed) *The World Today* (London 1994)
The Times Atlas of the World (London and New York, 8th ed 1990)
Tindall, G and Shi, DE *America, a Narrative History* (New York, 1996)
Twitchett, D and Fairbank, J (eds) *The Cambridge History of China* (15 vols, Cambridge and New York 1978–91)
Vincent, Mary and Stradling, R.A. *Cultural Atlas of Spain and Portugal* (London 1994, New York 1995)
Waller, Philip (ed) *Chronology of the 20th Century* (Oxford 1995)
Webster's New Geographical Dictionary (Springfield, Massachusetts, 1984)
Winter, JM *The Experience of World War I* (London and New York 1988)
Wintle, J *The Vietnam Wars* (London 1991)

Artwork
Artwork references have been assembled from a wide variety of sources. Any individual or institution who can demonstrate that copyright may have been infringed is invited to contact Andromeda Oxford Ltd.

Photographs
Map 6.09: ZEC/Dalkeith Poster Cards; 6.13: Popperfoto; 6.14: Andromeda Oxford Ltd; 6.16: Corbis; 6.19: Corbis-Bettmann/UPI; 6.22: Hulton Getty; 6.24: Saudi Aramco; 6.27: Hulton Getty